TERM FOR BODY PARTS AND FEATHERS

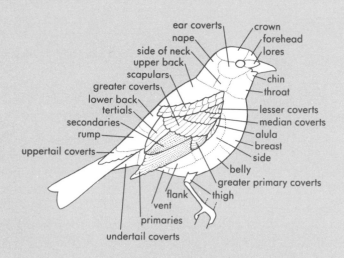

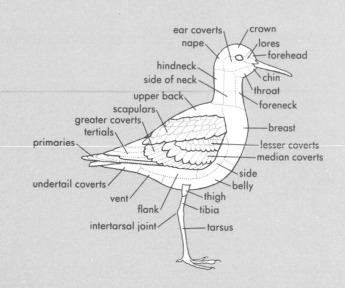

| HOUSE | PURPLE (eastern) | CASSIN'S (typical) | PURPLE (California) | CASSIN'S (short-billed) |

BILL SHAPES OF *CARPODACUS* FINCHES

| LEAST | HAMMOND'S | DUSKY | GRAY | BUFF-BREASTED |

| WESTERN | YELLOW-BELLIED | ACADIAN | WILLOW and ALDER |

BILL SHAPES OF *EMPIDONAX* FLYCATCHERS
(as seen from below)

POMARINE JAEGER

Adult YELLOW-BILLED LOON

PARASITIC JAEGER

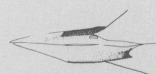

First-winter YELLOW-BILLED LOON

LONG-TAILED JAEGER

First-winter COMMON LOON

BILL SHAPES OF JAEGERS   **BILL SHAPES AND PATTERNS OF LOONS**

THE PETERSON FIELD GUIDES

Edited by Roger Tory Peterson

A Field Guide to Advanced Birding

Birding Challenges and How to Approach Them

Text and Illustrations by

KENN KAUFMAN

*Sponsored by the National Audubon Society,
the National Wildlife Federation,
and the Roger Tory Peterson Institute*

HOUGHTON MIFFLIN COMPANY • BOSTON

1990

For information about permission to reproduce selections from this
book, write to Permissions, Houghton Mifflin Company, 2 Park
Street, Boston, Massachusetts 02108.

Library of Congress Cataloging-in-Publication Data

Kaufman, Kenn.
  A field guide to advanced birding : birding challenges and how to
approach them / text and illustrations by Kenn Kaufman.
      p.   cm. — (The Peterson field guide series ; 39)
  "Sponsored by the National Audubon Society, the National
Wildlife Federation, and the Roger Tory Peterson Institute."
  Includes bibliographical references.
  ISBN 0-395-53517-4. — ISBN 0-395-53376-7 (pbk.). — ISBN
0-395-52282-X (pbk. prepack)
  1. Birds — North America — Identification.   2. Bird watching —
North America — Guide-books.   I. National Audubon
Society.   II. National Wildlife Federation.   III. Roger Tory
Peterson Institute.   IV. Title.   V. Series.
QL681.K38   1990
598'.072347 — dc20   89-71668
                              CIP

Printed in the United States of America

VB   10   9   8   7   6   5   4   3   2   1

EDITOR'S NOTE

Ludlow Griscom, a pioneer in the field identification of birds, was trained as a museum man, and because of his work among the specimen trays, he had masses of minutiae at his instant recall. Whenever he raised his binocular to look at a bird in the field, all of the minor details would fall into place, and he could name the bird with a speed and confidence that astonished the ornithological world of his day.

Griscom's expertise was the result of knowing enough to ignore most details and focus on the few key marks of each species. It was because of my close friendship with Griscom and his young disciples in the Linnaean Society that I was able to prepare my own *Field Guide to the Birds*, first published in 1934. Being academically trained as an artist, I was able to put it all down and give it form.

The "Peterson System," as it came to be known, was essentially a shortcut: by means of schematic drawings and little arrows it taught birdwatchers to look for those few diagnostic marks or patterns that would allow them to name almost every bird they saw. The very simplicity of this method, it has been suggested, was a major reason for the spectacular growth of birding.

As birding grew in popularity, and optical equipment became more sophisticated, it became inevitable that some active observers would not be satisfied just to name most of the birds most of the time. There are some groups of birds — some in winter plumage, some as immatures, some at all seasons — that are too subtle and variable to be identified with certainty by only the usual field marks. The level of detail necessary to solve every last problem in these groups has no place in the typical *Field Guide*, where it would serve only to confuse and discourage most birdwatchers.

With every new edition of my *Field Guides* I have struggled with the dilemma: how schematic should the drawings be? And how much detail should I include in the illustrations or in the text? There were no easy answers. If I included everything I knew, the books would swell well beyond the handy pocket size. If I mentioned some field marks briefly, without elaboration or warnings, birders might be misled; if I left some things out, some critical young birder would be sure to claim that I simply did not know these things. In general I have opted for the latter course, ignoring the handful of critics. But it has often seemed that the best solution would be to keep the *Field Guides* in their current fighting trim and to put the more detailed information into another book, a supplement of sorts.

The birding world has evolved to the point where there is now a ready audience for supplementary books, so we welcome *A Field Guide to Advanced Birding* to the Peterson Series. This field guide begins where the others leave off. If you have already determined that a certain fall warbler must be either a Pine or a Bay-breasted, for example, but the bird's field marks don't quite add up, this book offers a discussion of subtle points you can use — if you see them — to clinch the identification.

An effective field guide cannot be written by a large committee. There is too much risk of "flattening-out" of ideas. Therefore, although this book draws on the knowledge of many experts — and although it contains certain chapters written by specialists such as Claudia Wilds and Kevin Zimmer — most of the text and all of the drawings present challenging birds as seen through the eyes of Kenn Kaufman. A lifelong birder, Kenn made a splash as a top bird-lister while still in his teens, and then turned to more serious pursuits that ultimately led to his position as Associate Editor of *American Birds*, the field journal of the National Audubon Society. His writings on field identification appear regularly in that magazine, as well as in *Birding* (published by the American Birding Association) and other periodicals.

Aware of the special needs of less-experienced birders, Kenn Kaufman takes pains to explain basic things thoroughly and clearly. Why are immature gulls so confusing in early summer? What is the first thing to look for on an unknown warbler? When are the field marks of loons less reliable? How can you study hummingbird identification most efficiently? What kinds of field marks are most likely to change with the seasons? Insights like these could take years to work out on your own, but with this book you can accelerate the learning process.

This is a guide for all seasons, to be used in the field as well as at home. But you will probably find it most helpful to spend some time with it indoors, before your next encounter with the more puzzling birds. Study it whenever you plan to pursue sparrows in the winter fields, terns along the summer beaches, and any of the other complex groups. Such preparation will enhance your understanding and enjoyment of the challenges.

ROGER TORY PETERSON

ACKNOWLEDGMENTS

Although birds have been the focus of most of my waking hours since I was six years old, I could not have even attempted a field guide of this complexity without a lot of help.

In researching this guide I made heavy use of the resources at the University of Arizona in Tucson, including their excellent science library and specimen collection, and I appreciate the courtesy shown to me as an outsider. My particular thanks to Dr. Stephen M. Russell, who not only arranged for me to have extended access to the collection but also took the time to discuss a number of difficult bird groups on the basis of his own wide-ranging field experience.

My other major resource was the Academy of Natural Sciences of Philadelphia, where I worked in 1985 and 1986. In addition to an outstanding specimen collection, that institution houses VIREO (Visual Resources for Ornithology), a collection of tens of thousands of excellent bird *photographs*. The phenomenal value of VIREO to the study of field identification will continue to increase as the collection grows. My special thanks to Dr. Frank B. Gill, who made it possible for me to work at the Academy, and also to Crawford H. Greenewalt and J. P. Myers, two individuals who played crucial roles in the development of VIREO.

In addition to these two institutions, I visited a number of other collections in the course of this research. My sincere thanks to Ned K. Johnson of the Museum of Vertebrate Zoology, University of California at Berkeley; Luis F. Baptista of the California Academy of Sciences, San Francisco; Kimball L. Garrett of the Los Angeles County Museum, California; J. V. Remsen of the Louisiana State University Museum of Natural Science, Baton Rouge; Amadeo Rea of the San Diego Natural History Museum, California; George E. Watson and Gary R. Graves of the United States National Museum, Washington, D.C.; and Daniel D. Gibson of the University of Alaska Museum, Fairbanks; for allowing me to work with the collections in their care.

I owe an obvious debt of gratitude to Claudia P. Wilds and Kevin J. Zimmer, who wrote the chapters on dowitchers and on Thayer's Gull, respectively. Claudia, who serves as field identification editor for *Birding*, is widely respected for her scholarly work on difficult groups: she has solved many of the toughest problems for the rest of us. Kevin, whose fine book *The Western Bird Watcher* discussed many kinds of field problems, has recently been focusing on the most challenging of gulls. I am also indebted to Bret Whitney, with whom I co-authored a series of articles on *Empidonax* flycatchers for *Birding*; this book's chapter on *Empidonax* draws on many of Bret's ideas.

Some others went out of their way to help me. My parents, John and Joan Kaufman, furnished much practical advice on drawing materials, as well as years of moral support and an early background that emphasized both science and art. Janet Witzeman, my former co-editor of *Continental Birdlife*, was the first to urge me to put this material in book form, and she has been a constant source of sound advice. Rick Bowers, who learned to dread my phone calls, unfailingly responded to my requests for photographs, information, advice, critical readings, and so on. Elaine Cook, with her expertise in both information science and biology, taught me how to make the most of library resources; she also critiqued drafts of many chapters. Lydia Thompson, a talented bird artist, gave me much advice on illustration techniques. I also must single out a few authorities on bird identification with whom I have had countless hours of discussions over the last decade: Eirik A. T. Blom, William S. Clark, Jon Dunn, Davis W. Finch, P. J. Grant, Lars Jonsson, Paul Lehman, J. V. Remsen, Will Russell, Claudia Wilds, and Kevin J. Zimmer. As major contributors to our current knowledge they are all, in a way, contributors to this book; several of them also reviewed portions of the text or drawings. Any remaining errors are my responsibility, of course.

The number of birders from whom I have learned things must run into the thousands by now, and I wish I could thank them all. The following people gave me specific help (information, advice, photos, review of sections of text, etc.) on the birds in this book: my sincere thanks to Peter Alden, John C. Arvin, Stephen F. Bailey, Robert D. Barber, Tim Barksdale, Dan Brunton, Steve Cardiff, Rob Cardillo, Margaret Chalif, Charles T. Clark, Tom and Debbie Collazo, Doug Cook, Ross Chapin, the late Thomas H. Davis, William A. Davis, Bix Demaree, Carol de Waard, Susan Roney Drennan, Graham Dugas, Kim Eckert, Victor L. Emanuel, Bonnie B. Farmer, Al Ghiorso, Michael Godfrey, Sharon Goldwasser, Ruth Green, Daniel R. Heathcote, Tom Huels, Eugene Hunn, David T. Jones, Denny Jones, Lasse J. Laine, David Lambeth, Jeri Langham, Howard Langridge, Greg Lasley, Geoff LeBaron, Gerald Maisel, Nora Mays, Guy McCaskie, G. Scott Mills, Joseph Morlan, Killian Mullarney, Ron Naveen, Blair Nikula, Michael O'Brien, Bob Odear, Gerald Oreel, Arvil Parker, Ted Parker, Michael Patten, Dennis Paulson, Bruce Peterjohn, H. Douglas Pratt, Paul D. Pratt, Betty Randall, Phil Ranson, Robert Ridgely, Mark B. Robbins, Gary Rosenberg, Kenneth V. Rosenberg, Ruth Ogden Russell, Jeanne Skelly, Arnold Small, Al and Gwen Smalley, P. William Smith, Phoebe Snetsinger, Dave Sonneborn, Walter and Sally Spofford, Bobbie Squires, Rich Stallcup, David Stejskal, David Stemple, Doug Stotz, Rick Taylor, Scott B. Terrill, Stuart Tingley, James A. Tucker, Priscilla Tucker, Guy Tudor, Arnoud van den Berg, Richard Webster, Hal Wierenga, Sartor O. Williams, Eric Witmer, Robert A. Witzeman, David Wolf, Alan Wormington, Bob Yutzy, Barry Zimmer, and Dale A. Zimmerman.

It was a pleasure to work with Roger Tory Peterson, the man whose books fostered my own early interest in birds. The elegant simplicity of his popular field guides, as I soon learned, is distilled from an extraordinarily complex knowledge. Even though he was thoroughly occupied with bigger projects, Dr. Peterson took the time to lend insight on many of the most difficult groups; the book was greatly improved by his help.

I'm grateful to the staff of Houghton Mifflin Company. In particular, Harry Foster gave expert guidance from the beginning of the project. Barbara Stratton clarified and sharpened the book's final form, and Jay Howland reined in many a dangling participle.

My greatest thanks go to my wife Lynn. As a constant source of encouragement and inspiration, as an experienced birder with a keen eye for language and design, she improved the book in countless ways. In particular, with her supreme organizational skills, she quietly rearranged, collated, reorganized, weeded, and filed all the bits and pieces, so that ultimately it was no work at all for me to finish the project. Without Lynn, this field guide would still be a disconnected mass of drawings and paragraphs, not a completed book.

KENN KAUFMAN

CONTENTS

A Field Guide to
Advanced Birding

1

CHALLENGES IN BIRDING AND
HOW TO APPROACH THEM

Within the last few decades, birding has taken its place
among North America's favorite hobbies and sports. No one
questions its popularity today, but some might ask: Why did
it develop so recently? After all, birds — unlike video games
or model airplanes — have been around since the dawn of human civilization; so why didn't birding become popular cen-
turies ago?

The reason lies in the definition of birding itself. The word
"birdwatching" could mean any number of things, including
the simple act of watching a bird, any bird, without knowing
or caring what kind it is; but "birding" is generally understood to involve finding and identifying different species in
the wild. For it to be any fun, you must be able to name most
of the birds you encounter. So you need reliable information
on how to tell one bird from another. Many birders take such
information for granted today, but actually the process of determining the most reliable and consistent field marks for
each species and then publishing the facts is an ongoing process. This book represents a new step in that process.

Virtually all of North America's bird species were known
to science by the beginning of the twentieth century. But
naming them in the field remained an uncertain business.
Most binoculars were of poor quality, most bird books were
hefty volumes with few illustrations, and the only "acceptable" way of identifying a bird was to take it in hand and
compare it to extensive written keys or to specimens in a
museum.

Of course some ornithologists who studied museum specimens could later recognize the living bird outdoors. But bird
identification for the general public really arrived in 1934,
when Roger Tory Peterson brought out his first *Field Guide
to the Birds.* Simplicity was the keynote of the Peterson System. No matter that some female ducks, for example, were
plain and brown; the beginner could ignore them. It was

enough to know, with complete confidence, that the drake with the white face crescent was a Blue-winged Teal. No matter that some warblers in fall plumage were confusing; in spring, they all wore distinctive patterns. The original Peterson guides bypassed the technical details and made it possible for anyone to name most of the birds most of the time. The very simplicity of this approach has undoubtedly been a major factor in the tremendous growth of interest in birding.

By the 1960s there were millions of North Americans who claimed birdwatching as at least a casual hobby, and tens of thousands of serious enthusiasts who were out at all seasons identifying birds. And with so many birders in the field, it was inevitable that not everyone would be satisfied just to name most of the birds most of the time. Some of us wanted to go a few steps farther.

It was no challenge, for example, to identify Northern Waterthrushes if they looked the way they were "supposed" to, with obvious yellow tones. But what about those individuals that were more whitish below, like the Louisiana Waterthrush? And as for gulls: adults were not too difficult, but the young ones were more likely to wander out of range; how could we sort out all those motley immature gulls to find the rarities among them? Then there were those little look-alikes, the *Empidonax* flycatchers; we knew they had different voices, but how could we name a lone individual, away from its nesting habitat, if it would not sing?

These questions went beyond the limitations of the standard field guides. So the pioneers in modern birding have gone back to the technical volumes in the libraries, back to the specimens in the museum trays, and especially back to the field to look at the birds themselves. And these efforts have borne results. "Unidentifiable" birds are now routinely named in the field, and identifications that were once dubious at best can now be made with certainty ... because now we know what to look for. This kind of information has been spread by word of mouth; articles on some species groups have appeared in various periodicals; and bits and pieces of the new knowledge have trickled into the most recent bird guides. But up to now there has been no single source that birders could turn to for comprehensive information on all of the major identification challenges.

This book is designed to fill that niche. It is not meant to be a compendium of everything known about field identification; such a volume (if it would all fit in one volume) would be many times the bulk of this one. Nor is this book intended to replace any existing guide. By giving detailed attention to a selection of North America's top field problems, this book may serve as a useful supplement to your favorite field guide, enabling you to go a step further in the fascinating pursuit of bird identification.

Basic Rules of Field Identification

Most birds, fortunately, are easy to identify. However — and again I say, fortunately — they are not *all* easy. Some are moderately difficult to separate; a few are so similar to each other that they strain the abilities of the experts. So if you like a challenge, if you enjoy testing yourself against new questions, birding will never let you down.

When you delve into these challenging field problems, caution is the watchword. After all, some of these birds were regarded as simply unidentifiable in the field until recently; so you must be willing to take your time on them, and willing to admit it when you are uncertain of a bird's identity. These difficult identifications make up a whole new game; and the game has some important rules, as outlined below.

Check every field mark: Most birds can be identified at a glance by reference to one or two field marks, or diagnostic markings. But the birds in this book are those that require at least a second look. For these difficult species it is wise to check as many field characters as possible, and this becomes even more important when the bird involved is outside its normal range.

There are three major categories of field marks. Some are absolute: for example, Bird A has an eye-ring and Bird B does not. These are the best distinctions to use, because they are the easiest to confirm. (However, even the most "foolproof" character should not be relied upon completely by itself for identification. There are probably exceptions to every field mark.) Some field marks are relative: for example, Bird A has a longer tail, or a darker back, than Bird B. These differences are diagnostic only if you know both species well, or have both visible for comparison. Some field marks are only percentage characters: for example, Bird A usually (but not always) has dark lores, while Bird B usually does not (but sometimes does). These average differences are never diagnostic, but they may add minor support to an identification based on other characters.

In this book, absolute field marks are emphasized first, relative ones second. Nondiagnostic "percentage" characters are often mentioned to round out the picture, especially for the really difficult groups. But when you are dealing with an unfamiliar "problem" species, remember to check every detail; never rely only on what seems to be the best diagnostic mark.

Learn the common birds: Beginners are often tempted to ignore the common birds and go chasing off after rare ones. But ironically, experts are able to find rarities precisely because they know the common species so well. Topnotch birders may not necessarily have the biggest life lists or the quickest reflexes, but they have all spent lots of hours looking carefully at the common birds.

Suppose, for instance, that the only gulls usually in your area are Herring and Ring-billed. Maybe you can tell them apart at a glance . . . but it would be worth your while to do more than glance, to get well acquainted with these two. Study every detail of their plumage, their shapes, the way they fly. Consider not only the things that make them different from each other but also the points that would separate them from other species. With this background, you will know instantly what to look for if an odd gull shows up in your territory.

Consider shapes: Bird shapes are extremely important in identification. Roger Peterson made this point years ago by including charts of various bird silhouettes as endpapers in his field guides. Only recently have most birders really caught on to this idea. Shape is always an aid, and sometimes — when size is deceptive, when the light is bad, when the bird itself is a freak individual with aberrant markings — shape is the major factor that can keep you from getting off on the wrong track in your identification.

Unfortunately, shape is a difficult thing to learn from pictures. It is a struggle for even the best of bird illustrators to get shapes precisely right; and single photographs are often misleading. You may build up an accurate impression by studying large series of photographs, but for the most part, bird shapes must be learned in the field.

Some aspects of bird shape are obvious. For example, if the bill, neck, legs, or tail happen to be extremely long, you are likely to notice that immediately. But other points can be much more subtle. Look at the head: is the crown rounded, flat, peaked, double-peaked? What is the angle of the forehead relative to the base of the upper mandible? Does the head seem large or small for the size of the body? And the body itself: is it elongated, slender, chunky? Do not think only in terms of profiles: what shape is the head when viewed head-on or from behind? What shape is the body when seen from below? Look at the length of the wings: where do the wing-tips fall in relation to the tail? Look at the legs: their length, and thickness, are worth noticing not only on large wading birds but on songbirds as well. These are merely examples; there are innumerable other aspects of shape worth studying.

Adding to the overall impressions of shape are a bird's typical posture and mannerisms of behavior. Looking at the short tail of the Winter Wren, for example, we also note that it is often held up almost vertically above the back; looking at the long tail of Bewick's Wren, we also note that it is often flipped about expressively.

Keep in mind that the arrangement of the feathers may change a bird's apparent shape from moment to moment. The body feathers may be sleeked in when the bird is afraid, puffed out when the bird is cold; the crown feathers may be raised when the bird is excited. This is part of the reason why single photographs can mislead. But despite these temporary alterations, every species has a characteristic shape that will become evident after you watch it for a while.

It is important (and, perhaps, difficult) to realize that practically no two species are shaped exactly alike, even among groups of closely related birds. Things would be a lot easier for the illustrators of bird guides if this were not the case — if it were possible to draw just one warbler outline, for example, and then fill it in with the color patterns of various species. But there is no "standard" warbler shape. The Black-throated Blue looks bulkier than the Magnolia Warbler, but not nearly as bulky as the Connecticut Warbler. The tail of the American Redstart is relatively long, that of the Tennessee Warbler is relatively short. The bill of the Cape May Warbler is small and finely pointed, that of the Yellow-throated Warbler is relatively long and heavy, and that of the Worm-eating Warbler is long, sharply pointed, and thick at the base. Comparisons like these could be made for any other family of birds. In one confusing group after another — hawks, *Empidonax* flycatchers, sandpipers, even hummingbirds — shape differences among the species play an important role in identification.

Learn to see details: In using this book, you will find much discussion of very fine points — down to the patterns of individual feathers. Can such things be seen in the field? Yes, they can; but it takes concentration and practice (and, sometimes, good optical equipment). Do not be discouraged if you find that some of these fine details can be impossible to see under some conditions.

You can, and should, practice on common birds. Look at the Mourning Dove: it isn't merely plain brown all over; it has many subtle shadings of color. Look at the winter Starling: it has a surprisingly complex pattern. Practice analyzing and describing the plumage of common birds to sharpen your eye for detail.

Consider molt and wear: As a general rule, a healthy wild bird will replace (molt) every one of its feathers at least once a year. The reason is that feathers — remarkable as they are for their lightweight strength — do gradually wear out. If a bird did not shed its old feathers and grow in fresh ones, it would eventually lose its protective covering and its ability to fly. Except in those cases where a molt brings about a drastic change in color (as when a ptarmigan molts from summer brown to winter white), the effects of molt and wear are usually subtle; but they are worth considering in difficult identification problems, when we may already be dealing with subtle distinctions.

There is much variation among species in the timing and pattern of the molt, but many North American birds go through a complete molt in fall (replacing all the feathers) and another partial one in spring (replacing head and body feathers, but not most of those in the wings or tail). Feathers are replaced in orderly fashion, a few at a time.

The process of the molt itself may temporarily change the apparent shape or pattern of the wings or tail. A bird that normally has a square-tipped tail, for example, may appear fork-tailed if the central tail feathers have been shed. A bird that normally has white outer tail feathers may go through a stage of molt in which these feathers are missing. The molt of flight feathers in the wings may bring about similar changes in wing shape and pattern. Even the way a bird flies may be noticeably different — with faster wingbeats, for instance — when some of the flight feathers are missing.

Feather wear has two visible effects: fading of the colors and wearing away of the edges. Fading is rarely noticeable in the field for most species, but on some birds brown or gray plumage may become visibly paler as the season advances, and black plumage may take on a brownish cast. Abrasion of the edges, on the other hand, may be conspicuous when part of a bird's pattern is made up of contrasting edges or tips on individual feathers. For example, the white wing bars found on many songbirds are created by contrasting white tips on the dark median coverts and greater coverts; as the plumage becomes worn, these wing bars will become steadily narrower (or may disappear entirely if they were narrow to begin with). Such alterations of standard field marks need not be confusing if you are aware that molt and wear affect the feathers of every bird.

Avoid the common pitfalls: Memorizing field marks is not always enough. Under some circumstances it is possible to misidentify a bird even though you know what it is supposed to look like.

Two of these pitfalls involve errors in perception:

1. *Size judgment.* Although size is often quoted as a field mark, it can be a difficult one to use. I used to believe I could judge any bird's size quickly in the field; but I now think that what was happening was that shape and behavior told me what species the bird was, and my mind automatically filled in the known size. In traveling outside North America I find that my first impression of the size of an unfamiliar bird may be grossly incorrect. If you are looking at an unknown bird, do not make assumptions about its size unless you see it in direct comparison to something else.

2. *Color perception.* Beware the effects of light: your eyes can easily be tricked into misjudging color. Glare or shadow can make birds look paler or darker; low-angle morning or evening sun may intensify the warm colors, turning yellow birds to orange or red, white birds to pink. Even under normal conditions, the smooth surface of a bird's bill or eye may catch the light and momentarily look pale or white.

Any confusion caused by these perceptual errors can usually be resolved by simply taking a longer look. But stickier problems can be raised by birds that genuinely look odd . . . for any of several reasons:

3. *Abnormal color.* On rare occasions you may encounter a bird with abnormally pigmented plumage. Albinism, especially partial albinism, is the most frequent such condition. For this reason it is unsafe to identify a bird solely on the basis of a white area in the plumage. For example, an all-white finch-like bird doesn't *have* to be a McKay's Bunting;

it might be an albino House Sparrow. Other types of color aberrations, mostly very rare, produce birds that are abnormally dark (melanism), that are unusually pale all over (leucism or schizochroism), or that have excess reddish (erythrism) or yellow (xanthochroism) tones in the plumage. Aberrant colors can also appear on the bill, legs, or eyes, even on birds that are otherwise normally colored.

4. *Discolored plumage, legs, or bill.* Although aberrant pigmentation is rare, accidental discoloring or staining is not. Birds that feed on soft fruit may have dark stains around the base of the bill; birds that feed at blossoms may have the forehead, face, or throat dusted with yellow or red pollen. Waterbirds may have the legs or underparts discolored temporarily by mud (or permanently by oil or chemicals in the water).

5. *Bill deformities.* Because bill shape is often a field mark, it is important to note that an occasional bird develops a malformed bill. If the deformity is not serious enough to interfere with feeding, the bird may lead a normal life. The mandibles may be crossed, or one or both mandibles may be abnormally long; other kinds of deformities are also possible.

In cases of the three preceding types, an experienced birder can usually make a correct identification by pinpointing just what is odd about the bird and then taking into account all other clues. But there are three other categories of birds that simply cannot be identified by conventional clues ... because they do not belong to any species in your field guide:

6. *Hybrids.* Distinct species of wild birds seldom hybridize, but it has happened enough times that many different hybrid combinations have been reported. A hybrid's plumage pattern usually combines some features from both of the parent species, and in some cases this gives it an appearance resembling yet a third species. (For example, I know of a Dark-eyed Junco × White-throated Sparrow hybrid that was miscalled as a Black-chinned Sparrow, and a Northern Pintail × Greenwinged Teal that suggested a Baikal Teal.) It may be difficult or impossible to name these hybrids with certainty in the field, but you should resist the temptation to turn them into rare species.

7. *Escapees.* Exotic birds from all over the world are kept as zoo exhibits or pets in North America. Sometimes they escape, and some may live for weeks or even years in the wild. Not all such exotics look obviously "exotic"; some are superficially similar to North American species.

8. *Cosmic mind-benders.* On rare occasions, a strong-flying migratory bird may wind up literally thousands of

miles from where it is supposed to be. A few years ago, for example, birders in Maine found an odd streaky flycatcher. Looking through their bird guides, they decided that — even though it didn't look quite right — it had to be a Sulphur-bellied Flycatcher, a stray from the American Southwest. Photographs proved it was actually a Variegated Flycatcher from South America, the first ever recorded on this continent! The moral of this story is not that you need to memorize field marks for every species on the planet, but simply that you should avoid jumping to conclusions when an unfamiliar bird appears.

Question authority: Every so often, you may encounter a bird that doesn't add up — a bird with field marks that seem to contradict each other. Don't be too quick to conclude that an odd bird "has to be" a particular species just because some expert has endorsed a set of field marks. The expert may be wrong.

When I planned this book, I thought it would be easy. After all, wasn't I up-to-date on the latest discoveries about identification? Weren't there already articles in print on many of these groups? But when I started to write, I ran into problems. Some of the published information was incomplete or misleading; some of our "common knowledge" was just plain wrong. As I worked to double-check each fact, every chapter turned into a major research project. I found I had to spend many more hours in the field, in the museum, and in the library, looking for the truth about birds that I thought I "knew" already. As a result of this effort, I think I managed to avoid simply repeating false information from others. But I may well have introduced some of my own errors, or some misinterpretations, or some misleading claims; and I've undoubtedly missed some important field marks. Despite my best efforts, there are bound to be some mistakes in this book. Here's a birding challenge: find the errors. It's a good way to learn new things. For some of these difficult groups, there will always be room for refinements in our knowledge, and you can add to our understanding if you're willing to question the "experts."

Don't let it get you down: One obvious message of this book is that if you want to, you can make progress on identifying any of the most difficult North American birds. But I hope everyone will see the other side of the coin: you don't have to take on all these challenges.

If any group of birds leaves you confused, irritated, or uninterested, simply ignore that group. Maybe you'll want to look at them more closely next year, or maybe not; but it will always be acceptable to call them *"Empidonax* sp." or "unidentified small sandpipers" or "immature gulls, unidentified." After all, birding is something that should be thoroughly enjoyable. Don't let these tricky identification challenges keep you from having a good time in the field.

Document the problem bird: There are two kinds of problem birds. One is the bird that — even after reference to your field guides and this book — you are unable to name. The other is the bird that you have identified, but which is not supposed to occur in your area; then the problem lies in getting other birders to believe you.

In either case, what you need is documentation: evidence that can be examined by other authorities. Photographs are the best means of documenting a bird record today; preferably close-up photos, in color, from a variety of angles. In addition (or instead, if photography is impossible) you should sketch the bird and make a detailed written description. Try to note everything, not just the points that seem to be important field marks, and include comments on behavior and voice. Get other observers out to see the bird if at all possible, and ask them to take detailed notes as well.

This documentation may seem like a lot of trouble, but there are reasons why it is worth the effort. The subsequent research involved in naming a particularly tough bird will teach you a lot about the subject. You may turn up a fact about identification that is new to everyone, not only to yourself. And in taking steps to document a rarity, you are doing more than merely ensuring a checkmark on your list — because rare birds do have biological significance. The occurrence of a bird outside its known normal range is not a random event or a quirk of nature; it reflects the patterns of dispersal and, perhaps, the population trends of the species.

So if you learn how to identify the challenging species, then document your unusual finds, your birding can be both an exciting avocation and a real contribution to science.

How to Use This Book

As stated earlier, this book is intended to supplement the standard field guides. I am making the assumption that you will have some idea of a bird's identity before you turn to this book: that you will have narrowed it down at least to the family level. Therefore, you will find no discussion here of how to tell a gull from a shearwater or a flycatcher from a warbler. The book is arranged as a series of independent chapters, each one treating a group of similar species.

The species accounts vary in format to fit the complexity of the group under discussion. Separating Black-capped and Carolina chickadees, for example, requires a different approach from that used to untangle the eleven *Empidonax* flycatchers, and yet another approach is needed for naming female and immature hummingbirds. No single format would apply equally well in all these cases, and so I have made no attempt to cram all these differently shaped pegs into square holes.

Each chapter begins with a brief summary of the problem; this may serve to point out hidden pitfalls or sources of confusion peculiar to each group. Next I often present a section of "preliminary points." Here I cover important background information, which may include things like seasonal, geographical, or age-related variation in the birds; timing of the molt; or any other factors that will affect how you should interpret their field marks. For some of the more complicated groups, I talk about specific approaches to looking at or learning the birds. I sometimes discuss topics such as timing of migration, patterns of vagrancy, or details of distribution if they have an important bearing on identification. I usually omit basic range descriptions, however, since this information is readily available in the standard field guides.

In presenting field marks I have tried to list them in approximate order of importance, with the most significant or reliable ones first and minor supporting details last. This system often breaks down for groups of more than two species — the field mark that isolates one species may be useless in separating the others — and in these cases I have just attempted to find the simplest and clearest order in which to present the information.

Final chapter summaries, when they occur, also take various forms. And in many cases it is the captions for the illustrations that summarize a chapter's major points. If you have already read a chapter, you can use its picture captions or end-of-chapter summary to refresh your memory on that species group. But if you have not read the material, do not rely on the summaries alone. They are usually somewhat oversimplified to save space; the full chapter text always provides a more complete picture.

Some readers will probably protest that the format of this guide does not permit rapid reference and instant identification in the field. This is true. In this guide we are dealing with difficult birds, and simplifying the approach would automatically lead to errors.

As I said earlier, most birds are easy to identify. Roger Peterson showed the way with his first *Field Guide to the Birds*, breaking down tough problems with simple arrows, pointing out the shortcuts, showing everyone how they could name most of the birds they saw. Most — but not all. Peterson's field guides have always made the point that some birds are just too complex for "field guide treatment" and are best left unidentified by anyone except the expert. Unfortunately, some other recent bird books have glossed over the difficulties, leading beginners to an overconfidence that produces many wrong identifications. Any book that tries to tell you everything about a tough bird like Thayer's Gull, for example, in one-third of a page is definitely going to mislead you part of the time.

If you want to be accurate in your identifications, there are only two possible approaches: (1) Leave the difficult birds unnamed, or (2) take the time to learn the complexities of these groups. The other option — finding a shortcut, a "single diagnostic mark" to rely on — will lead you to misidentify birds at least part of the time.

Species Coverage

In choosing the species groups to treat in this guide, I have intentionally ignored most purely oceanic birds and most of those Asiatic species that stray to Alaska during migration. Both of these categories abound with identification challenges; but they are generally encountered by birders on organized trips, with experienced leaders who can comment on field marks. Therefore, I have largely omitted specialties of the open sea and of vagrant season in the Aleutians in favor of field problems that are more widespread in North America.

Probably no two birders would select exactly the same list of birds for a guide such as this one. (I would be happy to hear from anyone who has strong feelings about birds to be included in possible future editions of this book.) But different species groups are hard to identify for different reasons. My aim has been to choose a representative sampling of different *kinds* of field problems, and to discuss them very thoroughly. Reading a variety of these chapters should give you general insights that will increase your skill at identifying all birds, not just those treated in this guide.

In summary, then, this book is not just a list of field marks for difficult birds. This book is about *how* to learn to identify the most challenging birds, with detailed examples drawn from widespread problem groups.

Terminology and Bird Topography

Although I avoid technical jargon whenever possible, finding that it hinders communication more often than it helps, in this book it has been necessary to adopt some standard terms for the "parts of the bird," or bird topography. The reason is that in studying identification, we often have to focus on the details of a single group of feathers. If a field mark involves the greater coverts, we had better all be calling them "greater coverts" — because the alternative would be something like "that bunch of medium-sized feathers near the middle of the wing, in front of the flight feathers, where the second wing bar would be if this bird had wing bars." So I recommend that you take the time to learn the standard terminology. Not only will it make communication easier, it will also sharpen your awareness of the patterns of birds.

Head-pattern terms: Because of the arrangement of feather tracts on the head, certain elements of head pattern appear over and over in many groups of birds (Fig. 1). It is useful to have standard terms for these features.

The terms *median crown stripe* and *lateral crown stripe* are self-explanatory. However, they cannot be applied to all birds with patterned crowns. If the crown is uniformly finely streaked, for example, it would be wrong to designate one streak as "median" and another as "lateral."

The *moustachial*, *submoustachial*, and *malar stripes* are noticeable in the face patterns of many sparrows and other birds. These are most easily defined by their points of origin at the base of the bill. Of course, many birds show only one or two of these stripes; and on some birds you may need a close look at the face and bill to be sure just where the stripe falls. If you can't be certain, saying that a stripe exists in the *malar region* is better than guessing at its precise location.

Note that *eye-ring* indicates a contrastingly colored circle of feathers, while *orbital ring* (Fig. 2) indicates a narrow circle of bare skin around the eye. The latter is present on all birds, but it is rarely of importance in identification (indeed, rarely noticed) except when it contrasts with both the iris and the surrounding feathers.

The term *eyestripe* indicates a horizontal stripe at the level of the eye, while a stripe immediately above the eye is called the *supercilium* (or "eyebrow"). When the eyestripe exists only behind the eye, it is sometimes called the *postocular stripe;* when it exists only between the eye and the bill, it is sometimes called the *loral stripe.* But referring to these simply as sections of the eyestripe is equally acceptable.

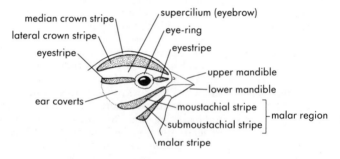

Fig. 1. Head-pattern terms.

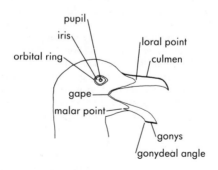

Fig. 2. Eye and bill terms.

Wing-structure terms: Wing structure is the most important aspect of bird topography to learn; you cannot begin to discuss wing pattern until you know these terms.

On the folded wing, the coverts of the secondaries are prominent. The coverts of the primaries are far less conspicuous, being largely folded out of sight. Therefore, *primary coverts* are labeled as such, while the term *coverts* (unmodified) is understood to mean the secondary coverts. Similarly, references to *coverts* and *primary coverts* indicate those on the upperside of the wing unless stated otherwise. In this way, the most awkward terms (such as *median underprimary coverts*) are reserved for the parts of the wing that we need to describe least often; and even these unwieldy terms are perfectly clear in meaning.

The two *wing bars* conspicuous on each wing of many songbirds are formed by contrasting pale tips to the *median coverts* and *greater coverts*. (In some species, only one of these sets of coverts is pale-tipped, forming a single wing bar.) For the sake of clarity it is best to restrict the term *wing bar* to this meaning, not applying it to other kinds of bars or stripes that may appear elsewhere on the wing.

Distinguishing among *tertials, secondaries,* and *primaries* on the folded wing requires some practice. On some birds (e.g., shorebirds, pipits, and grassland sparrows) the tertials are quite long, reaching practically to the ends of the longest primaries (and perhaps helping to protect the longer flight feathers from abrasion against the grass); on some birds they are relatively short and less conspicuous. The rest of the flight feathers are mostly hidden on the folded wing, except for the outer edges of the secondaries and the outer edges and tips of the outer primaries. On many birds these outer edges are contrastingly paler than the rest of the feather; but these pale edgings, being exposed to abrasion, are likely to be reduced as the plumage becomes older and more worn.

Do not expect to see all of the feather groups of the upperside of the folded wing on every bird. Parts of the wing are frequently obscured by overlapping breast and scapular feathers; this overlapping tendency reaches its extreme in ducks and some other swimming birds, in which practically the entire wing may be hidden among the body plumage. Also, the relative position and prominence of various feather groups on the folded wing vary among different families. The coverts make up a larger percentage of the visible wing on shorebirds than on sparrows, for example, but the shorebirds in turn are more likely to have more of the coverts hidden by the large

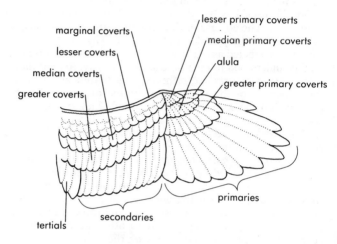

Fig. 3. Upperside of wing.

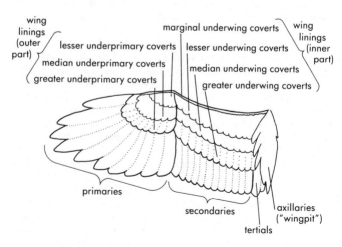

Fig. 4. Underside of wing.

scapulars. Experience with a number of groups will show you the extent of variability in wing structure.

Learning the groups of feathers on the spread wing is also important (Figs. 3 and 4). This is especially true for soaring birds, such as hawks and gulls, on which the details of the wing are clearly visible in flight. All of the coverts and primary coverts tend to be more sharply defined and easier to recognize the upperside of the wing than on the underside. An inclusive term for the entire area formed by the underwing coverts and underprimary coverts is *wing linings*; this term has sometimes been applied, incorrectly, to the whole undersurface of the wing.

The diagram of the spread upperwing shows the tertials, for clarity; but in the field these are routinely hidden by the scapulars, which spread out over the upperside of the base of the wing in flight.

Tail structure: A basic but essential point is that every bird's tail folds up with the *central* pair of tail feathers on top and the *outermost* pair on the bottom. Looking at the upperside of the folded tail (Fig. 5) you can see one feather of the central pair in its entirety, plus the outer edges of most of the others; looking at the underside, often you can see only the outermost pair.

On most birds the bases of the tail feathers are never visible, being hidden by the tail coverts. Recognizing the *uppertail coverts* as such may take some concentration: what looks at first glance like the "base of the tail" on the upperside of flying gulls, shorebirds, buteos, or other birds may of-

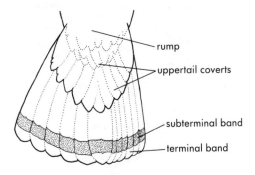

— rump

— uppertail coverts

— subterminal band

— terminal band

Fig. 5. Upperside of tail.

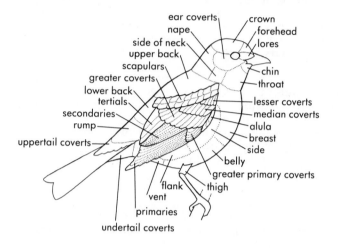

Fig. 6.

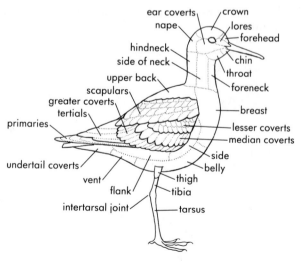

Fig. 7.

ten actually be the uppertail coverts. When these are contrastingly colored, they may be a significant part of the bird's flight pattern.

Body-plumage terms: The division of the underparts into *breast, belly, sides, flanks,* and *vent* (Figs. 6 and 7) is done for convenience in describing birds, and the dividing lines among these areas are positioned rather arbitrarily. (Some of these terms can be modified for more precise descriptions: "upper breast" or "lower belly," for example.) On the upperparts, however, the *scapulars* are well-defined tracts of feathers, distinct from the upper back. The scapulars tend to be less obvious on small birds than on large ones, but even among passerines the distinction between the scapulars and the upper back can have an important effect on the back patterns of some species.

Some alternate and miscellaneous terms:

Rectrix: Tail feather. Plural, **rectrices.**
Remex: Any one of the flight feathers of the wing (primaries, secondaries, or tertials). Plural, **remiges.**
Auriculars: Ear coverts.
Postocular: An adjective meaning "behind the eye," as in postocular stripe or postocular spot.
Interscapular region: The upper back (i.e., the area between the scapulars). The official British term for this area is "mantle," which has often been used in North America for the entire uppersurface of the wings and back (as in "dark-mantled gulls").
Ventral: Of the underparts.
Dorsal: Of the upperparts.

2

THE WINTER LOONS

RED-THROATED LOON *Gavia stellata*
ARCTIC LOON *Gavia arctica*
PACIFIC LOON *Gavia pacifica*
COMMON LOON *Gavia immer*
YELLOW-BILLED LOON *Gavia adamsii*

The problem: Immature loons and adults in winter plumage are all superficially similar, gray-brown above and whitish below. Most treatments of their identification have emphasized the distinctive bill shape of each species; unfortunately, bill shapes can be difficult to see at a distance, and difficult to judge without direct comparisons among species. Some other standard field marks, such as back pattern and bill color, are subject to variation with the bird's age. Problems have often surrounded claimed sightings of Pacific Loons in the East, Red-throated Loons inland, and Yellow-billed Loons practically anywhere.

A new dimension to the loon challenge resulted from the recent "split" of Arctic Loon and Pacific Loon, two forms that are closely similar to each other at *all* seasons.

Preliminary Points

The Arctic/Pacific Loon question: The Arctic Loon is extremely unlikely to be seen over most of North America, and it is also very similar to the Pacific Loon (differing from Common and Red-throated loons in most of the same field marks). Therefore, it is mostly ignored in this chapter. Notes on separating Arctic from Pacific appear at the end of this account.

Age variations: Winter loons are variable in appearance, sometimes enough so to affect their identification to species; and some of this variability is caused by differences among age groups.

In the larger species (Pacific, Common, and Yellow-billed), juveniles during their first winter have the back feathers (especially on the scapulars) rounded at the tips, with well-defined pale edges producing a conspicuous scalloped effect. On adults these feathers are broader and more square-tipped, with the pale edges faint, diffuse, or lacking. Adults also have white spots on the upperwing coverts, lacking in juveniles; but on a swimming loon the coverts are usually hidden by overlapping scapulars and side feathers. The postjuvenal molt of body feathers occurs gradually during the spring, followed by a more or less complete molt during summer and fall; the immatures look much like *winter* adults during their first summer and second winter, except that the white-spotted coverts on the upperwing do not begin to appear until late in the second winter. Other less consistent differences between juveniles and adults involve face and neck patterns (and in Yellow-billed Loon, importantly, the shape and color of the bill).

In the Red-throated Loon, juveniles and winter adults are difficult to separate in the field because the differences in their back patterns are more subtle. First-summer birds wear a plumage much like that of breeding adults, but duller, and in their second winter they attain adult winter plumage.

What to look for first: Instead of bill shape, look first at the *side of the neck.* In the Common Loon, the neck is *patterned,* with indentations of white back toward the dark hindneck, and forward extensions of dark feathering. In the Pacific Loon, the neck is *unpatterned,* with a sharp, straight, vertical division between light and dark. In the Yellow-billed Loon, the neck pattern is like that of the Common but usually with less contrast, and the Red-throated Loon has an unpatterned neck with a very vague division between light and dark. These things can be judged accurately at some distance, and they will immediately put you on the right track. *Face pattern* is the second major point to consider; follow up by looking at the shape (and posture) of the bill and head, relative darkness of the nape and back, and other things mentioned in the species accounts beyond.

Field Marks — Winter Loons

RED-THROATED LOON: Common in winter on Atlantic and Pacific coasts but less common southward; regular on Great Lakes, but otherwise rare to casual inland and on Gulf

Coast. Sometimes confused with Pacific Loon, rarely with Common Loon.

The Red-throated Loon (Fig. 8) has an *unpatterned neck;* the division between dark and light is not nearly so sharply defined as in the Pacific Loon. The Red-throated usually has a pale-looking face with *white or pale gray surrounding the eye.* The neck and lower part of the face are usually mostly white in winter adults, but in juveniles these areas are invaded by gray mottling or streaking; some juveniles seen early in winter are almost entirely dirty grayish on the head and neck, with very little white visible. The forehead may be quite pale in adults but is usually darker in juveniles (as dark as, or even somewhat darker than, the rest of the crown). At close range, the hindneck and crown show a finely *streaked* effect (especially in adults) that is not present in other loons.

In winter adults the upper back and scapular feathers are rounded at the tips, dark glossy gray, each feather with a pair of small, well-defined white spots near the tip. In juveniles these feathers are more pointed at the tips, dull dusty gray, with a pair of dull white spots or streaks tending to converge toward the point. This age difference is not apparent except at very close range, but it does tend to make juveniles look duller and less distinctly spotted above. Some bird books have emphasized "white spots on the back" as a field mark for winter Red-throateds, but this is helpful only if the bird is so close that actual feather details can be seen: juveniles and incompletely molted adults of all four of the other species can appear to have white-spotted or pale-spotted upperparts.

Bill shape is distinctive when seen well. The bill is narrow, with the *culmen* (upper ridge) *straight or even slightly concave* and the lower edge of the lower mandible angled slightly upward, creating an "upturned" look. This impression is enhanced by the bird's usual head posture, holding the bill *tilted slightly above the horizontal.* Note that the bill's "upturned" look becomes less obvious when the bill and head are held horizontally, as often happens. Head shape varies with the arrangement of feathers; the Red-throated occasionally shows a peaked forehead like that of the larger species, but usually its forehead looks very flat and the crown appears smoothly rounded or peaked toward the rear.

PACIFIC LOON: Abundant in winter on Pacific Coast, rare inland, casual to accidental in the East. In its Pacific wintering areas it tends to forage in deeper water than the other loons — so that while it may be the most numerous loon species offshore, it may be the one least often seen in harbors and along the immediate shoreline. It has been confused with both Common and Red-throated loons but is actually quite different from either.

The Pacific Loon (Fig. 9) has an "unpatterned" neck with a *sharp vertical division* between dark and light. The dark area of the hindneck usually extends forward in a point near the base of the throat; this is often connected across the throat in a variable "chinstrap" (especially in adults), a feature not apparent on other loons. The face pattern is distinctive: Pacifics (and Arctics) are the only loons with *no white or pale area above or in front of eye;* the dark gray of the crown extends down to enclose the eye. The face usually shows a *sharp division* between the white throat and ear coverts and the dark gray crown. A dark forehead and paler nape (silvery gray in adults, duller in juveniles) are typical of this species, but other loons may also have the nape paler than the forehead. Contrast with the pale nape helps to emphasize the *dark-backed appearance:* adult Pacifics are blacker-backed than other winter loons, with only faint paler edges to the feathers, although they have white spots on the wing coverts (usually concealed on swimming birds) and early or late in the winter they may have old or new squarish white spots on the scapulars (from breeding plumage). However, juvenile Pacifics have fairly prominent pale edges to the upper back and scapular feathers, so they do not look so dark above.

The Pacific Loon has a narrower and less angular bill than most Common Loons. It usually carries its head and bill horizontally, not uptilted as in Red-throated Loon. When the Pacific is alert its neck appears long and thin, but in a more relaxed posture the neck looks shorter and thicker. The Pacific is usually illustrated with a more smoothly rounded crown than the Common Loon, and indeed it often gives this impression, but appearance of head shape changes as feathers are raised or sleeked; the Pacific may just as often appear to have an angular forehead like the two larger species.

COMMON LOON: The most widespread loon in North America and the one most frequently seen on inland waters; sometimes outnumbered by Pacific or Red-throated in coastal areas. Has been confused with each of the other three species.

The Common Loon (Fig. 10) has a *patterned neck:* a single or double indentation of whitish back into the dark hind-

continued on p. 26

Size differences are sometimes helpful in direct comparisons; but apparent sizes of birds on open water are often deceptive.

winter adult   winter adult   early winter juvenile

Fig. 8. Red-throated Loon. The various head shapes shown depend on arrangement of feathers; they are not related to age. ID summary:
- Neck lacking strong pattern; light/dark division usually vague
- Pale face (usually) with light area surrounding eye
- Slender bill, with "upturned" lower mandible; often held above horizontal
- Finely streaked effect on hindneck and crown
- Tiny white or off-white spots on upper back and scapulars

winter adult   juvenile

Fig. 9. Pacific Loon. Head shape varies with arrangement of feathers; it is not related to age. ID summary:
- Sharp vertical division between dark and light on neck
- No light area in front of, or above, eye
- Sharp division between white ear coverts and dark crown
- Bill narrow and straight, held horizontally
- Forehead often darker than nape
- Adults: blackish back; often a dark "chinstrap"

winter adult   juvenile

Fig. 10. Common Loon. ID summary:
• Heavily patterned side of neck
• Ear coverts mostly dark
• Light area in front of and/or above eye (sometimes obscure)
• Nape usually as dark as, or darker than, upper back
• Heavy, rather angular bill

winter adult   juvenile

Fig. 11. Yellow-billed Loon. ID Summary: much like Common Loon, differing as follows:
• Outer half of culmen entirely pale (discernible only at close range)
• Often an isolated dark spot on ear coverts
• Often with paler head and neck, less distinct neck pattern
• Proportionately thick neck and large bill may make head seem small
• Adults: back may appear more strongly cross-banded
• See text for details of bill structure

neck, and an incomplete dark collar that extends forward into the white at the base of the neck; this is a good distinction from Pacific and Red-throated. So is the face pattern: the Common has *white around the eye* — not always surrounding the eye completely, but at least some pale area separating the eye from the darkness of the crown. In juveniles, the area *below* the eye is often washed with gray. As an extension of the dark area of the crown and hindneck, the *ear coverts are fairly dark*. This region includes some diffuse lighter and darker areas, so the division between the ear coverts and the white throat may appear irregular and indefinite. The hindneck often looks darker than the back (the opposite of the usual effect in Pacific Loon).

The bill is heavier, thicker, and more angular than those of the smaller species. (Young Common Loons, however, may have slightly smaller bills than adults, so a smaller-billed loon seen with Commons may not necessarily be a different species.) The Common typically carries its head and bill horizontally, and the neck often appears somewhat slumped.

YELLOW-BILLED LOON: Winters regularly in southern Alaskan waters and in very small numbers south to Washington; stragglers reach California almost annually; accidental as far east as the Great Lakes. Away from the breeding grounds and southern Alaska should be identified with extreme caution, with attention to every possible field character. Yellow-billed (Fig. 11) most resembles Common Loon, with patterned neck and heavy bill, but is even larger and bulkier and thus is unlikely to be confused with the two smaller species.

Paleness of the bill is not a good field mark: many winter Commons (especially juveniles) have mostly pale bills; most winter Yellow-billeds have at least some duskiness near the base of the bill; and some juvenile Yellow-billeds during their first autumn can have mostly dark bills that lighten gradually as the season progresses. However, the *pale culmen* (upper ridge of the upper mandible) is diagnostic for Yellow-billed. In Common Loon the culmen is dark to the tip, or very near the tip, but in Yellow-billed the culmen is pale for at least the outer half, usually the outer two-thirds, with only the basal section dark. A close view or careful study is necessary to verify this mark, because the dark culmen area on a Common tends to become very narrow toward the tip of the bill and may be hard to see against a background of dark water.

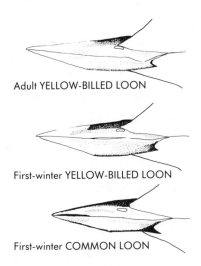

Adult YELLOW-BILLED LOON

First-winter YELLOW-BILLED LOON

First-winter COMMON LOON

Fig. 12. Comparative bill shapes and patterns.

The *"upturned" appearance of the bill* is an important mark that requires some detailed discussion (Fig. 12). The "upturn" is mostly an illusion, because the angle in the lower mandible (gonydeal angle) is only very slightly more pronounced in Yellow-billed than in Common Loon. The culmen of the adult Yellow-billed is *nearly straight*, making the lower mandible appear more angled by comparison; but juveniles have more decurved culmens, so their bill shape is less distinctive. However, Yellow-billeds of both age groups often *hold the bill tilted above the horizontal*, adding to the "upturned" look. Here are some other aspects of bill shape that can be seen at close range. In adult Yellow-billeds the cutting edge of the upper mandible dips sharply downward near the base, producing a "smile." In some immature Yellow-billeds there is a stage during development of the bill when a long narrow gap appears between the mandibles (but on rare occasions this occurs in the Common Loon as well). In both age groups, the lower edge of the lower mandible near the base of the bill is usually slightly convex in the Yellow-billed, concave in the Common. The chin feathering extends farther forward in the Yellow-billed than in the Common Loon.

Yellow-billed Loons (especially juveniles) tend to have a *paler head and neck* than Commons. The whitish area above and before the eye is usually wider. The ear-coverts area is generally paler than the center of the crown and nape, but in the middle of this pale region there is usually a *dark ear spot*, which is an excellent field mark. In the Common Loon, by comparison, the diffuse darker areas on the sides of the head rarely (if ever) create the impression of an isolated dark ear spot.

Experienced observers may notice that Yellow-billed has a *thicker neck* than Common Loon; thus the head looks proportionately smaller, and this in turn emphasizes the large bill. Another subtle distinction is that Yellow-billed has a smaller eye than Common Loon. Believe it or not, this actually can be noticed in the field!

The Problem of Pacific vs. Arctic

Arctic Loon breeds across northern Europe and Asia, and barely reaches extreme western Alaska as a breeder. The Siberian race, *G. a. viridigularis*, is the only form known to occur in North America, although the west European *G. a. arctica* would be a possible (if doubtful) stray across the Atlantic. Comments below apply only to the Siberian race of Arctic.

Summer plumage: Birders visiting the Seward Peninsula in western Alaska in summer naturally hope to encounter the Arctic Loon. The race that occurs there, as suggested by its name of *viridigularis*, has a green gloss on the throat instead of the purple usually shown by the Pacific Loon. Unfortunately, this is not enough for identification, because color of iridescence can be tricky in brief or distant views — and even with an excellent view, some Pacific Loons have green throats. Further field marks are needed.

The Arctic is a larger bird than the Pacific, with almost no overlap. This size difference would have little value for a lone bird, but if an Arctic were seen with Pacifics it should stand out as being at least 10 percent larger. Difference in bill size is even greater, so Arctics should look proportionately larger-billed. Nape color is an additional clue. Pacifics in breeding plumage are usually very pale gray, almost silvery, on the nape, contrasting with the blackish of the face. Some Pacifics are not as pale there as others. Arctics are regularly darker on the nape than the average Pacific, showing less contrast with the face. A swimming Arctic also often shows a white patch on the rear flanks, just above the waterline, which seems to be usually absent on Pacific Loon. The black and white vertical stripes on the side of the neck in summer may be more noticeable on Arctic Loon.

Winter plumage: So far, no one has come up with a certain way of separating the species in the field in winter. Supposedly, Arctics generally lack the dark "chinstrap" shown by many Pacifics. The white flank patch mentioned above is equally apparent in winter. And the size differences described above would, of course, apply in winter as well. However, field identification of these two species in winter should be considered an unresolved challenge that all of us have to look forward to.

3

THE WESTERN GREBE COMPLEX

WESTERN GREBE *Aechmophorus occidentalis*
CLARK'S GREBE *Aechmophorus clarkii*

The problem: These two very similar birds are both common over much of western North America. But for many years they had been regarded as constituting just one species, Western Grebe. Most birders were not even aware of the existence of two forms until the early 1980s — shortly before the two were formally split in 1985. Some scientists are still not convinced that the two forms are actually separate species.

In breeding plumage, Western and Clark's grebes can be distinguished easily with a good view of the face pattern. But problems arise in fall and winter, when the face patterns of both can be less distinct, approaching an intermediate condition.

Preliminary Points

General range: The relative distributions of these two species are not yet fully understood. Their breeding ranges may overlap almost completely. But Clark's is apparently very scarce at the northern end of the range, in Canada; it gradually becomes more common farther south, but remains less common than Western in most of the United States, with some local exceptions. Many older sight records of vagrants in eastern North America cannot be assigned to either species, owing to a lack of precise details, but Western may be more likely than Clark's to show up in the East.

Size: Both of these grebes tend to be larger toward the northern end of their ranges, and smaller toward the south. In both, males average larger (and proportionately larger-billed) than females. At some sites in the United States, Westerns average larger than Clark's — possibly because these areas were colonized by Westerns from populations in the north, and Clark's from smaller populations in the south — but size could never be considered a field mark.

Seasonal change: Grebes seem to be undergoing at least a slight molt at all seasons. But in general, adults of these two grebes are in breeding plumage in North America at least from April to July, and in nonbreeding plumage at least from October to February. Young birds are likely to have more indistinct or intermediate face patterns during their first winter; but by the following summer most will have face patterns like adults, with a few exceptions (possibly birds hatched late in the previous year).

The Mexican populations: Scientists who still question whether Western and Clark's are actually separate species point to uncertainties about the populations breeding in Mexico. In Mexico both forms are essentially the same size, smaller than their counterparts north of the border, and there seem to be many birds with intermediate plumage characters. These intermediate birds may be simply in nonbreeding plumage (the timing of the nesting season in Mexico is not well understood), or they may be hybrids.

Field Marks — Western Grebe vs. Clark's Grebe

Bill color: This is apparently the most consistent character for adults at all seasons. In Western Grebe, the bill is a dull greenish yellow, with a broad and diffuse blackish ridge on the upper mandible and some blackish suffusion on the lower mandible. In Clark's Grebe, the bill is bright orange-yellow, with a very narrow and sharply defined dark ridge on the upper mandible. However, when Westerns are viewed in bright, low-angle sunlight (morning or evening, with the sun behind the observer), their bills may look lighter and brighter than they really are.

Face pattern — adults in breeding season: In considering the facial markings of these two grebes, we should avoid being distracted by the fact that both show a very narrow strip of bare skin from the eye to the base of the upper mandible; this strip may look lighter or darker than the surrounding feathers.

Face pattern (Fig. 13) is a reliable mark for almost all adults at least from April through July. In Western Grebe, the dark area from the crown extends down to the area below the eye. This region may be black, dark gray, or medium gray on some birds; but there is no *white* on the lores, above the eye, or directly behind the eye. On Clark's Grebe in summer, the lores, a narrow strip above the eye, and the area behind the eye are almost always clear white, contrasting with the black crown. Some Clark's in summer may have some pale gray feathers in the area behind and above the eye, but these birds are white on the lores and immediately above and below the eye.

Only a very few summer birds are intermediate, with gray faces down through the eye, and whitish gray lores. If their bill colors are also uncertain, these birds may be hybrids.

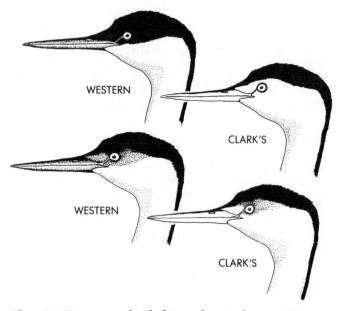

Fig. 13. Western and Clark's grebes. *Left:* two Western Grebes, showing the variation in darkness of the face; paler birds (like the lower figure) may be more frequent in winter. *Right:* two Clark's Grebes. Most immature Clark's, and many adults in winter, resemble the lower figure (with extensive gray on the face, although the lores remain white).

Face pattern — other seasons: The distinction in face patterns is less clear in winter. At that season apparently a higher percentage of Westerns have gray, rather than black, on the face. Most Clark's in winter have some gray behind the eye connecting to the black of the crown (this is especially prevalent in immatures). Almost all Clark's will still have white lores, as opposed to the gray lores in Westerns. However, some winter birds look truly intermediate in face pattern, and can be named only if diagnostic bill colors can be clearly seen. Many winter birds seen at a distance will not be safely identifiable.

Flank and back color: On Western Grebe, the flanks and back tend to be uniformly dark or blackish. On Clark's Grebe, the flanks usually have extensive light flecking, and the back may be slightly paler than on Western. But these areas are sufficiently variable that flank and back color should be considered only a minor field mark.

Voice: The advertising call of the male Western Grebe is a far-carrying, reedy, two-noted *crik crick*, with the second note sounding a bit higher. The total call lasts about one-half second. This call in Clark's Grebe is very similar in tone quality, length, and pitch, but it is all one up-slurred note without a break: *criiiick*. Both species also give a variety of other notes.

Downy young: The downy young of Clark's Grebes are whitish all over, while those of Westerns are gray above and white below.

4

MEDIUM-SIZED WHITE HERONS

SNOWY EGRET *Egretta thula*
LITTLE BLUE HERON *Egretta caerulea* (immature)
REDDISH EGRET *Egretta rufescens* (white morph)

The problem: Adults of these three species are so distinctive that they will seldom create problems in identification. Immatures, however, can be surprisingly tricky. The colors of the feet, legs, bill, and bare facial skin, which provide diagnostic marks for adults, are less distinctive and more variable on young birds. This often leads to confusion between the white immature Little Blue Heron and the immature Snowy Egret.

The white morph of the Reddish Egret is far less common than the dark morph, and when white individuals are still in immature stages, they may be overlooked or misidentified. The dark-morph immature is occasionally confused with adult Little Blue Heron.

Field Marks — Snowy Egret vs. Little Blue Heron

Leg color: The Snowy Egret's well-known pattern of black legs and yellow toes applies only to adults. On immature Snowies the legs are mostly yellowish green, with a stripe of black down the front of each leg, and the toes are often dull greenish yellow, not bright yellow. It takes a close look to see the difference between this pattern and the plain greenish legs and feet of the immature Little Blue Heron.

Bill and face color: Most Snowy Egrets have black bills, but a minority of immatures have a pale base to the bill — extending up to one-half or even two-thirds of its length — which appears very similar to the pattern of the immature Little Blue. More helpful is the color of the bare skin on the face in the loral area, between the eye and the base of the bill. In Little Blue Heron this area is gray; in Snowy Egret it is bright yellow. A possible pitfall is that the young Little Blue may show some yellow right at the base of the bill, so it is important to look at the color of the facial skin itself.

Bill shape: The difference is subtle, but the bill of Little Blue Heron tends to be stouter toward the base than that of Snowy Egret, and it often looks somewhat more decurved.

Dusky wingtips: The plumage of Snowy Egret is all white at all stages, but the Little Blue is never pure white: even in the youngest immatures, the tips of the outer primaries are gray. This gray area is not especially dark and not sharply contrasted, so it can be difficult to see, but it would be essential in identifying a young Little Blue out of range.

Behavior: Although it should never be used as the main diagnostic point for any heron, feeding behavior can be surprisingly helpful for separating these two species. Snowy Egrets when foraging tend to be active, wading in the shallows with many shuffling motions of the feet to stir things up. Little Blues usually move more slowly, and they are often seen standing still in fairly deep water, neck outstretched and leaning far forward, looking intently down at the water.

The posture in flight can sometimes provide a minor clue. All herons typically fly with their heads hunched back onto their shoulders, but they may occasionally fly short distances with their necks fully extended. Little Blue Heron has a tendency to fly with its neck extended more often than Snowy Egret or most other herons.

Field Marks — Snowy Egret vs. Reddish Egret

The juvenile white-morph Reddish Egret lacks the shaggy neck plumes and bicolored bill pattern of the adult. Dark-billed and dark-legged, it has no obvious field marks, and at a distance it might be passed off as a Snowy Egret by the unwary.

For an observer familiar with both species, differences in shape will be the most obvious distinctions. The Reddish Egret is a larger bird with a somewhat longer neck. Its legs are proportionately much longer, giving the bird its rangy look. The bill of Reddish Egret is long and straight and appears *heavy*, because it is relatively thick for almost its entire length rather than tapering toward a fine point. Besides these structural points, the lores on the Reddish are medium to dark gray (never bright yellow as on the Snowy), and its legs are usually blackish or dark gray (not mostly yellowish green as on the Snowy).

In areas where Reddish Egret occurs regularly, identifying a white immature should not be too tricky. But if you encounter such a bird out of range, it will be a challenge to prove the record. Even a perfect description will leave your local records committee wondering whether you might have seen a discolored Snowy Egret, with the colors of its lores and legs somehow dulled. To establish the subtle points of leg length and bill shape, it is almost essential that stray Reddish Egrets be photographed.

Field Marks — Reddish Egret vs. Little Blue Heron

Confusion of these two species is unlikely. Beginners may occasionally be misled by the strongly bicolored bill of Little Blue Heron, vaguely similar to the pattern of adult Reddish Egret (in the immature Little Blue, the bill base may even be pink). Thus, the immature Little Blue might be mistaken for the white-morph Reddish Egret, while the adult might be mistaken for the dark morph. Conversely, immature Reddish Egrets may occasionally be passed off as Little Blue Herons.

On Little Blue, the pale base of the bill usually blends evenly into the black tip; on Reddish Egret, the demarcation is an abrupt line separating pink and black. And any Reddish Egret old enough to show this bill pattern (immatures and perhaps some winter adults have black bills) will also have shaggy plumes on the head and neck, far more obvious than on even the adult Little Blue.

The structural differences mentioned above for Snowy vs. Reddish egrets also help to separate the latter from Little Blue Heron. Thus, Reddish Egret will have proportionately longer legs, a longer neck, and a long straight bill that looks heavy practically all the way to the tip.

Hybrids and Outlanders

Little Blue Heron × Snowy Egret: This hybrid combination has been reported several times. Adults should be recogniz-

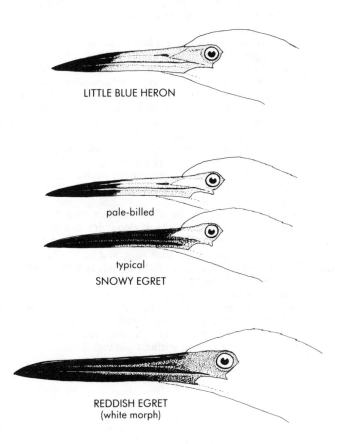

Fig. 14. Heads of immature herons. *Top:* immature Little Blue Heron, with bill extensively pale and rather thick at the base. The pale base may be tinged with gray, blue, pink, or even yellow, but the lores are gray. *Center:* two examples of immature Snowy Egret. The upper bird shows the extreme for paleness on the bill, while the lower bird is more typical. On both examples the bill is slightly thinner than in Little Blue, and the lores are bright yellow. *Bottom:* immature white-morph Reddish Egret. The bill is long, straight, and looks heavy for most of its length, and it is all dark at first; the lores are also usually fairly dark.

able by their intermediate appearance, but immatures probably would be impossible to identify in the field.

Old World species: Thornier problems involve the Little Egret (*Egretta garzetta*), which has strayed to eastern Canada and the West Indies, and the Western Reef-Heron (*Egretta gularis*), which has been reported once in Massachusetts and several times recently in the West Indies. Little Egret is extremely similar to Snowy Egret. It is supposed to differ in having lores that are gray-green, not yellow. But its lores reportedly turn orange at the beginning of the breeding season, and on the other hand, some observers think it is possible that Snowy Egret may very rarely have gray or green lores. There are probably structural differences between the two species; any possible Little Egret on this continent should be thoroughly photographed.

Western Reef-Heron, in the West African race that has strayed to the New World, occurs in two color morphs. The dark morph is a slaty bird with a white throat, and it has black legs with yellow toes; it may suggest a Snowy Egret × Little Blue Heron hybrid. The white morph is superficially much like a Snowy Egret or Little Egret. In both morphs, the reef-heron has a bill that tends to look quite heavy and is horn-colored or brown, not black. But identification of Western Reef-Herons (especially white-morph birds) out of range should be considered extremely difficult, and records are most unlikely to be accepted without photographs.

5

THE DARK IBISES

GLOSSY IBIS *Plegadis falcinellus*
WHITE-FACED IBIS *Plegadis chihi*

The problem: Their distinctive shape and color make it easy to separate these dark ibises from all other birds, even at a great distance. But separating these two from *each other* is far more difficult. Most of the differences between them involve minor details of the face pattern, requiring a close view (Fig. 15). And all of these differences vary with season and with age.

The normal ranges of the two species overlap only in a limited area along the Gulf Coast. Both species wander, however; over large parts of the Midwest, a stray ibis could easily belong to either species.

Preliminary Points

Seasonal variation: In both species, most adults are in full alternate plumage (breeding plumage) only from early spring to midsummer. The color of the bare facial skin is at its brightest only during the breeding season. In basic (nonbreeding) plumage, adults have a dark gray-brown head and neck, with numerous narrow white streaks, and dull-colored facial skin.

Age variations: In both species, juveniles are mostly dull gray-brown, with pale markings on the head and throat and glossy greenish on the wings. They start their postjuvenal molt shortly after leaving the nest. In first basic (first-winter) plumage they are much like winter adults, but usually duller, paler brown on the head, neck, and underparts. One-year-old birds in spring may look much like adults, but with duller, mottled head and neck.

In summary, only adults in alternate plumage have the rich chestnut head and neck, and breeding-season field marks should not be expected on other individuals.

Field Marks — Glossy Ibis vs. White-faced Ibis

Facial skin color: The bare skin of the face, from the base of the bill back to the eye, is mostly dull charcoal in both species on immatures and winter adults. On breeding adults, this skin develops brighter colors: blood-red to pinkish red on White-faced Ibis; blue-black, with very pale blue edges, on Glossy Ibis.

The pale edging on Glossy Ibis is worth studying for two reasons: (1) Superficially, this pale skin border resembles the white feather border on breeding White-faced Ibises; and (2) adult Glossy Ibises generally retain at least a hint of this pale edging all year, providing a potential field mark at all seasons. It may take a close view to tell feathers from bare skin, but the *shape* of the pale border on Glossy is quite consistent. The upper border widens between the eye and the bill; it connects narrowly across the forehead, but does not encircle the back of the eye. The lower border curves narrowly down against the base of the lower mandible. The color of this bare skin is bright pale blue during the breeding season, dull gray at other times.

Head feathers: For part of the breeding season, the adult White-faced Ibis has a border of white feathers surrounding the bare facial skin. The exact shape of this white area is variable, but it is frequently large and conspicuous, and (unlike the bare-skin border on Glossy) it encircles the back of the eye. This white face pattern is diagnostic for adults (barring the remote possibility of a Glossy with partial albinism around the head). Note that *juveniles* of either species may have whitish feathers on the face, but these birds will have the head and neck pale grayish brown, not rich chestnut.

Eye color: The most consistent year-round field mark for the adult White-faced Ibis is the *red iris*. In Glossy Ibis (and in the immature White-faced) the iris is dark brown. The timing of the change in eye color on the young White-faced is not fully established, but at least some of the immatures show red eyes by December of their first year.

If you can clearly see red eyes, the bird is a White-faced.

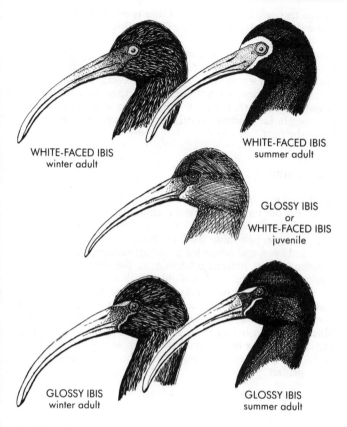

WHITE-FACED IBIS
winter adult

WHITE-FACED IBIS
summer adult

GLOSSY IBIS
or
WHITE-FACED IBIS
juvenile

GLOSSY IBIS
winter adult

GLOSSY IBIS
summer adult

Fig. 15.

However, if the eyes seem dark, it does not necessarily mean the bird is a Glossy — because on some White-faced Ibises, the red eye color may not have developed yet or may simply be hard to see.

Leg color: Both species have dull gray-green legs for most of the year. For part of the breeding season, the legs of White-faced Ibis turn bright red. Those of Glossy Ibis remain gray-green or turn reddish around the intertarsal joint only. But this distinction has limited value as a field mark, because a White-faced with bright red legs will have other obvious field marks too, while a White-faced in a transitional stage could show the same leg pattern as a Glossy Ibis.

Size: White-faced Ibis averages slightly smaller than Glossy Ibis. This difference is not significant in the field, because both species vary in size (with males averaging larger than females), and there is much overlap. Furthermore, immatures may be smaller than adults; they may not attain full adult bill length, for example, until three to six months after they leave the nest.

Quick Summary

Adults in the breeding season (with rich chestnut head and neck) can be recognized by a combination of characters of face pattern: Glossy has dark eyes and blue-black facial skin with narrow, pale blue borders; White-faced has red facial skin, red eyes, and white feathers surrounding the bare face.

Juveniles are indistinguishable in the field, and winter adults often will be unidentifiable. With a close view of winter ibises, one with obviously red eyes and plain blackish facial skin will be a White-faced; a Glossy can be named with confidence if it has a very clear indication, in pale gray, of the blue facial-skin border from summer and if the eyes are definitely dark. If a bird's facial-skin trim is not clearly delineated and if the eyes are not obviously red, it must be left unidentified.

6

THE SCAUP

GREATER SCAUP *Aythya marila*
LESSER SCAUP *Aythya affinis*

The problem: The two scaup species are practically identical in pattern. The size difference between them is not strikingly obvious even when the two are together; when they are seen separately (as often happens), size is no help at all in identification. Furthermore, two of the best-known field marks are tricky: the extension of the white wing stripe onto the primaries is variable in both species, and the color of the head gloss in males varies according to light conditions.

Preliminary Points

Seasonal change: Scaup are mainly seen by birders, and illustrated in field guides, in their "winter" plumages (which males wear for most of the year, females for about half the year). Males of both species wear "eclipse plumage" from midsummer into early fall; in this plumage they look somewhat like winter females but have a dingier appearance, much less white around the base of the bill, and sometimes paler upperparts. Females wear a "summer plumage" from spring (or even late winter) into early fall; it is not strongly different from winter plumage, but the bill may become darker, the white patch around the base of the bill may become smaller and less sharply defined, and a diffuse white spot or crescent usually appears on the ear coverts. Some females (especially Greaters?) may show traces of this white ear spot all winter.

Age variations: Young scaup in their first autumn are molting almost continuously and may be into their third generation of head and body feathers by midwinter. During autumn, therefore, their plumage patterns can be highly variable, but by early winter they can be readily identified as to sex. First-winter males are patterned approximately like adult males but are much duller: the head has little gloss, the back pattern is coarser, and the flanks may be darker. First-winter females are much like adult females but tend to have less white feathering around the base of the bill. In both sexes of both species the eye is brown in young birds, lightening to yellow in adults.

The value of practice: Birders experienced with scaup tend to base their identifications largely on head and bill shapes. This chapter describes and illustrates these marks carefully as a guide to what to look for, but there is no substitute for practice in seeing the differences. If you are fortunate enough to visit a pond or bay where both species are present, it would be most worthwhile to spend a few hours with a telescope studying their head and bill shapes from all angles, watching the apparent changes in head shape in both species. This kind of study will prepare you for identifying the scaup when only one species or the other is present.

Field Marks — Greater Scaup vs. Lesser Scaup

Head shape: The apparent head shape of any bird changes as the feathers are raised or depressed. Nevertheless, I find head shape (Fig. 16) to be the most consistently useful field mark for scaup. Of the two species, Lesser Scaup has much longer, thicker crown feathering, creating the appearance of a peak

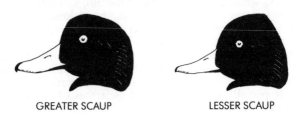

GREATER SCAUP   LESSER SCAUP

Fig. 16. Head and bill shapes of adult male scaup (adult females are similar). Note the position of the highest point on the crown.

or point toward the rear of the crown. On Greater Scaup the highest part of the crown is a more smoothly rounded peak toward the *front* of the head. This may seem like a subtle character, but with practice it can be seen even on sleeping birds.

I have never seen a Greater Scaup appear to have the Lesser's head shape even temporarily, but the peak on the Lesser's crown is often (or even usually) sleeked down, briefly, just before or after a dive. Head shape may also appear odd on a bird in the midst of molting the head feathers.

Bill shape: This character is less variable but more subtle than head shape. The bill of the Greater looks a little deeper at the base and larger, proportionately, than that of the Lesser. Viewed from the side, the upper outline of the bill makes a slightly straighter line on Greater Scaup, a slightly more concave line on Lesser Scaup, especially toward the base.

Size of bill nail: In keeping with the larger bill of Greater Scaup, the nail at the tip of its upper mandible is noticeably and proportionately larger than that of Lesser Scaup (Fig. 17). This is visible only at fairly close range, but at least on males the pattern of the bill tip adds to the effect: in Lesser, the nail is black, sharply outlined against the pale blue; in Greater, the black usually spreads out somewhat beyond the nail onto

GREATER SCAUP

LESSER SCAUP

Fig. 17. Bills of adult male scaup, one-half life size, as viewed from directly above. Compare the relative size of the nail at the tip of the bill. These represent typical individuals, but not all Greaters have the nail as large as the one shown.

the rest of the bill tip. This seems to be more variable on females, and harder to see at any rate, since their bills tend to be darker overall.

Wing pattern: This is the best scaup field mark for birders who lack comparative experience with the birds' head and bill shapes. Of course, wing pattern can be seen only on flying birds, and occasionally when a bird on the water raises its wings. As illustrated in the standard field guides, the white wing stripe on Greater Scaup typically extends out from the secondaries onto the inner six primaries, so that this white stripe reaches more than halfway from the bend in the wing to the wingtip. In Lesser Scaup, the white stripe typically extends only across the secondaries and cuts off sharply at the primaries, which are gray. Unfortunately there are a few exceptions, and about 5 percent of scaup show a wing pattern that is intermediate or approaches the condition of the opposite species. Lessers with "extra" white are mostly adult males, and Greaters that have less extensive white than average are mostly females. Keep this in mind when viewing a scaup with a suspicious wing pattern.

Color of head gloss: If you have ever noticed that drake Mallards can look purple-headed in some lights, then you already know there are dangers in relying on iridescent head colors as field marks. Never use head color as a major field mark for a lone drake scaup, or even for groups of them at a distance or in poor light. But don't dismiss head color entirely, either: when you can see both species together in good direct sunlight, the head sheen in adult males — greenish in Greaters, purple in Lessers — can serve as a good quick field mark.

Flank pattern: On adult male Greaters, the flank feathers are often a nearly immaculate white. On adult male Lessers, these feathers often have extensive fine vermiculations of gray, which are almost never visible as such in the field but may give the flank a clouded appearance. Because light conditions affect this so much, the whiter flanks of Greater Scaup are rarely helpful in identification except when you can see the two species together.

Back pattern: The backs and scapulars of adult males of both species are finely barred with black and white zigzags that blend to a pale gray when seen at any distance. These markings are finer in Greater Scaup than in Lesser (and finer still in European populations of Greater), and this can be a minor supporting character at close range. However, first-winter males of either species may have coarser back markings than adult males.

Size: Greater Scaup average nearly 10 percent larger than Lessers. But because there is individual variation, and because females average smaller than males, the size difference is no aid to identification when the two species are seen separately and only a minor point when they can be directly compared.

Face pattern in females: It has been suggested that female Greaters have more white around the base of the bill than female Lessers. This appears to be true on average but the difference is slight, and I do not find this a very helpful field mark.

A Note on Hybrids

More than members of most bird families, different species of ducks often interbreed. This is something to keep in mind when trying to name odd individuals. Once I went to look at a reported Greater Scaup and found, sure enough, a duck that was noticeably different from all the Lesser Scaup on the pond; but it was evidently a scaup × Ring-necked Duck hybrid. Years ago in Britain, what would have been their first Lesser Scaup was finally determined to be a Tufted Duck × Common Pochard. Several other hybrid combinations involving scaup-like ducks of the genus *Aythya* have been reported. Although I have not heard of any definite crosses between Greater Scaup and Lesser Scaup, identifying such a bird would certainly be a challenge! The message is that not every scaup can be safely named, and you should be willing to let a bird go if it doesn't look quite right.

7

BRIEF NOTES ON OTHER DUCKS

Among the ducks, males usually wear gaudy patterns, while females tend to be more subtly marked. Birders often learn the males first and then put off studying the females, generally identifying them by reference to the males they accompany. But naming every male duck on a pond will not necessarily give you a complete tally of every species present.

Most female ducks are fairly easy to identify if you concentrate on bill color, bill shape, and head shape. These points alone will separate almost all North American species. Bill color is especially helpful in identifying the females of dabbling ducks, but it is often different in females than in males, contrary to what one might expect.

Scoters: Female-plumaged Surf Scoters can be confused with either White-winged or Black scoters, under different conditions.

The face pattern of female Surf Scoters includes a dark crown, darker than the rest of the head, and two roundish white spots on the face: one before and one behind the eye. Many White-wingeds (especially immature females) share the two whitish spots on the face; and since their white wing patches are often invisible when the birds are swimming, they may be confused with Surf Scoters.

However, because of the arrangement of feathering at the base of the bill, the *shape* of the forward pale spot differs. On White-winged, the feathering extends well forward onto the bill; when the pale spot is present, it is usually *egg-shaped* and extends some distance forward into the bill region. On Surf Scoter, the feathering ends abruptly at the base of the bill, so the forward white spot also ends there — often as a sharp *vertical* line. Also, White-winged almost never shows a contrasting darker cap: aside from the whitish spots (which are often virtually or completely absent in adult females), the sides of the head are nearly as dark as the crown. Surf Scoter is a little smaller than White-winged, and has a long, sloping forehead; White-winged has a slightly more rounded head (Fig. 18).

When female Surf Scoters are in worn plumage, the dark separation between the fore and aft pale spots on the face may fade into obscurity, so that the only obvious pattern on the head is the contrast of pale face and dark crown. In this condition, the Surf may be mistaken for the female Black Scoter. However, Black Scoter does not have the grossly enlarged bill of Surf Scoter: its smaller bill and steeper forehead give it a very different profile. And with a careful study, even Surf Scoters in very worn plumage will not show quite the neat two-toned face pattern of female Black Scoters.

Common and Red-breasted mergansers: Females of these two species are usually not difficult to identify. The female Common has a rich chestnut face and neck, sharply set off from the white throat, while the female Red-breasted has a duller rufous-brown head grading into the whitish throat and foreneck. However, when Commons are in worn or eclipse plumage their heads can be quite dull, and throat pattern can be less reliable.

Bill shape provides a good clue in all plumages (Fig. 19). The bill of the Red-breasted is thinner than that of the Common for most of its length, and because the Red-breasted also has a steeper forehead, the junction of bill and head looks noticeably *concave*. The Common Merganser has both a thicker-based bill and a flatter forehead, so the junction of bill and head often looks practically *straight*. Emphasizing

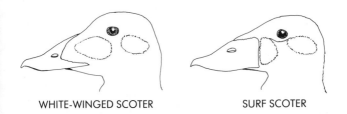

WHITE-WINGED SCOTER   SURF SCOTER

Fig. 18. Female-plumaged White-winged and Surf Scoters, to compare feathering at the base of the bill, and shape of the forward pale spot on the face. Note also head shapes, and the dark-capped appearance of the Surf Scoter.

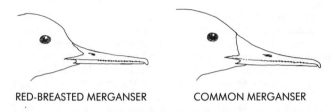

RED-BREASTED MERGANSER   COMMON MERGANSER

Fig. 19. Female-plumaged Red-breasted and Common mergansers, to compare bill shape, head shape, and pattern of feathering at the base of the bill.

the difference in bill thickness is the feathering at the base of the upper mandible. On the Red-breasted the feathering extends forward as a point onto the bill, while the Common has no such extension, so that the Common shows much more *exposed bill surface* at the base. The overall effect of this can be seen from a surprising distance. With a very close look, one might notice that the nostril is farther from the base of the bill on the Common than on the Red-breasted.

8

THE ACCIPITERS

SHARP-SHINNED HAWK *Accipiter striatus*
COOPER'S HAWK *Accipiter cooperii*
NORTHERN GOSHAWK *Accipiter gentilis*

The problem: The accipiters are the most consistently difficult to identify of North American hawks. The adult Northern Goshawk has a distinctive plumage pattern, but adults of
the other two species are patterned almost alike, and immatures of all three are very similar to each other. Size differences are not very helpful as field marks, partly because size
is so difficult to judge in the field, and partly because size
variations *within* each species are nearly as great as the size
differences *between* any two of them. The often-quoted field
mark of tail shape is subject to some confusing variation, and
other differences in flight silhouette may vary from moment
to moment depending upon the flying conditions. To top off
the problem, accipiters (when they are not migrating) stay
inside the forest more than most hawks, making them harder
to see well.

Preliminary Points

The need for caution: As recently as the late 1970s, some
ornithologists were still insisting that accipiters could not be
identified in the field, because it appeared that each well-
known field mark was subject to variations or exceptions.
This extreme view has been altered by further study of identification, but the need for caution is still apparent. Accipiters can be named with confidence only if several different
field marks are seen well. No single field mark is foolproof
by itself. No expert can name every bird seen — some views
of accipiters are just too brief or too distant. The real expert
knows when to say, "I don't know."

The value of practice: Use of shape and flight style (adding up to the "jizz," or "gestalt") as field marks demands some comparative experience. If you can get to one of those favored spots on a coast, lake shore, or ridge where raptors concentrate in migration, study as many accipiters as you can, constantly analyzing and refining your impressions. But when you try to use these characters elsewhere, remember that the surroundings can have an effect: an accipiter wintering or nesting in the woods may not behave like one cruising down a ridge or a beach.

General Field Marks — Accipiters (All Ages)

Size: In the hand, size is diagnostic: there is no size overlap among the species. In the field, size alone can rarely be used

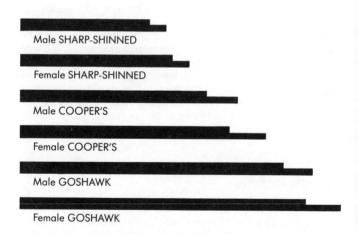

Male SHARP-SHINNED

Female SHARP-SHINNED

Male COOPER'S

Female COOPER'S

Male GOSHAWK

Female GOSHAWK

Fig. 20. Size comparison of adult accipiters. Total length, from tip of bill to tip of tail. The stepped-down section at the end of each bar shows the range from smallest to largest birds in each category; most individuals will fall between the extremes shown. Notice the great amount of variation within each species, practically overshadowing the differences among the species; size alone is a very poor field mark for these birds.

for identification. But since direct comparisons are sometimes possible, I include a graph of relative sizes (Fig. 20).

Females average noticeably larger than males (and in the Sharp-shinned Hawk all females are larger than all males). I give the separate data here only to show the amount of size variation in each species. Unless you are a raptor specialist, I don't recommend trying to guess the sexes of accipiters in the field — although it can be obvious when both members of a pair are seen, e.g., near the nest.

Tail shape: Some observers have claimed this to be the best diagnostic difference between Cooper's and Sharp-shinned, while others have argued that it is worthless. The truth seems to fall between these extremes. Tail shape is a useful difference between the two, at least part of the time, but because it varies it should be used with great caution.

On Cooper's Hawk the outer pairs of tail feathers are progressively shorter than the central pair; the tail looks more or less smoothly rounded, whether it is folded or spread. On the Sharp-shinned Hawk all the tail feathers are roughly the same length, so that when the tail is folded it appears square-tipped, slightly rounded, or slightly notched. When the tail is spread widely the tip looks rounded, of course, but not as much so as on a Cooper's in the same position. The appearance of "corners" on the tail remains more obvious on the Sharp-shinned, because the outer tail feathers themselves are more smoothly rounded on the Cooper's, while the Sharp-shinned has definite angles on the outer corners of these feathers.

Molt must be considered in any discussion of tail shape. Accipiters go through their annual molt in summer, so in late summer to early fall (until the tail feathers are fully grown) they may have misleading tail shapes. If the central tail feathers are missing, or not full-grown, an otherwise rounded tail may look notched or squared; if the outer tail feathers are not full-grown, the tail will look more rounded than normal. Usually a tail in molt will look somewhat irregular in shape, warning the observer that something is amiss.

In summary, a neatly square-tipped tail is a pretty sure sign of a Sharp-shinned, but a rounded tail does not necessarily indicate a Cooper's. Judging that a tail is rounded enough for Cooper's requires some comparative experience. Tail shape should be used only in combination with other field marks.

The Goshawk's tail is somewhat rounded, more so than in most Sharp-shinneds, but less so than in a Cooper's Hawk.

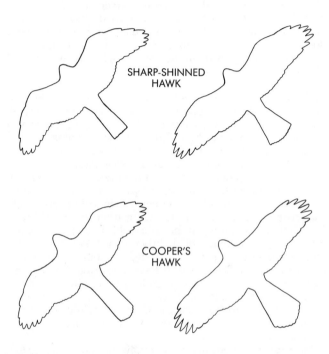

Fig. 21. Flight silhouettes. Here the great size differences among the species are ignored; they are intentionally drawn the same approximate size, scaled by wingspread, to emphasize the differences in shape.

Sharp-shinned Hawk: The head is relatively small and the wings are usually held with the "wrist" somewhat forward, so that the head hardly projects beyond the leading edge of the wing. The tail is square-tipped or slightly notched when folded and appears moderately rounded when spread.

Cooper's Hawk: The wings are relatively short — so that here, scaled to the same wingspread as the other two, the bird looks large-bodied and long-tailed. The head is large and the leading edge of the wing is usually held "flatter" than in the Sharp-shinned; the head projects well out in front of the wings. The tail is rounded, more obviously so when spread.

Head size and extension: For experienced hawk-watchers, the relatively larger head is a good way to distinguish a Cooper's from a Sharp-shinned Hawk. This distinction is especially apparent in flight because of the usual wing positions of each species. The Sharp-shinned tends to hold the "wrist" farther forward, so the head barely extends in front of the wings. Cooper's holds the wing with the leading edge appearing "flatter" in outline, so the longer head *extends well out in front of the wings*. The Goshawk is closer to Sharp-shinned than to Cooper's in this characteristic. Of course, even when the bird is gliding its wing position can change from one moment to the next, so a brief look can be misleading; but if you have a reasonably long view and some prior experience this is a very good mark.

Judging head size on perched birds is more difficult; but with a good view, the *eye* on the small head of the Sharp-shinned looks relatively *large* and *centrally positioned* on the face. The eye of Cooper's is actually a bit larger, but (because of the size of the head) it *looks relatively smaller* and is set farther forward on the face. The head of the Sharp-shinned also tends to be more rounded, the head of the Cooper's slightly more squarish.

Relative wing and tail lengths: If the human eye were capable of accurately gauging body size, wing length, and tail length on a flying accipiter, we might detect the following propor-

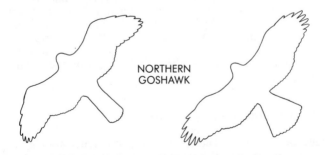

NORTHERN GOSHAWK

Fig. 21, continued. Northern Goshawk: As in Sharp-shinned, the head barely projects out in front of the leading edge of the wings. The tail is relatively short and somewhat rounded at the tip. When soaring, this species has a very buteo-like silhouette.

tions. *In relation to body size,* Cooper's has a proportionately longer tail while Sharp-shinned has proportionately longer wings. Comparing the two larger species, Cooper's has slightly shorter wings relative to its body size, but the Goshawk's tail is proportionately quite a bit shorter (by about 10 percent on average).

In actual practice, the eye tends to analyze mainly tail length, comparing it to an overall impression of size which is based mostly on wingspread (Fig. 21). Therefore, Cooper's Hawk looks *proportionately longer-tailed* than the other two: with practice this can be a helpful character. The bulky, rather broad-winged Goshawk looks distinctly *short-tailed* for an accipiter.

Leg thickness: With a good view of a perched accipiter, the thickness of the exposed tarsus is a helpful mark. On the Sharp-shinned the tarsus is thin, almost pencil-like, and this makes the bird look proportionately long-legged. The tarsus of Cooper's is at least twice as thick, so it does not look nearly as long in proportion. The Goshawk's tarsus is very thick, often making the bird look short-legged for its size.

Flight style: All three accipiters normally fly with a repeated pattern of several rapid flaps followed by a glide. Subtle differences among the species, however, can be helpful clues for experienced hawk-watchers. The wingbeats of Sharp-shinned are quite rapid, and it appears very buoyant in flight. Cooper's looks heavier, with slightly slower wingbeats; it may appear to use its tail more actively in maneuvering. The wingbeats of Goshawk are still slower, and its flight looks more powerful, purposeful, and direct. Of course, these descriptions will not have a lot of meaning until you have watched the birds yourself, carefully studying and comparing their flight styles.

Plumage Differences — Adults

Back and cap color: There is no useful difference among the species in the overall blue-gray tone of the upperparts, although in all three species females average slightly duller and browner above than males. However, *crown color* and *contrast* can help to separate Cooper's and Sharp-shinned hawks (Fig. 22). Cooper's has a *blackish cap*, contrasting abruptly with the paler nape and upper back. The crown of the Sharp-

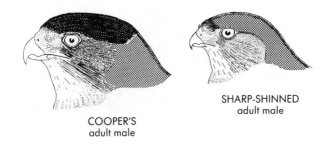

SHARP-SHINNED
adult male

COOPER'S
adult male

Fig. 22. Head patterns of adult males. The dark cap of Cooper's may be somewhat less obvious on females. Notice also the size and positioning of the eye: although it is actually larger on Cooper's, on Sharp-shinned it appears proportionately larger and more centrally located on the face.

shinned is slaty blue (males) or dusky gray (females), sometimes a little darker than the upper back but not showing a line of sharp contrast. The Goshawk's head pattern is very different, with a blackish cap and ear coverts setting off a white supercilium.

Breast color: In Cooper's and Sharp-shinned hawks the breast is narrowly barred with rufous and white. There is no useful difference between the species, but the females of both average paler and duller below than males. The Goshawk is immediately separated by its *gray* breast, finely and rather obscurely barred. But beware: the drab female Cooper's may also look gray-breasted at first glance.

Tail pattern: In fall, when they are in fresh plumage, Cooper's Hawk has a proportionately *broader white band* at the tip of the tail than Sharp-shinned Hawk (Fig. 23). The difference is most apparent from above, but it can also be discerned from below. Use of this field mark requires some practice, because the narrow white terminal band on an adult Sharp-shinned's tail can stand out conspicuously against the blackish subterminal band: the mark of a Cooper's is the width of this white band, not merely its presence. Wear on the plumage makes this mark less reliable by spring; and by early summer, shortly before the molt begins, either species may be left with virtually no white tip on the tail.

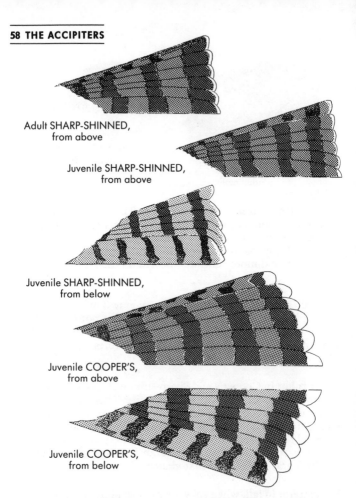

Adult SHARP-SHINNED,
from above

Juvenile SHARP-SHINNED,
from above

Juvenile SHARP-SHINNED,
from below

Juvenile COOPER'S,
from above

Juvenile COOPER'S,
from below

Fig. 23. Tail patterns of Sharp-shinned and Cooper's hawks, as they appear in fresh plumage (autumn). Notice the slight difference in pattern between adult and juvenile Sharp-shinneds, and how this affects the appearance of the white terminal band. From above, this band is more conspicuous (but still narrow) in adults; from below, juveniles can give the illusion of having broad pale terminal bands. Be aware of these pitfalls when using the broad white terminal band of Cooper's Hawk as a field mark. *Note:* The tip of the tail is often slightly more rounded than shown in female Sharp-shinned Hawks.

Goshawks can have white tail tips nearly as broad proportionately as those of Cooper's Hawk. A field mark that is occasionally useful is that the dark crossbands on the tail of the adult Goshawk usually show far *less contrast* than those of the two smaller species, so that in some views the tail can appear practically uniform.

Plumage Differences — Juveniles

Accipiters wear juvenal plumage for about a year, from the time they leave the nest until the following summer; their second-winter plumage is very much like that of the adults. Juveniles (Fig. 25) differ from adults in having brown upperparts and streaked underparts (and in being very slightly longer-tailed and shorter-winged, proportionately, species for species).

Tail tip: As in adults, juvenile Cooper's Hawks in fresh plumage have broader white tips to the tail feathers than do Sharpshinneds. Use this mark with caution, however, because in *juvenile* Sharp-shinneds (unlike adults) there is a noticeable pale area beyond the last dark tail band (see Fig. 23). As seen from below, this can be tricky: light coming through this pale area can make the tail look extensively pale-tipped in bright sunlight. Seen from above, however, the actual narrow white tip to the juvenile Sharp-shinned's tail is made even less noticeable by this medium gray area that separates it from direct contrast against the last dark tail band. Juvenile Goshawks have proportionately more white at the tail tip than Sharp-shinneds but less than Cooper's Hawks.

Because of wear, this field mark becomes difficult to use for juveniles after late fall.

Tail banding: On each feather of a juvenile Goshawk's tail, each dark crossband is shaped like a shallow V or chevron across the inner web of the feather; when the tail is fully spread it shows a *neat zigzag pattern*, especially as seen from below (Fig. 24). On the other two species, the crossbands on most of the tail feathers run straight across, so that the fully spread tail shows a more *evenly banded effect.* When the tail is *not* spread this difference is not apparent from below, because the outermost tail feathers may have irregular bands on all three species.

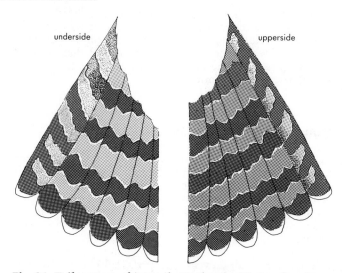

underside   upperside

Fig. 24. Tail pattern of juvenile Goshawk. Notice the zigzag pattern of the bands (especially noticeable from below, but only when the tail is spread) and their contrasting pale borders (especially noticeable from above). When seen from below with the tail folded, not spread, all three accipiters have irregular tail bands.

The Goshawk's tail bands are often made even more conspicuous by narrow *pale margins* that set them off from the ground color of the rest of the tail; these are usually best developed on the upperside but may also show on the underside of the tail. The other two species may rarely show traces of this effect on some tail feathers, but not as clearly as on the Goshawk.

Breast pattern: Typical juvenile Cooper's Hawks have the breast rather narrowly and *sharply striped with blackish brown* on a whitish background. On typical juvenile Sharpshinneds, the streaks tend to be *broader,* more teardrop-shaped, and *paler brown* or dull reddish brown on a more buffy white background; and the streaking usually extends farther down onto the belly than on Cooper's. But this difference is useful only for well-marked individuals at one extreme or the other. Both species are variable, and some Sharpshinneds in particular approach rather closely the pattern of the typical Cooper's. The streaks of the juvenile Goshawk are heavy and sharply defined like those of the typical Cooper's; they usually extend well down onto the belly and show up as heavy spots on the flanks and thighs.

Undertail coverts: On all three species the undertail coverts are basically white. On Sharp-shinneds they are always unmarked; on Cooper's they are usually unmarked but sometimes lightly streaked; and on Goshawk juveniles they almost always show *heavy streaks or spots*, at least near the tips of the feathers.

SHARP-
SHINNED
HAWK

COOPER'S
HAWK

NORTHERN
GOSHAWK

Fig. 25. Juvenile accipiters, to compare patterns of the underparts. The extreme pattern shown here for Sharp-shinned (with broad reddish brown streaks and some crossbars on a buffy white background) is diagnostic, but many Sharp-shinneds have an intermediate pattern grading toward that shown for Cooper's (with more sharply defined streaks on a whiter background). Notice that the streaking tends to end higher on the underparts on Cooper's than on the other two. Heavy markings on the undertail coverts are diagnostic for the Goshawk, but many Cooper's are lightly streaked in this area. Notice also the shape of the legs and feet: the tarsus appears very long and thin in Sharp-shinned Hawks (of all ages), proportionately shorter and thicker in the other two species.

Back pattern: The upper back and scapulars may appear more uniform on juvenile Sharp-shinneds than on Cooper's: the edgings to these feathers tend to be narrower and darker (chestnut to rufous) on Sharp-shinned, broader and often paler (rufous to buff) on Cooper's. White areas are more often apparent on the back of Cooper's Hawk, although the Sharp-shinned also has concealed white areas on the back that show up if the feathers are disarranged. This difference between the species is variable enough that it is only a minor field mark.

The juvenile Goshawk tends to be a little paler and more variegated above than the other two species, with edgings of buff, pale rufous, and whitish.

Head pattern: The juvenile Goshawk has a whitish supercilium that usually broadens behind the eye. On some individuals this is quite conspicuous. However, juvenile Cooper's Hawks (and Sharp-shinneds) also have light supercilia; usually these are narrow, but on some birds they are as broad and noticeable as on some Goshawks. So the Goshawk's white supercilium is only a minor field mark at best for juveniles.

The crown tends to be more uniformly dark in Sharp-shinneds, more strongly variegated with light and dark in Goshawks, with Cooper's intermediate between these extremes. However, this too is variable in juveniles of all three species.

Field Marks — Goshawk vs. Gyrfalcon

The Gyrfalcon (*Falco rusticolus*) is sometimes confused with the Goshawk, especially the juvenile, and especially in areas where either of these large northern raptors is a rare wanderer. Although they are not closely related, they are superficially similar in size and bulk; the difference between the rounded wingtips of the Goshawk and the more pointed ones of the Gyrfalcon may not be evident in some views. Part of the problem, too, is psychological. With birds as potentially exciting as one of these, it is harder to admit it when your view has not been good enough.

Adult Gyrfalcons (of the most frequently seen gray morph) are usually lightly marked with spots or streaks on the breast and barred on the flanks and undertail coverts, while juveniles are heavily streaked in these areas. Thus it is only the juveniles of Gyrfalcon and Goshawk that are likely to be confused; obvious plumage characters should separate the adults in any reasonably good views.

Here are some field marks for distinguishing juvenile Gyrfalcons and Goshawks:

Tail pattern and shape: The Gyrfalcon's tail is more densely and narrowly barred; the light bars are usually narrower than or equal in width to the dark bars, and all are very even-edged. The effect is very unlike the broad zigzag tail bands of the juvenile Goshawk (Fig. 24). The difference in tail shape is more subtle, but the Gyrfalcon's tail usually looks less substantial; when folded, it tends to narrow somewhat toward the tip, while the Goshawk's tail usually appears to broaden toward the tip. The Gyrfalcon's tail is roughly square-tipped when folded, slightly rounded when spread, while the Goshawk's tail is distinctly rounded or somewhat wedge-shaped at the tip (more obviously so when spread).

Overall color: The juvenile Goshawk always has warm brown tones; the juvenile Gyrfalcon is more of a brownish gray. However, because of the tricky effects of winter light, this color difference can be surprisingly indistinct; it should never be used as a major point for identifying these birds.

Color of bare parts: In the juvenile Gyrfalcon, the legs, feet, and cere (bare fleshy area at the base of the upper mandible) are blue-gray to greenish gray. In all Goshawks (and in adult Gyrfalcons) these areas are yellow.

Wing shape and flight style: Although it is generally true that the wingtips are rounded in accipiters and pointed in falcons, the wing shapes of these two large species can be deceptive. Both species sometimes soar, with wings and tail fully spread, and in this position the Gyrfalcon's wingtips appear very rounded. Even in normal flight the Gyr's wingtips are somewhat more rounded, less pointed, than those of most typical falcons. And when the Goshawk is flapping or gliding with the wings partially pulled in, its wingtips can look rather pointed. Therefore, use of wing shape as a field mark requires consideration of the flying conditions.

The Goshawk's normal flight style consists of several deep, quick flaps, followed by a flat-winged glide. The Gyrfalcon usually flies with steady, shallow wingbeats, occasionally broken by long bouts of soaring.

At most times and places south of the Arctic, the Gyrfalcon is the rarer of these two species. It should always be identified with special caution, and with attention to as many field characters as possible.

9

BASICS OF SHOREBIRD
IDENTIFICATION

Learning to recognize most shorebirds, members of the sand-piper and plover families, can be a distinct challenge. Most shorebird species occur in two or three noticeably different plumages. Most of these plumages lack obvious field marks; they tend to be subtly patterned in brown or gray. And it is unsafe to base an identification on assumptions of what bird "should" be there, because many shorebirds are long-distance migrants and can show up far from their normal ranges. For these reasons, beginners are often confused or frustrated by these birds.

But — for exactly the same reasons — it seems that most experts love the shorebirds. When you have studied and learned these birds, when you realize that you can name everything out there on the flats, the sense of accomplishment is very rewarding . . . and you begin to see that those subtle plumage patterns are really beautiful.

Getting started is the hardest part. With a daunting array of similar birds massed on the mud flats, and with an equally daunting array on the pages of the field guide, birders may be uncertain where to begin with shorebirds. The following pointers may be helpful.

Look at shape: I cannot overemphasize the importance of shape in recognizing shorebirds. Shape provides up to 90 per-cent of the evidence in our sight identifications. To prove this to yourself, pull out your favorite field guide and compare: what are the field marks for separating the winter-plumaged adult Stilt Sandpiper and Red Knot? Or the winter Long-billed Dowitcher and Dunlin? Or, to carry it to an extreme, the winter Western Sandpiper and Willet? There are size dif-ferences, of course, which are especially useful when the birds are seen together, and there are differences in flight pat-tern. But solitary standing birds are just grayish above and whitish below, and all the obvious field marks that come to mind involve shape: bill length, leg length, neck length, the overall shape of the head and body.

While the difference in silhouette between the elongate Stilt Sandpiper and the dumpy Dunlin will be immediately obvious, experienced shorebird-watchers use a host of more subtle shape clues, such as the precise shape of the bill tip, the angle of the forehead, the size of the head relative to the size of the body, the length of the wingtips, and so on. If you make a conscious study of these subtleties on various shore-birds, you'll be able to use them subconsciously later, for very rapid identifications.

In looking at shape, of course, be aware of how much a bird's posture may change its apparent shape. In a flock of one species, an agitated bird may crane its neck, sleek down its feathers, stand more erect, and thus appear to be a totally different shape from its fellows. Simply watching for a while is the best way to understand and allow for such variations.

Many shorebirds are more distinctive in breeding plumage than at other seasons. If you have a chance to see birds like the Red Knot, Dunlin, or Stilt Sandpiper in spring, take time to study their shapes and postures; you will then find them easier to recognize when you see them in fall.

Separate the age groups: During fall migration, identifying the species of any difficult shorebird usually requires identi-fying it to age *first*. This is not as complicated as it might sound. Juveniles differ from adults in predictable ways, mainly involving the freshness of the plumage and the pat-terns on edges of feathers on the upperparts and wings. Once you learn to separate adults and juveniles in a few species, the others will be much easier.

The "fall" migration of shorebirds begins before the Fourth of July in several species. The first southbound birds are all adults. Juveniles of many species begin to appear by late July or early August. (The timing described here, however, does not apply as well to shorebirds that nest south of the Arctic, like Wilson's Phalarope, which may begin fall migration by the middle of June!) Over most of North America, August is the best time to study the differences between adults and ju-veniles.

As a rule, adult shorebirds molt from breeding plumage to winter plumage after they start their southward migration and mainly after they arrive on the wintering grounds. When they appear at our latitudes in late summer, they are wearing feathers they have had for some time; colors have begun to fade, edges are abraded, patterns are less distinct. Juveniles, however, come south in brand-new plumage. All their feathers are very fresh, and this is emphasized in many species by sharply defined pale edges, or pale spots along the edges, on the scapulars, coverts, and tertials. (Knowing the various feather groups obviously helps here; see "Terminology and Bird Topography" in chapter 1.)

So in late summer, juvenile shorebirds are generally very crisp-looking birds, often with sharply defined and neatly spaced pale edgings that give the effect of bright lines, scales, or scallops on the upperparts and wings. Older birds are generally duller on the upperparts, with the borders of feathers less clearly defined because pale edges have been worn away and any contrast has been reduced by fading. See Figs. 31, 32, and 33 in chapters 11 and 12 for comparisons: compare the worn adult Sharp-tailed Sandpiper with the fresh juvenile of that species, or look at the late-summer adult Western Sandpiper as compared to juvenile Western and Semipalmated.

Naming any tough shorebird with confidence in fall, then, demands aging it first. Birders who ignore this principle may run into serious difficulties. For example, there have been a few cases of Least Sandpiper being misidentified as Little Stint, an extremely rare vagrant from Eurasia. Juveniles of the two species are not at all similar to each other; adults of the two species are easily distinguished from each other; but *juvenile* Least Sandpipers in fresh plumage have bright foxy-rufous tones, rather like the color of spring *adult* Little Stints. This would never pose a problem in identification if the age of the bird were considered first.

In some species, such as Common Snipe and several plovers, the differences between adults and juveniles are subtle at best. By late fall, in most species, age differences have become less significant, and aging usually has little effect on specific identification in winter or spring.

Consider unfamiliar plumages of familiar birds: An offbeat problem sometimes crops up when birders run into an old familiar shorebird in a new plumage. For example, we are so accustomed to seeing the Sanderling in its whitish winter plumage that we may be thrown off by its bright breeding plumage, which sometimes gets it mistaken for a Rufous-necked Stint.

Study voice: Learning the calls of shorebirds can be a challenge. It takes a lot of concentration to be sure, on a crowded mud flat, which birds are making which calls. But learning them is well worthwhile. When studying large groups of shorebirds, I often hear the uncommon species before I see them, especially if they are flying over or just arriving. Some shorebirds are more easily identified by voice than by any visual point; for a few species in certain plumages, voice is the *only* reliable distinction.

Beware of leg color: Many bird guides point to leg color as a major field mark for various groups of shorebirds. And it's true that for beginners, struggling for any clue, this is a worthwhile straw to clutch. But at advanced levels of shorebird identification it is not very important. No expert uses leg color to separate Least and Semipalmated sandpipers, for example; it is much easier to tell these two apart by bill shape; head and body shape, overall plumage color, and differences in pattern.

One problem with leg color is variability. In some species the legs run the gamut from brown to green to yellow, or even to orange; other species are more consistent but in rare instances may have the "wrong" leg color. Another problem is that the feet and legs are especially subject to discoloration by mud or muck. Also, leg color can be hard to see on the smaller species: the "yellow" legs of the Least Sandpiper, which may actually be dull greenish brown, often simply look dark in the field.

Of course, leg color should be carefully determined on any mystery shorebird. But using it as a major step in the narrowing-down process would be sure to mislead you part of the time.

10

THE DOWITCHERS

Text by Claudia Wilds

SHORT-BILLED DOWITCHER *Limnodromus griseus*
LONG-BILLED DOWITCHER *Limnodromus scolopaceus*

The problem: The two species of dowitcher are so similar — and Short-billed Dowitchers in breeding plumage are so variable — that they were considered one species by most ornithologists until 1950. Despite their names, there is so much overlap in their bill lengths (and in other measurements) that only a small percentage can be identified in the field by any means other than details of plumage and differences in voice. Most treatments do not take into account the three races of Short-billed Dowitcher, which require attention to different features in breeding plumage relative to the Long-billed Dowitcher in different parts of North America. Information on the distinctive juvenal plumage, in which the two species are readily identified, has not been readily accessible to most birders.

Preliminary Points

Variations due to age and season: The first decision to make is whether the bird is in breeding plumage (from April to August); nonbreeding plumage (both species from September to March, a few Short-billed Dowitchers all year); juvenal plumage (August to October); or in molt between two plumages (adults from March to early May and from late July to early September; juveniles from October to December). This chapter describes and treats these plumages separately.

Regional variations: While there is only one form of Long-billed Dowitcher, there are three subspecies or races of Short-billed Dowitcher, which are quite distinctive from each other in breeding plumage. The nominate race, *griseus*, breeds in

Canada east of Hudson Bay and migrates along the Atlantic Coast. North of New Jersey this is the only race seen in spring and by far the most common one in fall. The inland race, *hendersoni*, breeds in Canada west of Hudson Bay; its broad migration route lies across the continent from the eastern Great Plains to the Atlantic Coast, where it is the most common race from Virginia south. (Thus observers on the East Coast, especially south of New York, must cope with both these races.) The Pacific Coast race, *caurinus*, breeds in southern coastal Alaska and migrates west of the Rockies. Both *hendersoni* and *caurinus* may occur close to the Rockies and in the western Great Plains, where Short-billed Dowitchers are rare.

Size and proportions: Long-billed Dowitcher females are on the average larger, with longer bills and legs, than Short-billed Dowitchers of both sexes, but both species are very variable in size. In a potentially mixed flock, it certainly pays to look closely at the birds that appear noticeably larger than the rest, but it is dangerous to call any but an extra-large bird with an extra-long bill a Long-billed Dowitcher on these grounds alone. Until you have put in so many hours studying Short-billed Dowitchers that you are confident that you know the full range of variation in size and bill length of that species, it is probably best not to use these features as diagnostic at all.

Tail pattern: A good look at a dowitcher's tail feathers, normally possible only when the bird is preening or when it is flying directly away, can be diagnostic (Fig. 26). (The tail feathers of a standing bird are usually concealed by the barred uppertail coverts, which are much the same in both species, and by the tertials and primaries of the folded wing.) On all dowitchers the tail is barred black and white, or black and cinnamon: the cinnamon is present in breeding plumage on a majority of Long-billed Dowitchers and a minority of Short-billed Dowitchers. Most Long-billeds have narrow light bars, less than half as wide as the dark bars; they are never wider than the dark bars. Short-billeds are more variable, but most have light bars as wide as or wider than the dark bars. If you can decide that the light bars are *much* narrower than the dark bars, you are looking at a Long-billed. If you are sure the light bars are *wider* than the dark bars, you have a Short-billed. In between, this character is not safe to use.

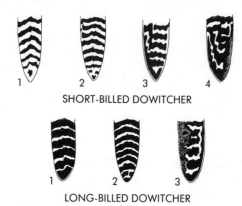

SHORT-BILLED DOWITCHER

LONG-BILLED DOWITCHER

Fig. 26. Patterns of tail feathers in dowitchers. These are tracings of the uppersides of central tail feathers from Short-billed (upper four) and Long-billed (lower three) dowitchers. The extreme pattern shown at left (number 1) for each species is diagnostic but uncommon; the patterns shown at number 2 are more typical. Short-billed Dowitchers are quite variable in their tail patterns; those shown at right (numbers 3 and 4) are not uncommon. Long-billed Dowitchers are less variable, and the pattern shown at right (number 3) is rare. However, there is enough variation in both species that tail pattern cannot be used as a field mark for some dowitchers.

Dowitchers — Nonbreeding plumage

In this plumage (Fig. 27) dowitchers of both species are brownish gray on the upperparts, throat, and breast, and white on the belly. In direct comparison the Long-billed Dowitcher is darker above and on the breast; the gray usually extends farther down toward the belly and the barring on the flanks may not be as heavy as on a Short-billed Dowitcher. If you cannot judge the tail pattern or hear the call, however, it is almost always dangerous to label a dowitcher in nonbreeding plumage.

SHORT-BILLED
DOWITCHER

LONG-BILLED
DOWITCHER

Fig. 27. Dowitchers in winter (basic) plumage. *Left,* Short-billed; *right,* Long-billed. The color and pattern of the throat and breast are sometimes helpful clues at close range. On the Short-billed these areas tend to be lighter overall, with fine streaks and speckles that may extend down onto the white upper belly and sides. On the Long-billed these areas tend to be a smoother and darker gray, with this color extending farther down (onto the lower breast/upper belly) and ending more abruptly. Many individuals are not as well marked as those shown here; generally this character alone is not safe for identification.

Dowitchers — Breeding plumage

In this plumage (Fig. 28) the key features to check are the background color of the lower breast and belly; the pattern, density, and distribution of the dark markings on the underparts; and, in the range of *hendersoni*, the brightness of the upperparts.

Short-billed Dowitcher: *L. g. griseus* has a white belly and often a white lower breast. The orange-red or brownish red of the underparts is confined to the throat and breast and perhaps a wash on the undertail coverts. This subspecies has medium to heavy spotting on the breast and is often strongly barred on the sides and flanks. The entire breast may be covered with fine, scallopy bars, and the belly may be barred and

SHORT-BILLED
(*griseus*)

SHORT-BILLED
(*hendersoni*)

SHORT-BILLED
(*caurinus*)

LONG-BILLED

Fig. 28. Dowitchers in breeding (alternate) plumage. Short-billed Dowitcher: *Upper left, L. g. griseus.* Extensive white belly area; breast usually heavily spotted or barred, sides and flanks often heavily barred. Upperparts with narrow rusty edges. *Upper right, L. g. hendersoni.* Underparts mostly orange-red, with very little white; breast usually lightly marked with roundish spots; sides and flanks may be lightly barred. Upperparts with broad rusty edges. *Lower left, L. g. caurinus.* Almost always has white belly, heavy spotting on breast, coarse barring on sides (a few patterned more like *hendersoni*). Upperparts with narrow rusty edges. *Lower right,* **Long-billed Dowitcher:** Underparts uniformly brownish red (with white barring in very fresh plumage). Foreneck and breast densely spotted, sides and flanks barred, center of belly unmarked. Upperparts with narrow dark rusty edges, some narrow white tips.

Note: Birds are shown as they would appear about mid-May, when most of the coverts of the wings may still be gray-brown. At the height of the breeding season, e.g., late June, most of the coverts may be patterned like the scapulars.

spotted. The dark feathers of the upperparts have narrow rusty edges and gray or rusty tips.

L. g. hendersoni in breeding plumage is largely or entirely orange-red or brownish red below, with white, if present, confined to the center of the lower belly and vent. Typical birds of this race look somewhat paler behind the legs than before them, but the underparts may be quite uniform. The foreneck and belly are lightly spotted, the center of the breast is a little more spotted, and the sides of the breast moderately spotted. The marks on the sides of the breast may look like short dashes or chevrons but are usually round. The sides and flanks may be lightly barred, and the undertail coverts are usually spotted. The upperparts have broad rusty feather edges, making a bird in full breeding plumage look very bright.

L. g. caurinus in breeding plumage almost always has a solid area of white on the belly and undertail coverts, is heavily spotted on the breast, and is coarsely barred on the sides. The individuals that are all-red below are much more lightly marked, resembling *hendersoni*. The upperparts have narrow edges, like those of a Long-billed Dowitcher but more orange.

Long-billed Dowitcher: In breeding plumage the underparts are uniformly brownish red except in very fresh plumage (up to mid-May), when the white tips of the feathers form white bars across the red; the white disappears with wear. The foreneck and breast are densely spotted but the center of the belly is clear. The sides of the breast, the sides, the flanks, and usually the undertail coverts are marked by narrow bars, often chevronlike. All these marks except those on the sides of the breast and perhaps the undertail coverts have normally worn away by late July. The upperparts have narrow feather edgings of deep rusty red, with white tips on the back and scapulars.

Dowitchers — Juvenal Plumage

Short-billed Dowitcher: Just when the adults are looking really worn and faded and the upperparts are frayed and drab, about the beginning of August, the first brightly marked juveniles appear south of the breeding grounds (Fig. 29).

They are instantly recognizable by the broad, neat, reddish buff edges of the back feathers, scapulars, and tertials, forming a bold crisscross pattern across the dark feather centers. The tertials are marked internally by conspicuous loops, streaks, or (most often) "tiger-stripe" barring of the same reddish buff. (Juveniles of the two more easterly races are indistinguishable in the field; *caurinus* juveniles have narrower, redder feather edges but their tertials show the unmistakable Short-billed pattern.)

The underparts are richly washed with reddish orange over the underlying winter pattern of gray breast and white belly; the throat and breast are marked by fine dark streaks and speckles, usually visible only at close range.

Though the reddish tone of the upperparts gradually fades to a light buff, this plumage is largely intact well into October, and the tertials may be identifiable until spring.

Fig. 29. Juvenile dowitchers. The scapulars and tertials (see detailed enlargements) provide the best field marks. On Short-billed juveniles these feathers are broadly edged with reddish buff, and the tertials and some of the scapulars have extensive internal markings of the same color. On Long-billed juveniles the scapulars have narrow (often scalloped) edges of dark rust, and the tertials have narrow, very even pale edges. Also note that fresh juvenile Short-billeds have the underparts washed with warm reddish orange, with fine dark streaking on the throat and breast; juvenile Long-billeds are duller and grayer below, usually without any breast streaks.

Long-billed Dowitcher: The Long-billed juveniles first arrive in the Pacific Northwest in early September but are extremely scarce farther south and east until the last third of the month. (By then the adults of both species are in gray nonbreeding plumage.)

The Long-billed juvenile is much darker above than the Short-billed juvenile; the feather edging is narrower and is more chestnut-red when fresh. On the back feathers and scapulars the edging is often scalloped, on the tertials very even. Internally the tertials are normally plain; on a minority of birds, a pair of small reddish spots or short streaks can be seen near the tip.

The underparts are duller than those of the Short-billed juvenile: grayer on the throat and breast, and less rusty overall. The streaks and speckles are lacking or nearly so.

As the juvenile molts in October and November, the small dark scapulars that remain become conspicuous against the large, gray scapulars of nonbreeding plumage. These feathers and some of the tertials may be retained into the new year, allowing specific identification as long as they are present.

Voice

When details of plumage are of no help in making a decision, a call provides the only reliable clue.

Short-billed Dowitcher: The *tututu* described in most bird guides works very well, as long as you are aware of the variations. As a flight call it is clear and mellow and may be shorter by a syllable or two, sounding much like the call of a Lesser Yellowlegs; as an alarm call it is lower and harsher, reminiscent of the call of a Ruddy Turnstone, and may be expanded into several syllables. Especially in spring, you may hear a *tiddle-whee* as well. Feeding flocks are generally silent unless they are disturbed, but you may occasionally hear a single *tu* or *t'tu*.

Long-billed Dowitcher: The high thin *kee* or *keek*, uttered usually as a single or triple note, serves as both a contact call in a feeding flock and a normal flight call. When a bird is alarmed, the call becomes louder and more strident but does not otherwise change in quality. Long-billeds also emit a harsh, high rattle. They are generally much more talkative than Short-billeds.

11

SHARP-TAILED AND PECTORAL SANDPIPERS

SHARP-TAILED SANDPIPER *Calidris acuminata*
PECTORAL SANDPIPER *Calidris melanotos*

The problem: Sharp-tailed Sandpiper, an Old World species closely related to our Pectoral Sandpiper, is a regular visitor to Alaska and the Pacific Northwest. It has also occurred farther afield, including the Atlantic Coast, and could probably turn up practically anywhere in North America.

Most Sharp-taileds found on this continent are juveniles. These birds are quite distinctive, but overly optimistic birders may be misled by juvenile Pectorals that superficially approach the appearance of Sharp-tailed.

Adult Sharp-tailed Sandpipers are usually distinctive in full breeding plumage. However, at a certain stage of molt from breeding to winter plumage, they can be remarkably similar to Pectoral Sandpipers; they may be overlooked at such times.

Preliminary Points

Variation in Pectoral Sandpiper: Seasonal change in Pectoral is slight, other than changes from fresh to worn plumage. But some seasonal tendencies are worth noting. The throat and lower face are streaked (often heavily) on breeding adults, mostly unmarked on other plumages. Breast markings are heaviest and darkest on breeding males, more uniformly streaked on females, and often more lightly streaked on juveniles. The supercilium (eyebrow) is often cleaner and more conspicuous on juveniles, more obscured by mottling on adults. Juveniles may show more obvious rusty tones on the crown. Thus, juvenile Pectorals differ from adults in some ways that make them slightly more like Sharp-taileds.

Variation in Sharp-tailed Sandpiper: Unlike Pectoral Sandpiper, the Sharp-tailed has three distinctly different plumages that vary dramatically in the pattern of the underparts. They are described in some detail below.

General Field Marks — Sharp-tailed Sandpiper vs. Pectoral Sandpiper

Shape and related points: The two species are roughly the same size on average. Sharp-tailed averages shorter-billed (by about 15 percent); but there is much overlap, so this is only a minor aid. In both species, males average larger and longer-billed than females. The bill of Sharp-tailed, besides being shorter, often looks straighter and darker, with only a small pale area at the base of the lower mandible. Sharp-tailed also usually appears to have a flatter crown, and it often looks shorter-necked and slightly heavier-bodied. The body shape and hunched posture may create the illusion that Sharp-tailed has shorter legs than Pectoral, but its legs actually average very slightly longer.

Voice: The typical call of Pectoral is a hoarse, low *chrrrt*, sometimes doubled or tripled. Sharp-tailed gives a more musical *trreep* or *tree-reap*. Both species call most often in flight.

Field Marks — Juvenile Sharp-tailed Sandpiper

Peak passage of juvenile Sharp-tailed in the Northwest occurs from late September to early October; reports of juveniles south of Alaska before September should be reviewed with great care.

As with most shorebirds, field marks for juveniles do not work for adults, so it's crucial to determine age first (Fig. 30). Adults in fall (both Sharp-tailed and Pectoral) are in worn plumage, with abraded feathers and reduced contrast on the scapulars and wings, unlike juveniles with their fresh plumage and bright feather edgings.

The most obvious field mark for juvenile Sharp-tailed is the breast pattern and color. The breast is heavily streaked at the sides, but only very *lightly streaked* toward the center, and the upper breast is washed with a *warm orange-buff* that may extend down onto the flanks. (Juvenile Pectoral may also have a buff wash on the breast and flanks, but it has conspic-

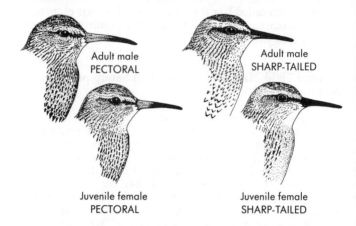

Adult male
PECTORAL

Adult male
SHARP-TAILED

Juvenile female
PECTORAL

Juvenile female
SHARP-TAILED

Fig. 30. Age differences in Pectoral and Sharp-tailed sandpipers. *Left*, Pectoral Sandpipers (adult male in summer, above; juvenile female in fall, below). Juvenile has paler supercilium, lighter streaking on breast, whiter throat. *Right*, Sharp-tailed Sandpipers (adult male in summer, above; juvenile female in fall, below). Differences between age groups in pattern of underparts is obvious. Compared to Pectoral, Sharp-tailed tends to have shorter, darker bill, broader supercilium, more obvious eye-ring, and usually flatter crown. In both species, males usually have longer bills than females.

uous streaking down to an abrupt demarcation on the lower breast.) Juvenile Sharp-tailed has a striking face pattern, with a *broad supercilium* (eyebrow) that tends to become wider and whiter behind the eye. On the Pectoral, the supercilium is usually duller and more mottled, and usually narrows somewhat behind the eye. Sharp-taileds of all ages usually show a more obvious *white eye-ring* than Pectorals, and on juvenile Sharp-taileds this eye-ring is usually set off only by the broad rufous-brown eyestripe, while the rest of the face looks quite pale. The bright *chestnut cap*, set off by the paler nape and broad supercilium, is conspicuous on Sharp-tailed — but not diagnostic, since Pectorals often have chestnut on the crown as well. In pattern of the upperparts, Sharp-tailed is not very different from Pectoral: the feathers are blackish with conspicuous buff, rufous, or whitish edges on the back, scapulars, and tertials. On Sharp-tailed the two white stripes on the scapulars may be less obvious, and the coverts may show less contrast than on Pectoral, but these are not major field marks.

The only likely source for confusion would be the occasional young Pectoral that has both a fairly bright chestnut crown and relatively light streaking on the breast. The way to prevent this error is to study any suspected Sharp-tailed thoroughly, checking all points rather than a few "key" marks.

Field Marks — Adult Sharp-tailed Sandpiper

In North America there are still very few records of adult Sharp-taileds outside of Alaska. Evidently spring adults are exceedingly rare out of range. However, Britain now has quite a few records of adults in late summer and fall; such birds may be overlooked to some extent in North America.

Fig. 31. Juvenile Pectoral Sandpiper compared to three stages of Sharp-tailed Sandpiper. *Lower left,* juvenile; *lower right,* adult in full breeding plumage; *upper right,* adult in molt from breeding to winter plumage, as it might appear in late summer or early fall.

Breeding plumage: Sharp-tails in anything close to breeding plumage should be easily recognized by the broad, shallow V-shaped or crescent markings extending down the sides and flanks. These birds usually look more distinctly spotted with black on the face, and more spotted (less streaked) on the upper breast, than Pectoral Sandpipers. Like the juvenile, the adult Sharp-tailed usually has a more obvious eye-ring and broader supercilium (eyebrow) than the Pectoral.

Transitional plumage: Sharp-taileds in molt from breeding to winter plumage are potentially very tricky. They can lose most of the broad chevrons on the sides and flanks while retaining most of the streaking on the chest, and thus appear much like Pectorals. Birds in molt can be quite variable, and a suspected adult Sharp-tailed in fall must be viewed with care. First, of course, study the amount of wear to be certain the bird is an adult. Then consider the pattern of the underparts. Molting Sharp-taileds will look uneven or "messy" because the incoming plumage is quite different from the pattern it replaces. (On molting Pectorals, the new pattern matches the old, so birds in transition are less obvious.) A molting Sharp-tailed will probably never duplicate the sharp cutoff on the breast that is the trademark of the Pectoral — it will have the pattern broken up by white toward the center of the breast, or the remains of some dark chevrons on the flanks, or, more probably, both. Look for distinctive aspects of face pattern — eye-ring, bill color, broad supercilium. The relative brightness of the cap and back, sometimes claimed as a field mark, is probably too variable in both species to be useful.

Winter plumage: Sharp-tailed normally winters in and near Australia, but it has been known to winter in California. Winter plumage is duller than other plumages in Sharp-tailed, with broad, buffy gray edgings on the upperparts and a pale gray wash crossed by fine black streaking across the breast. The face retains suggestions of summer pattern (broad supercilium, eye-ring, some chestnut on crown). Young Sharp-taileds may molt into first-winter plumage (much like adult winter plumage) by late fall.

Comparisons to Other Species

RUFF (*Philomachus pugnax*): The female Ruff ("Reeve") is not much larger than the Sharp-tailed Sandpiper, and in juvenal plumage it wears similar colors: rufous tinges on the upperparts and buff (sometimes bright orange-buff) on the breast. However, the female Ruff is longer-legged, and it has a longer neck between the rather bulky body and the small head. The face usually looks quite plain on the juvenile Ruff, lacking the strong pattern of the Sharp-tailed.

COX'S SANDPIPER *(Calidris paramelanotos):* One of the world's least-known shorebirds, described from the wintering range (Australia) in 1982, Cox's Sandpiper has sparked debate as to whether it is a species or a well-marked hybrid. Whatever it is, it astounded the birding world by straying to *Massachusetts* in 1987. It looks quite like a Pectoral Sandpiper but with a much longer bill; for more information, see Bibliography.

12

SEMIPALMATED AND WESTERN SANDPIPERS

WESTERN SANDPIPER *Calidris mauri*
SEMIPALMATED SANDPIPER *Calidris pusilla*

The problem: For many years, birders separated these two species on the basis of bill length. Few observers questioned the accuracy of this method, even though the average differences involved mere millimeters, and it had already been shown that there was some *overlap* in bill length between the species. The bubble finally burst in the mid-1970s, when ornithologist Allan Phillips pointed out that almost *all* of the hundreds of Semipalmated Sandpipers reported on this continent in winter were probably misidentified — they were mostly Western Sandpipers.

Winter, admittedly, is by far the most difficult season for distinguishing these two species. At other seasons, there are plumage characters that can be diagnostic for identification. But these characters must be applied with caution, and with an appreciation for the way that these small sandpipers rapidly change in appearance during the year.

Preliminary Points

Ruling out other species: In addition to the three small "peeps" regular on this continent (Least, Western, and Semipalmated), four other species occur in Eurasia. All four of the latter have been recorded in North America: numerous times in Alaska, extremely rarely elsewhere. One of those (Temminck's Stint) is distinctive in a number of ways, and another (Long-toed Stint) is quite similar to Least Sandpiper. That leaves two (Little Stint and Rufous-necked Stint) that are very similar to Semipalmated Sandpiper, especially in juvenal and winter plumages.

One point that immediately separates these two outlanders from our species is a detail of foot structure. Semipalmated Sandpiper is named for the fact that it (like Western, but unlike other small *Calidris* species) has "semi-palmations," partial webs, limited to the area near the base of the toes. You can actually see these in the field, with a close approach and careful study. A valuable educational project for any North American birder: go out and look at the feet of Semi or Western, whichever you have readily available, and see this webbing for yourself — then look for the lack of it on a Least Sandpiper. (Beware of the effects of mud caked on the toes, which can make any bird look web-footed.) Once you have observed the partial webbing on Semi and Western, you may be ready to recognize the lack of it on a stray stint.

Be forewarned, however, that the "stint fever" that has come to North America recently has produced many dubious records. An odd-looking small sandpiper is still extremely likely to be one of our species, not a stray. To avoid adding to the problem, I am not even describing any of the vagrants in this book. An excellent reference, however, is the Veit and Jonsson paper noted in the Bibliography.

Bright-plumaged adult vagrants from other continents might be picked out, with caution, by anyone. But you should not even look for vagrant stints in *other* plumages until you are sure that you know Semipalmated and Western sandpipers from A to Z.

General Field Marks — All Ages

Bill shape: The *typical* bill shapes of these two species are visibly different, and this can allow for rapid identification of some individuals. The classic Semipalmated bill is short, straight, blunt, and slightly expanded at the tip. The classic Western bill looks thinner at the tip, partly because the bill is longer; it is somewhat drooped toward the tip as well. With practice, you can recognize these extremes easily.

Unfortunately, there is much variation. In both species, females average longer-billed than males. There is also a geographic trend in bill length in Semipalmated, with the longest-billed individuals at the eastern end of the breeding range. Some female Semis from eastern Canada are actually longer-billed than some male Westerns; throughout their ranges, many individuals will be "too close to call" on this character. However, the Semis that migrate through western North America are likely to be among the *shortest*-billed individuals, which is some help to birders there.

Voice: Small sandpipers are capable of making a great variety of call notes — for an example of this, try listening carefully to Least Sandpipers in a place where they are common. Generally the loudest and most recognizable calls are those given in flight, while birds on the ground give softer and more variable sounds; but even the flight calls can vary substantially. Taking that into account, Western and Semipalmated do differ in their most typical calls. Western gives a *kreeip*, less drawn out and with more of a "strained" or "squeezed" quality than the call of Least Sandpiper. Semipalmated has a short, rough *cherrt* that sounds lower-pitched. This voice difference is not diagnostic by itself — Westerns, in particular, give many abbreviated calls that sound much like those of Semipalmateds — and to use voice even as a minor field mark, you must listen to a particular individual for some time.

Overall shape and behavior: Shape differences between the two species are very slight, but with typical individuals we may notice that Western tends to be very slightly longer-legged and has a slightly larger, more squarish-looking head. Semipalmated looks a little more compact in most dimensions and has a slightly more rounded head, but its wingtips are at least as long as (or longer than) those of Western.

Feeding behavior is variable in both, but there is a slight tendency for Semipalmated to do more delicate picking at the surface while Western does more probing (as one might expect from the difference in bill length). Western is more often found wading in belly-deep water.

Field Marks — Summer Adults

Separating adults of these two species in full alternate (breeding) plumage, as seen in late spring, is not too difficult (Fig. 32). Birders who rely too heavily on a sense of overall color may misidentify some Semipalmateds as Westerns: it is true that Western generally has brighter colors, but some Semis are more warmly colored than others and may look pale rufous around the upperparts, face, and sides of the crown. However, such birds are likely to have an overall brown cast. The rufous color on Western is *brighter* and shows strong *contrast* against the rest of the plumage — rufous scapulars against gray wing coverts, rufous face markings against pale gray nape and breast. Western in this plumage also usually

WESTERN SANDPIPER   SEMIPALMATED SANDPIPER

Fig. 32. Adult sandpipers in breeding plumage.

has a paler look to the face, with a wider and cleaner supercilium. Both species have some dark arrowhead-shaped marks on the underparts, but in Western these are larger and more conspicuous and extend much farther down the flanks.

Field Marks — Juveniles

When fresh juveniles of both species first arrive south of the breeding grounds (late July to early August in most areas), they are not too difficult to separate (Fig. 33). To learn these birds in juvenal plumage, look at them as early in the season as possible; they become more difficult later on.

Overall color: The fresh juvenile Semipalmated gives the first impression of being *all one color*, a beautiful soft buffy gray, with some individuals having a pale rufous suffusion throughout. On closer inspection, this overall unicolored look turns out to be made up of buffy white or pale rufous-buff edgings to the gray feathers of the wings, scapulars, back, and head. The fresh juvenile Western has a *two-colored* look: at first it is chestnut-rufous and pale buffy gray; later it becomes more simply rufous and gray. The key is the *contrast* between the upper scapulars (which are black with deep chestnut edges) and the lower scapulars (which are extensively gray). Thus the two or three upper rows of scapulars stand out as a contrasting dark patch, the most richly colored part of the bird.

WESTERN   SEMIPALMATED

Fig. 33. Sandpipers in fresh juvenal plumage. Notice the strong contrast created by the upper scapulars of the Western.

Face pattern: The facial expression is a very good mark on typical birds. The Semipalmated usually shows a little more contrast in the face. It has darker lores, darker ear coverts, and a more contrasting dark cap, showing up a narrow pale eye-ring and making the pale supercilium stand out prominently. These aspects, combined with the short bill, may explain why the face of a typical juvenile Semi looks vaguely "plover-like." The Western generally has a paler face overall. Although the forward part of the Western's supercilium is actually wider and its forehead is whiter, these areas do not stand out because there is less contrast. It shows less of a "capped" look, and its eye-ring is usually inconspicuous.

Change in appearance: By late August or early September, wear and fading have already begun to affect the appearance of these juveniles. The colors have become duller, and the pale edgings have become narrower and less contrasty.

Timing of the molt may affect the identification of these young birds. Juvenile Westerns begin to molt much earlier — as early as the first part of August, when they are still migrating in North America. As the strongly patterned juvenal feathers are replaced by the gray of winter plumage, these Westerns begin to take on a grayer and plainer appearance, but the contrast between this gray and the retained rufous continues to make them look different from any plumage of Semipalmated. Often the last feathers to be molted are the forward scapulars, so that a young Western that has almost completed the molt to first-winter may be mostly gray with a spot of rufous on the shoulder.

Juvenile Semipalmateds, although they may fade considerably, generally do *not* actually begin to molt into first-winter plumage until after they have reached the wintering grounds — which are to the south of us. But after early September, it can take a close look to see the difference between juvenal plumage that has largely faded and juvenal plumage that has largely been replaced. To learn to recognize these birds in the latter part of the season, it is tremendously helpful to go out shorebirding regularly from late July into the fall — you will get to follow the gradual changes in the appearance of these sandpipers.

Field Marks — Winter

Identifying a Semipalmated Sandpiper in midwinter in North America is nearly impossible given the state of current knowledge. Here are some thoughts, however, for those who would like to try to establish some criteria.

For starters, it would be helpful (although it would not be enough) to find a "classic" short-billed individual. If the bird consistently gave short, low-pitched calls, that would be helpful as well. It would be worth trying to get tape recordings of the calls of any such problem bird. Unfortunately, the best way to induce a small sandpiper to call is to flush it, and if you make the bird fly, it may fly away for good.

Plumage differences between Western and Semipalmated in winter are very slight and variable. Semipalmated tends to be just a little darker and browner on the upperparts, and its forehead and face may be darker. The narrow eye-ring may continue to be a little more noticeable on winter Semipalmated than on Western. The sides of the chest may tend to be slightly more finely streaked in Western, more blurry in Semipalmated. Even with all these points in mind, a sight identification may be open to question; but if you are sure you have found a Semipalmated in winter on this continent, by all means document it thoroughly.

13

THE JAEGERS

POMARINE JAEGER *Stercorarius pomarinus*
PARASITIC JAEGER *Stercorarius parasiticus*
LONG-TAILED JAEGER *Stercorarius longicaudus*

The problem: Although there are only three species of jaegers, telling them apart is a challenge that has innumerable angles and complications.

Adult jaegers, despite the variability of their plumage patterns, can usually be identified by the shapes of their central rectrices (tail feathers). However, Parasitic Jaegers with unusually long central tail feathers are often mistaken for Long-taileds; the same error has been made with adult Pomarines at odd angles. On the other hand, Long-tailed Jaegers with shorter central rectrices are sometimes passed off as Parasitics. And in any of the three species, the central tail feathers may be broken off or missing, so knowledge of other field marks is essential.

Immatures are much more difficult. Jaegers probably take about four years to reach adulthood, going through a series of distinct plumages. But the sequence of these plumages is still poorly understood — and research on them is difficult, because the birds may spend their early years entirely at sea. To make matters worse, at every age there is a great amount of individual variation, which blurs the distinctions among age groups and among species. It becomes difficult to find any one field mark for one species that cannot be matched by some individuals of some age group of another species.

There are two kinds of situations in which jaegers, especially immatures, pose problems:

1. *At sea.* Viewing conditions cause much of the difficulty here. Strange light conditions, motion of the boat, and distance all work against the observer, making fine details almost impossible to see. On the positive side, a good boat trip may let you encounter numbers of jaegers; and if some of

them are "easy" adults, they can provide you with a basis for comparing the shapes and flight styles of the others.

2. *Inland.* Aside from their regular passage on the Great Lakes, a few jaegers turn up every year well inland in North America. These birds may remain at small lakes for several days, allowing fairly close approach and good views. But for inland observers, who rarely see jaegers, such a bird can be a major source of frustration: it may remain unidentified (or uncertainly identified) even after a lengthy study. Because such a bird probably also represents a significant record wherever it turns up, an identification based on general size impressions is not likely to be accepted; more solid criteria are needed.

General Field Marks — Jaegers (All Ages)

Size: Most books used by birders indicate a bird's size by a measurement of total length, from tip of the bill to tip of the tail. This can produce very misleading impressions of size for jaegers, because of the varying lengths of the elongated central tail feathers. (A short-tailed Pomarine Jaeger, for example, can be much shorter in overall length than a Long-tailed Jaeger, even though the Pomarine is clearly the larger bird.) Wingspread, even though it is a rough measurement at best, is a better index of size for field use.

wingspread of:	is about equal to that of:
Pomarine	Ring-billed Gull, Heermann's Gull
Parasitic	Laughing Gull, Mew Gull
Long-tailed	Black-legged Kittiwake, Common Black-headed Gull

This is useful *only* with direct comparisons, as when a jaeger is chasing a gull; it doesn't work with lone birds. For example, it would take rather odd perceptions to say that a lone Pomarine Jaeger "looked about the size of a Ring-billed Gull" — seen alone, the Pomarine's bulky shape and powerful flight actually create the illusion of a substantially larger bird.

Shape and flight style: Once you have plenty of experience with jaegers and you are out at sea or on the tundra where you can expect them, you may find that you can identify many at a distance by their characteristic shape and flight action. Some bird guides offer lengthy descriptions of these aspects, supporting the idea of naming the birds by "jizz," or general impression. This does sound like a lot more fun than studying fine details of plumage and structure. Unfortunately, however, until you have done your own observing, reading such descriptions is not very helpful. To recognize jaeger species by general impression, you have to see the birds for yourself and study them repeatedly.

When you see a jaeger that can be identified with certainty — a well-marked adult, for example — watch it for as long as possible, studying its shape (Fig. 34) and its action in flight, and try to store this image for comparison with other individuals.

Pomarine looks heavier than the other two, with a bulky body, thick neck, and broad-based wings. Its wingbeats in normal flight are relatively slow and deep, like the action of a large gull. Parasitic is not so broad-winged and has a slimmer neck and body, although it can often look very bulky, at least temporarily. Its wingbeats in normal flight are quicker than those of Pomarine, broken by short glides, and its flight may bring to mind the flight of a falcon. Long-tailed has the slimmest body and smallest head of these three. The narrow wings contribute to the impression of a *long* tail, even without the central streamers. Its wingbeats in normal flight are buoyant, and the action may bring to mind a medium-sized tern. Any of the three species, of course, will "shift into high gear" when chasing other birds, changing their flight action. And bill shape (discussed in detail under juveniles) contributes to the overall look of each species.

White primary shafts: There are differences among the species in the number of outer primaries that have white shafts. Many birders are aware of this detail, but it has been misinterpreted remarkably often, even in print. The distinction applies only to the *shafts* of the primaries, *not* to the surfaces of the feathers themselves. Because of the way the primaries overlap, none of the shafts except the outermost is visible from the underside of the wing, so this character has no effect on the amount of paleness visible on the primaries from below.

Focusing on the upperside of the outermost primaries, Long-tailed Jaeger shows two primary shafts that are white

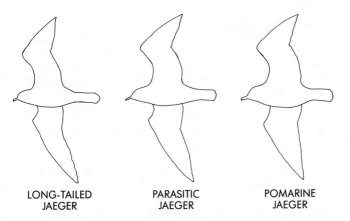

LONG-TAILED
JAEGER

PARASITIC
JAEGER

POMARINE
JAEGER

Fig. 34. Flight silhouettes of jaegers. Although there are distinct *differences* in size among the three jaegers, here they are all drawn the *same* size — and with their elongated central tail feathers broken off — to emphasize differences in overall shape. Long-tailed is the slimmest of the three, and its wings are relatively narrow at the base, so that the extension of body and tail behind the wings is noticeable; even without the elongated central feathers, the tail looks long. At the opposite extreme, Pomarine is heavy-bodied, thick-necked, and broad-winged. Parasitic is intermediate in shape between the other two, but its impression in the field is usually closer to that of Long-tailed.

(or pale ivory) for most of their length. The next shaft inward is sometimes pale brown (and may look whitish in some lights). The rest of the primary shafts are dark brown; but because their surfaces are glossy, they may momentarily catch the light and look whitish, especially toward their bases.

In Parasitic Jaeger the number of pure white primary shafts varies from three to six; in Pomarine it is usually more than five. However, when the wing is less than fully spread, even a Pomarine can appear to have only one or two white shafts. Thus, despite the prominence that has sometimes been given to this characteristic, the number of white primary shafts is rarely much help in field identification.

Field Marks — Adults

As noted at the beginning of this chapter, identifying adults solely by the shape of the central tail feathers can lead to errors. To be comfortable with naming even adult jaegers, it helps to know other field marks. The following is a brief review of some aspects of plumage pattern that can be helpful.

Adult jaegers molt into a winter (basic) plumage that is less distinctly marked than the summer (alternate) plumage. This is a complication in *describing* adult plumages, but it is not usually a major problem *in the field* in North America. Winter adults usually have barring on the rump and undertail coverts, narrow light barring on the back, more extensive and uneven dark markings on the underparts, less sharply defined black caps, and shorter central tail feathers than summer adults. (All but the last of these points applies mostly to light-morph birds; dark birds show less change.) Thus, in a number of ways, adults in basic plumage look like subadult birds.

The molt to basic plumage takes place mostly after the adults have moved south from the breeding range. The molt back into alternate (breeding) plumage takes place mostly before spring migration. Long-tailed Jaeger — which migrates south early, molts late in fall, and winters below the equator — is very unlikely to be seen in full basic plumage in North American waters. On the other hand, many adult Pomarine Jaegers go through the year without molting into full alternate plumage; they wear many barred basic feathers through the spring and summer, adding to the excessive variation in adult Pomarines.

The notes on adults below apply mainly to their appearance in spring, summer, and early fall. I'll also refer occasionally to their basic (winter) plumage.

Color morphs: Most Pomarine Jaegers are of the light morph; dark birds rarely make up more than 20 percent of a breeding population. In Parasitic, the ratio of dark to light birds is extremely variable: dark birds can make up anything from 0 to 95 percent of a breeding population. Adult Long-taileds in summer show very little variation. The dark morph in adults is exceedingly rare and has seldom been documented.

Although it is convenient to speak of light- and dark-morph jaegers, this conventional distinction can also be misleading, since it implies that all fit neatly into these two categories. Actually, Pomarine and Parasitic jaegers are quite variable, with many intermediates.

Pattern of underparts: In summer plumage, Long-tailed is the least variable of the three in pattern of the underparts. Its throat and chest are immaculate white, with the gray from the undertail coverts extending forward as far as the lower breast. In full winter (basic) plumage it may develop a dark chestband, but this plumage is unlikely to be seen in North America.

The underparts of adult Parasitic vary from light (with or without a dark chestband) to very dark. But in summer plumage, the underparts of this species tend to look *smooth*, without barring or mottling; the chestband, if present, is a wash of smooth gray. By comparison, adult Pomarine is far less smoothly marked on the underparts. Light-morph adults usually have dark barring along the sides and flanks, under the wings; the chestband, usually but *not always* present, is mottled or barred, not smooth. The darkest Pomarines still look mottled, not the evenly dark smoky gray of the darkest adult Parasitics. Adding to the varied look of summer Pomarines is the fact that many of them retain some winter (basic) plumage, so that their undertail coverts or even their entire underparts may be heavily barred.

Head pattern (Fig. 35): The adult Long-tailed Jaeger has a rather small black cap, sharply defined and neat in outline. The black is more extensive on the light-morph Pomarine, often creating the effect of a ragged-edged hood. The light-morph Parasitic has a blackish or charcoal cap, intermediate in extent between those of the other two species, often looking less sharply defined at the edges.

The pattern of the malar area (extending back from the base of the lower mandible) contributes much to the overall head pattern of adults. In Long-tailed, only the base of this area is black, and the rest is white (or yellowish white) like the throat; the sharp edge of the black in the malar area connects evenly with the black edge of the cap. In light-morph Parasitic, the malar area is variable. It may be whitish with a gray smudge in the center, or it may be gray, shading toward black at the center; but it almost always pales somewhat toward the base of the bill. In adult Pomarine the entire malar tract is typically black, creating a "heavy-jawed" appearance and emphasizing the heavy bill.

In most adult Parasitics, the cap pales noticeably toward

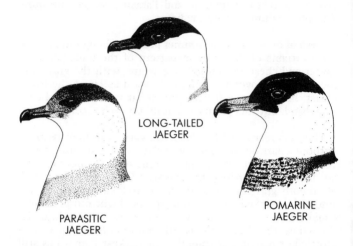

Fig. 35. Jaeger head patterns on light-morph adults in spring and summer. Parasitic has a cap that becomes paler toward the base of the bill, especially in the malar region; its dark chestband, when present, is usually relatively smooth. Long-tailed has a very neatly defined black cap, and in summer it never has a dark chestband. Pomarine has a black cap that is usually strongly developed in the malar region; its dark chestband, when present, is often more mottled or barred than that of Parasitic Jaeger.

the base of the upper mandible, going from blackish at mid-crown to smoky gray at the sides of the forehead to whitish at the point where the feathering meets the bill. This pattern does not occur in the other two species, although light Pomarines sometimes have a narrow light area where the feathers meet the upper mandible.

Color of upperparts: The darkness of the back and the upperside of the wings is variable in both Pomarine and Parasitic, but both species are very dark there, and Pomarine is often virtually black on the back. Long-tailed is consistently medium gray on the back and wing coverts, paler than most Parasitics. On all three species the secondaries are black, but only on Long-tailed do the secondaries create an obvious *dark trailing edge* (because of the contrast against the paler coverts). This trailing edge rarely contrasts on Parasitic, and almost never on Pomarine.

Field Marks — Juveniles

The difference between "juvenile" and "immature" takes on particular importance with jaegers. As I've noted, it may take four years for the birds to achieve full adult plumage, and they are extremely variable for most of that time; but they are *juveniles* (i.e., in juvenal plumage) only from the time they fledge until their first winter. Jaegers in their first southward migration are juveniles, and they differ from later immature plumages in important ways.

Jaegers in far-inland areas tend to show up in fall, and most are either adults or juveniles, not intermediate-age immatures. Trying to figure out a juvenile jaeger (Fig. 36) can be a frustrating experience for an inland birder. In several cases, birders have studied, photographed, and identified a juvenile jaeger — only to find out years later that the photos proved the bird to be not the species they had thought. Obviously, sightings that are *not* backed up by photos are open to considerable doubt, even if they cannot be so clearly disproven.

General appearance: Among autumn immature jaegers, juveniles are the ones with the neatest, cleanest appearance. Older immatures may be in molt, with a combination of old and new feathers in the wings, or feathers missing from the wings or tail, but juveniles are in uniformly fresh plumage. Their general color tends toward *brown* or gray-brown. Their dark upperparts and wings, except on the darkest individuals, have neatly arranged pale barring. Winter adults and older immatures may also have some pale bars on the back, but the pattern on the *wings* of juveniles is distinctive, with neat pale tips on the coverts creating a precise barred or scalloped effect (which carries over onto the scapulars).

A few of the darkest juveniles may lack all pale markings and look uniformly sooty all over. Identifying these birds as juveniles will be very difficult without an excellent view (to be sure of the very fresh condition of the plumage), and of course naming them to species will also be quite a challenge.

Central tail feathers: Given a good view, preferably from directly above or below (not always the easiest angle to achieve), the shape of the central tail feathers on a juvenile jaeger makes an excellent clue (Fig. 37). These central feathers extend slightly past the rest of the tail, and on fall juveniles the tail should still be in good condition and the shapes easy to discern.

On Pomarine juveniles the central tail feathers barely ex-

Fig. 36. Juvenile Parasitic Jaeger in early autumn. This bird shows several of the characteristics typical of juvenile jaegers. Most important is the pattern of the back and wings, with sharply defined pale tips on the coverts and the scapular feathers, creating a neatly barred or scalloped effect; older jaegers (even adults) in basic plumage often have some barring on the back, but they do not duplicate this wing pattern. Also typical of juveniles (though not diagnostic for this age group) are the overall dusky look, the strong barring on the undertail coverts, and the vague barring on the rest of the underparts.

Points on this bird that are good indications for Parasitic, although not diagnostic, are the pale nape; the streaking on the head; the pale feathering in the malar region, creating little contrast against the bill; and the very irregular pattern of the barring on the undertail coverts. Almost diagnostic for juvenile Parasitic are the conspicuous pale tips on the outer primaries, very rarely shown by juveniles of the other species.

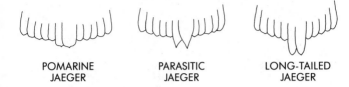

POMARINE
JAEGER

PARASITIC
JAEGER

LONG-TAILED
JAEGER

Fig. 37. Central tail feathers of juvenile jaegers, as viewed from the upperside; see text for discussion.

tend past the others, and they are generally blunt, looking squarish or rounded with only slight points showing. The short, broad extension that they create may be overlooked altogether in a casual view. On Parasitic juveniles, the central feathers extend more obviously; they vary from slightly to noticeably longer, and taper to a sharp point. On Long-tailed juveniles these feathers are often noticeably long, extending up to an inch past the rest of the tail. They may have fine spiky points, but their overall shape is distinctly *rounded* at the tip; and they often have *whitish marks* at the tip, which are usually lacking in the other two species. It is important to remember that these characters apply only to first-autumn juveniles. After early winter, wear on the feathers will make these shapes unreliable, and in older birds the tail shapes are different.

Bill shape and color: The shape of the bill is worth noting for any jaeger, but it is described in this section because it may be especially helpful for young birds out of range. Close-up photos that show the precise shape of the bill may provide the clincher for identifying a difficult young jaeger. The color and pattern of the bill are more variable but also worth noting.

Pomarine has a long and heavy bill, with a heavy hooked nail at the tip of the upper mandible. The *gonydeal angle* on the lower mandible is usually prominent. The base of the bill is almost always pale in juveniles, contrasting sharply with the black tip; the size and pattern of the bill may bring to mind a first-winter Glaucous Gull. (The bill base is often somewhat pale in older Pomarines as well.)

Parasitic is variable in bill size. Some large-billed individuals might suggest Pomarine, although they rarely show such

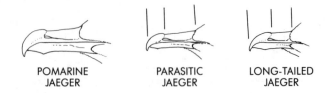

POMARINE JAEGER   PARASITIC JAEGER   LONG-TAILED JAEGER

Fig. 38. Bill shapes of jaegers. Only the closest of views or best of photos will reveal this kind of detail, but these subtleties can be very helpful on difficult individuals. Especially on Parasitic vs. Long-tailed, look at the length of the nail on the upper mandible (from the tip of the bill to the back of the nail) and compare that to the length of the rest of the upper mandible; the different ratio is apparent. Also note the gonydeal angle (on the lower mandible): it is most prominent on Pomarine, and it is set farthest back proportionately on Long-tailed.

an obvious gonydeal angle. Small-billed Parasitics might suggest Long-taileds. However, there are small but definite differences in bill shape between Long-tailed and Parasitic (see Fig. 38). On Long-tailed, the basal section of the upper mandible is *shorter* and the nail on the bill tip is *longer* than on Parasitic. Either of these factors would be obscure by itself, but the different *ratio* between them is noticeable. On the lower mandible, the distance from the tip back to the gonydeal angle (which can be hard to see) is longer on Long-tailed even though the bill is shorter, creating again a different ratio.

General plumage color: Although juvenile jaegers are as variable as adults, each of the three species has some general tendencies in color and pattern that can be very helpful in identification.

Juvenile Parasitic Jaeger is typically the most colorful of the three, usually warm brown with edgings of rufous and golden-buff that give the back and wings a strongly scalloped effect. The underparts are usually barred (except on the darkest birds), but the bars are very uneven or wavy except on the flanks. The head usually shows a pale nape and streaked face.

Juvenile Long-tailed is usually much grayer. Its upperparts

are marked with narrow whitish edgings, which often look straighter (less curved or scalloped) than on the other two species. Its chest is often very uniform dark brownish gray, but the uppertail coverts, undertail coverts, and flanks are usually heavily barred with black and white.

Juvenile Pomarine is usually brown in tone but darker and duller than Parasitic, with buff-white bars on the back and a uniformly dark head. When it has barred underparts, the bars tend to be stronger and more even than on Parasitic.

Head pattern: Mentioned briefly above, this is frequently a good clue. On Parasitic the *nape* is usually *very pale* brown or buff, and the face and nape usually have noticeable dark *streaks*. The juvenile Parasitic's malar area (next to the base of the lower mandible) is usually pale, creating little contrast with the bill. On juvenile Pomarine the head is usually darker and more uniform, without an obvious pale area on the nape, and the head may be very lightly barred but is *almost never streaked*. The Pomarine's *malar area* is usually quite dark, helping to emphasize the pale base of the bill. Juvenile Long-tailed has a variable head pattern; it sometimes looks almost white-headed, but its nape is usually at least somewhat pale and it usually has some fine streaking on the face.

Wing-pattern details: The great majority of juvenile Parasitics (except a few of the darkest individuals, and very rarely others) have *buff tips* on the outer primaries that look like conspicuous *pale chevrons* on the wingtip when the wing is folded. Pomarine and Long-tailed almost never show this effect, or show it only very faintly, so it is a strong indication for Parasitic.

Some sources have mentioned a pale area at the base of the underprimary coverts on juvenile Pomarine, forming a narrow pale crescent on the underwing, just beyond the bend of the wing, that is separate from the extensive pale bases of the undersides of the primaries themselves. In my experience this is not especially helpful — Pomarine juveniles usually do have this mark, but many juvenile Long-taileds and some juvenile Parasitics can have a strong suggestion of it, so it becomes a matter of degree and may be hard to judge under some conditions.

Uppertail coverts and undertail coverts: Almost all juvenile jaegers (except perhaps the darkest ones) have conspicuous barring on the tail coverts. However, the pattern of this varies. On both Pomarine and Long-tailed, the bars run more or less straight across the feathers, creating a pattern of even barring. On Parasitic, the bars on each feather are usually irregular, producing a pattern of wavy or uneven bars. Color is a slight clue here as well: the barring on the uppertail coverts and undertail coverts tends toward black and white in Long-tailed, toward chocolate and cinnamon-buff in Parasitic, with Pomarine usually somewhere between these extremes.

Field Marks — Older Immatures

Like some of the larger gulls, jaegers probably take up to four years to reach adult plumage. Unlike gulls, however, jaegers are not easy to age. Light-morph jaegers tend to become lighter and more adultlike in pattern as they mature, but telling the age of a given bird (between juvenile and adult) will be at least partly guesswork.

Beyond juvenal plumage, young jaegers have the central tail feathers shaped like those of adults at the tips, but much shorter. Otherwise, because of their extreme variation, there are almost no plumage characters for separating the species.

Fortunately, these intermediate-aged birds rarely show up inland, and at sea they are routinely identified (by observers familiar with the species) by their shape and flight style. Perhaps the worst jaeger problems involve the immatures in very worn plumage that sometimes show up on southern beaches in early summer. The best approach with one of these birds is to try to get close-up photographs that show the overall shape of the bird, its size compared to other species if possible, and especially the shape of the bill.

Comparisons to Other Species

HEERMANN'S GULL: Surprising as it may seem to birders unfamiliar with Pacific Coast species, Heermann's Gull is not infrequently mistaken for a jaeger — if only temporarily. There are two major reasons for this. (1) Heermann's seems to be even more pushy than most gulls and is often seen chasing other species. (2) Heermann's overall grayish appearance is suggestive; moreover, it has an uncommon but regular plumage variant in which there are white patches on the primary coverts, recalling the white that often shows at the bases of the outer primaries themselves on jaegers. It is little wonder that a dark bird with white wing-flashes, in hot pursuit of another bird just offshore, may be momentarily mistaken for a jaeger (or even a skua!).

SKUAS: Dark Pomarine Jaegers seen on offshore trips are sometimes misidentified as skuas by hopeful observers. However, the reverse almost never happens — a real skua is most unlikely to be passed off as a mere jaeger.

Skuas are larger and bulkier than Pomarine Jaegers, even thicker-necked and more barrel-chested; their wings are very broad and in normal flight look more rounded at the tips. The breadth of the wings helps to accentuate the skuas' short-tailed look. Broad, crescent-shaped white patches at the base of the primaries are very conspicuous on both the underside and the upperside of the wings. Dark young Pomarines often have a great amount of white at the base of the primaries on the underside, but they rarely if ever show such extensive and well-defined white patches on the wings' upper surface.

The taxonomy of skuas is still being debated, and the field identification of some of the southern ocean forms is still a major problem. The two species recognized from North American waters so far are Great Skua (*Catharacta skua*) and South Polar Skua (*Catharacta maccormicki*), but several other forms (species?) are possible. Some sources of information are listed in the Bibliography.

14

BASICS OF LEARNING THE GULLS

Yes, the key phrase here is: *learning* the gulls. That is not what most birders want, of course. Most of us would like to have a quick reference that would allow us to go out cold and identify the first odd gull we see. Unfortunately, it doesn't work that way.

The problem is that gulls are too variable for that approach. Since all gulls go through various plumages before they reach adulthood, the 25 or so North American species (plus a few recognizable subspecies) present nearly 200 different plumages. Even that number could be manageable — but each of these plumage classes of each species is affected by a large amount of variation. Most gulls are gradually and continuously changing in appearance throughout at least their first two years of life, and no two individuals look exactly alike even at the same age. And then there are various hybrid combinations, some of which are relatively frequent. For a field guide to cover all this variation adequately would take at least 2,000 illustrations. We would never have time to flip through the book and find the picture to match our odd gull before the bird flew away. In other words, there will never be a quick solution that will allow the beginner to identify every gull immediately. If you want to identify gulls tomorrow, you'll have to take the time today to learn the basics — to *learn* the gulls.

A good start would be to go back and read "Basic rules of field identification" in chapter 1. All of these rules apply particularly well to gulls, and all of the "common pitfalls" listed are especially prevalent in this subfamily. But there are a few additional points to consider.

Approaches to Gull Study

Start in winter: Unless you live in an area where no water remains unfrozen through the cold months, winter (especially early winter) is the time to work on learning gulls. That is when most are in their freshest plumage, and when the distinctions among various age groups are most apparent. During fall and spring their patterns are complicated by molt. In summer, the plumage of some gulls (especially one-year-old immatures) may become incredibly worn and faded.

Work your way up: On your first serious attempts to study gulls, don't try to name every bird in a mixed flock or zero in on something complicated like Thayer's Gull. It is better to start by studying a gull with a simpler plumage sequence, such as Bonaparte's or Ring-billed. Don't be discouraged if you have to leave many birds unidentified at first. Build your familiarity with the easier gulls before you take on the tough ones.

Understand plumage sequences: If you want to identify gulls with confidence, it is essential that you absorb some basics of how and why their appearance changes as they grow up.

An excellent species to start with is the Ring-billed Gull, which has a relatively straightforward plumage sequence and is available to birders in most parts of North America. In this chapter a two-page spread of illustrations (Fig. 39) follows the full sequence of plumages, from juvenal to adult, of one Ring-billed. As you study this, keep these points in mind.

Two kinds of changes affect plumage. The most obvious abrupt changes are caused by *molt*, when certain feathers are dropped and new ones grow in their place. More gradual and constant change is caused by *wear* and fading of the feathers.

Among gulls, molt occurs mainly during specific periods of the year. The head and body plumage is molted twice annually, once in late winter and spring, once in late summer and fall. Most gull species continue to show head and neck patterns that are different in winter than in summer, even after they are adult, and these two molts bring about these two seasonal appearances. The wing and tail feathers are generally replaced only once per year, in the late-summer annual molt.

Because their feathers are held longer, the tail and especially the wings are subject to the effects of wear and fading. This is particularly noticeable on first-year gulls. By the time a gull is one year old (in first-summer plumage), black areas in the wings may have faded to pale brown, brown areas may have faded to beige, and gray areas to white. Especially among the larger gulls, first-summer birds may be extremely pale and devoid of any distinct markings. This is why reports

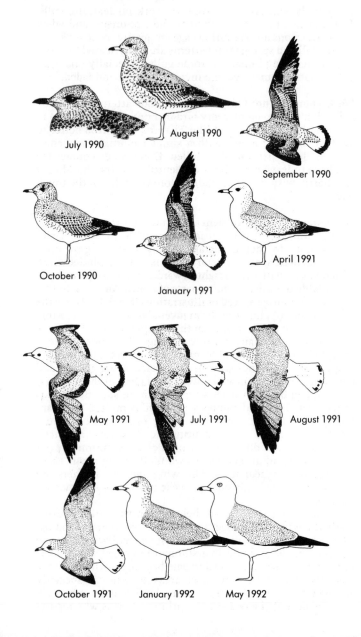

July 1990

August 1990

September 1990

October 1990

January 1991

April 1991

May 1991

July 1991

August 1991

October 1991

January 1992

May 1992

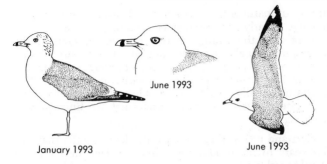

June 1993

January 1993   June 1993

Fig. 39. Tracing the plumage sequence of Ring-billed Gull, with an individual hatched in 1990. In *July 1990* it is in juvenal plumage. This plumage is rapidly replaced; by *August* and *September 1990* the bird is already molting the head and body feathers to first-winter plumage. By *October 1990* the bird is in first-winter plumage. There is little molt between now and *January 1991,* when the bird is still in first-winter plumage, but wear is reducing the contrast in the wings. The molt to first-summer plumage, which occurs early in spring, involves only head and body plumage, leaving those areas much whiter; by *April 1991* the gull is in first-summer plumage. By this time its wings are becoming very worn and faded. In late *May 1991* the bird has just begun to molt, having dropped the innermost primaries. The molt is in progress in *July 1991,* with the inner four primaries fresh, the fifth half-grown, the sixth missing, and the rest old and worn; molt of the other wing and tail feathers (and body feathers) is proceeding in a less orderly sequence. By *August 1991* the molt is nearly completed, but the outermost primaries are not yet full-grown. In *October 1991* and *January 1992* the bird is in second-winter plumage. It looks much like the adult but with extra black on the primary coverts, usually on the tail, and sometimes on the secondaries; the white spots on the wingtip are reduced. Seen in *May 1992,* in second-summer plumage, the bird could easily be taken for an adult. In the following months, the bird will again go through a complete molt, but the changes brought about this time will be less dramatic. After this molt, through the fall and winter (including *January 1993*) the bird will be in third-winter (adult winter) plumage; by late spring (and including *June 1993*) the bird will be in third-summer (adult summer) plumage. Changes hereafter will be limited to alternation between summer and winter adult plumages.

of pale immatures like Glaucous or Thayer's gulls seen out of range in early summer may be open to question.

Note that the timing of the molt varies considerably among individuals. It is not unusual, in late winter, to see gulls in winter plumage and summer plumage standing side by side. Immatures generally molt earlier in the season than adults (especially in fall), since adults usually delay their complete annual molt until after they are finished with breeding.

Understand ratios of age groups: In viewing gulls that take 3½ years to reach adulthood, like the Herring Gull, you should be able to separate four plumage types in winter: first-winter, second-winter, third-winter, and fourth-winter/adult. At first thought, one might expect all four of these age groups to be about equally common; but in practice, first-winter and adult gulls are generally the most common, second-winter are less numerous, and third-winter are rather scarce. (In a species that matures in its third winter, like Ring-billed, the second-winter gulls will be the least numerous).

With a little more thought, the reasons become apparent. Life in the wild poses many hazards for a Herring Gull. Many of those first-winter birds will not live to see a second winter, and even fewer will survive to their third winter. Somewhat fewer than that will make it to the fourth winter, of course; but at that point the Herring Gull is in adult plumage, and the combination of fourth-winter with all subsequent winter plumages (the birds may live for more than 20 years) makes the adult plumage relatively common.

A further complication is that different age groups may have different patterns of dispersal. Among some northerly species, immatures may move farther south than adults. Conversely, adults of some species may wander farther afield than young birds. So the ratios of various age groups in a given locality may be different from those in the population as a whole.

Look at flying birds: Once most birders resign themselves to studying a gull flock, they concentrate on the perched or swimming birds and ignore the ones in flight. This is understandable, perhaps, but it is also unfortunate, because in general gulls are much *more difficult* to identify at rest than in flight. Many of the best field marks, especially for immatures, involve details of pattern of the wings and tail. These details are partially or wholly obscured when the wings are folded.

Although it may seem very difficult at first, concentrate on *seeing* details on flying gulls. Concentrate on the upperside of the wings and tail — the pattern of the underside is usually less distinctive, and the groupings of feathers on the underside of the wings are less well defined. Study the wing pattern, and practice picking out and describing the various tracts of wing feathers. If you hope to become adept at finding and identifying rare gulls, this is an essential step.

Use shapes: If you want to report a rare gull, subtleties of shape are the *last* things to note in your description. But for separating the common gulls in your area, close study of shapes can allow you to make very quick identifications.

On the Pacific Coast, where many kinds occur together, I find that (after a few minutes of gull-watching to refresh my memory) I can instantly recognize most of the local species in flight just by silhouette. For example, the California Gulls look distinctively long-billed, small-headed, long-winged, and slim-bodied, different from any other gull there. But I would never report a California Gull out of range on the basis of silhouette.

Look at facial expressions: Although little attention is given to the facial expressions of gulls in most field guides (including this one), I find that in practice I use this aspect a lot for

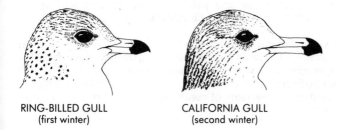

RING-BILLED GULL
(first winter)

CALIFORNIA GULL
(second winter)

Fig. 40. Comparing facial expressions. This example involves first-winter Ring-billed Gull and second-winter California Gull. In terms of pattern (including head and bill pattern) these two can be rather similar. But there is enough difference in *shape* of the head and bill to give each a distinctive "look" on the face.

naming nonflying gulls. The precise shape of the bill (and its pattern), the usual shape of the head, and the typical pattern of dark markings on the head of an immature or winter-plumaged bird, all combine to create a characteristic "expression" (Fig. 40) that may allow you to identify many common gulls very quickly.

However, this kind of field mark also breaks down very quickly when the bird in question is not a typical individual. A slight difference in markings can change the whole facial expression; a different pattern on the bill can change the appearance of bill *shape* in a major way. I suggest that you use facial impressions as field marks only for typical individuals of common species, and seek more concrete evidence for any gull that is atypical or possibly rare.

Beware of special pitfalls: For many adult or near-adult gulls, the darkness of the gray on the back is a significant field mark. This can be a tricky thing to judge, however, especially on a lone bird. Seen on a bright background like snow or white sand, a gull can look very dark-backed; conversely, bright light from above can wash out the gray to paler tones. Even when several gulls of one species are standing together, one that is turned to a different angle from the observer may seem to have a different shade of gray.

A gull that has nearly finished its annual complete molt presents another kind of problem. Such a gull may not appear to be in molt (see the bird labeled "August 1991" in Figure 39); but because its outermost primaries are not yet full-grown, the shape and pattern of the wingtip will appear strange. Watch out for such birds in early fall.

Expect variations: Study of a large flock of gulls can give one a new appreciation for the endless variability of nature. That appreciation may be worth more than any number of correct identifications. If you study variation, you'll be prepared to separate the variants of common species from the true rarities.

15

FRANKLIN'S AND LAUGHING GULLS

FRANKLIN'S GULL *Larus pipixcan*
LAUGHING GULL *Larus atricilla*

The problem: In North America the Laughing Gull is mainly coastal while the Franklin's is a summer bird of the interior, so their normal ranges overlap only near the Texas coast in migration season. However, each is known to wander widely, and either could show up practically anywhere on the continent.

In the past there was much confusion over identification of immatures. Actually, young birds in their first autumn are easily separated. More difficult are Laughing Gulls at slightly later stages, which may be confused with younger Franklin's. The biggest problem involves one-year-old Franklin's Gulls in summer, which are often misidentified as *adult* Laughing Gulls.

General Field Marks — All Ages

Bill shape: For a birder with experience and good views, the difference in bill shape between the two species is striking (Fig. 41). Laughing has a longer bill that often looks somewhat curved, or drooped and thickened, toward the tip. Franklin's has a shorter, straighter bill that appears to be of even thickness.

Overall shape and flight style: Complementing its larger bill, Laughing is a larger bird overall, with a longer and heavier head and longer wings. Its wingbeats are relatively deep and powerful, and its wingtips usually look quite pointed. Franklin's is a more petite bird in most ways, with a smaller and more rounded head. Its wings are noticeably shorter, its wingtips often look more rounded, and it flies with shallower

LAUGHING
GULL

FRANKLIN'S
GULL

Fig. 41. Comparison of bill shape and head shape in Laughing Gull and Franklin's Gull (in first-winter plumages).

wingbeats, giving an overall effect in flight that is more delicate and buoyant. (Of course, the flight style of either species may be affected if they are in heavy molt of the wing and tail feathers.)

Field Marks — Juvenile/First-Winter Birds

Ways to separate these two species in their first-autumn plumage have been covered in recent field guides, but a review of some points (Fig. 42) may be helpful.

Both are variably dusky-headed in juvenal plumage, but by early fall Franklin's shows a distinctive *head pattern* of blackish from the ear coverts across the upper nape, forming a "scarf" or "half-hood," while Laughing is more extensively gray-brown on the face. *Tail pattern* is diagnostic if seen well: Franklin's has a neat black subterminal band that does not extend to the outermost tail feathers (which are all white), while Laughing has a broader black band going all the way across the tail (the center of the tail is pale gray in both species). The upperside of the wings is more heavily marked with black and dark brown on Laughing Gull; Franklin's becomes cleaner and grayer rather early on. The breast, sides, and underwings are usually a clean white on Franklin's, while Laughing is usually washed with gray-brown on the body and heavily marked with dusky on the underwing.

The differences described above apply during the first fall and early winter. By the following spring, the young of both species will have changed in appearance. The change in Franklin's is striking: the Franklin's Gull undergoes a complete molt and comes north with fresh wing and tail feathers, having lost most of the dark markings in the tail and on the inner part of the wing. The Laughing Gull molts only head and body feathers at this time, so its appearance changes less.

One result is that one-year-old Laughings in spring can look superficially more similar to first-autumn Franklin's. Wear and fading on the inner parts of the wings can make these areas paler and more uniform; the birds may become much whiter on the neck and underparts; and some develop a "half-hood" like the young Franklin's. The broad dark tail band remains, but if tail feathers are accidentally lost, the replacement feathers that grow in will be white. I have seen young Laughings that had lost the outermost tail feathers and had grown white ones in their place, making a crude copy of the first-winter Franklin's tail pattern. To avoid being misled by these deceptively clean-cut Laughing Gulls, it is important to read the calendar: the resemblance (albeit a slight one) is between first-*autumn* Franklin's Gulls and first-*spring* Laughing Gulls.

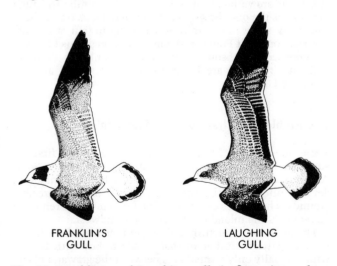

FRANKLIN'S
GULL

LAUGHING
GULL

Fig. 42. Franklin's and Laughing gulls in first-winter plumage, as they would appear about October. Earlier in the fall (in juvenal plumage), Franklin's would show more dark mottling on the back and more dusky marking on the head, while Laughing would be extensively dark brown on the head and chest, and sharply scaled brown and buff on the back and scapulars.

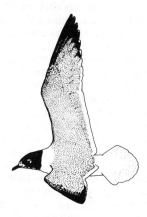

Fig. 43. One-year-old Franklin's Gull in midsummer. Birds at this age are variable, and most are not so similar to Laughing Gull as the one shown; most have less black on the head, and many show more white in the wingtip (but still much less than on adult Franklin's). But even though this bird is an extreme example, some first-summer Franklin's Gulls do look like this and are likely to be misidentified as adult Laughing Gulls.

The Problem of First-Summer Franklin's

Some one-year-old Franklin's Gulls, during their first full summer, may remain on the wintering grounds in South America. Others come to North America, but they may wander the interior of the continent away from the breeding grounds. These birds are responsible for many false reports of Laughing Gulls inland in the West and Midwest.

The most easily identified first-summer Franklin's have a wingtip pattern similar to that of adults but with far less white (usually only a small area between the gray and black), and a half-hooded effect like that shown here (Fig. 42) for first-winter birds. The tail at this age is already very pale gray, like that of the adult. The overall effect might suggest an adult Franklin's in winter plumage but with reduced white in the wingtip.

However, the variation in wing pattern produces some birds in which gray meets black on the wingtip with no obvious white in between — superficially very much like the pattern seen on adult Laughing Gull. Also, many first-summer Franklin's develop a lot of black on the head, sometimes forming almost a complete hood. Birds with this combination (Fig. 43) are very likely to be misidentified as Laughing Gulls.

The best way to avoid this error is to be cautious in claiming what appears to be an "obvious" adult Laughing out of range, especially in late spring and summer. Study the wing-tip pattern to see if there may be some paler area between the gray and the black. Look to see if the hood is really solid black, without any white feathers on the forehead or throat. Look at the white crescents above and below the eye — these tend to be a little wider on Franklin's than on Laughing at any age. In particular, study the shape of the bill. Photographs that show an exact profile of the bill, or the shape of the wings in flight, will be most helpful in establishing the record.

16

THE THAYER'S GULL COMPLEX

Text by Kevin J. Zimmer

THAYER'S GULL *Larus thayeri*
HERRING GULL *Larus argentatus*
ICELAND GULL *Larus glaucoides*
KUMLIEN'S (ICELAND) GULL *Larus glaucoides kumlieni*
GLAUCOUS-WINGED GULL *Larus glaucescens*
GLAUCOUS-WINGED × WESTERN GULL *L. glaucescens × L. occidentalis*

The problem: As the study of gull taxonomy and identification becomes increasingly sophisticated, we are discovering that we actually know less about these birds than we thought we did several years ago. Thayer's Gull is a perfect case in point. Originally described as a separate species, it was later lumped with Herring Gull, and this status as a race of Herring was maintained into the 1970s. In 1973 the American Ornithologists' Union, largely in response to work by Neal Smith, restored Thayer's Gull to full species status. Birders were suddenly confronted with another gull to identify.

In 1980 Paul Lehman synthesized the existing knowledge of identification of Thayer's Gull. Like any pioneering treatise on identification, this article unleashed a horde of birders who had previously lacked the knowledge and confidence to name Thayer's in the field. Armed with enthusiasm and new field marks (and ignoring Lehman's many cautions), these birders were soon finding Thayer's Gulls everywhere. Or were they? Photos of many of these "records" revealed that all too often, Herring Gulls were being mistaken for Thayer's Gulls.

Further complicating the picture is our evolving knowledge of the variation in Iceland Gulls, and rampant speculation that researchers will soon be pushing to re-lump Thayer's Gull — this time with Iceland Gull. As if all this were not enough, birders must also face up to the confusion cre-

ated by frequent hybrids, particularly Glaucous-winged ×
Western crosses.

In short, the problem of identifying Thayer's Gull has not
gone away; it has, perhaps, become even more difficult.

Preliminary Points

Distributional notes: Thayer's Gull breeds from the northern
Northwest Territories (Banks, Melville, Bathurst, and Elles-
mere islands) south and east to Victoria and Baffin islands,
western Greenland, and the northern edge of the Hudson Bay
region. Most Thayer's winter along the Pacific Coast from
southern British Columbia south to central Baja, with
smaller numbers wintering in southern Alaska, the Gulf of
St. Lawrence, the Great Lakes, and along the Atlantic Coast
south to Florida. Thayer's has been reported casually from
the Gulf Coast and almost throughout the interior of the continent. This is a bird that could turn up anywhere!

The Kumlien's race of Iceland Gull (*L. g. kumlieni*) breeds
in the Baffin Island region and in extreme northwestern Que-
bec. On Baffin Island it is reported to interbreed with Thayer's Gulls in mixed colonies. It winters from southern Labra-
dor, Newfoundland, and the Gulf of St. Lawrence south to the
middle Atlantic Coast (sometimes as far as Florida) and along
the Great Lakes to Minnesota. It is casually reported from
the prairie provinces of Canada, the plains states, and the
Rockies west to British Columbia. Several recent records
from the Pacific Coast are still under review. The true status
of this form in the interior is clouded by the difficulty of separating it from Thayer's Gull.

Iceland Gulls of the nominate race (*L. g. glaucoides*) breed
in Greenland and seem to winter mostly in Greenland, Iceland, and northwest Europe. Winter occurrence in North
America is supported by only a few specimens (mostly from
northeastern Canada).

General notes: Nominate Iceland, Kumlien's Iceland, and
Thayer's gulls represent a trend from east to west of increasing size and darker pigmentation. This variation is arguably
clinal (showing gradual change over a geographic area), so
true discontinuities — breaks in the cline — are difficult to
discern. Herring Gull lies at the far end of this spectrum, averaging both larger and darker than the other forms. Although the ends of this chain (Herring and nominate Iceland)

are not difficult to separate, the distinctions in the middle can be treacherous. Thus, our greatest difficulties are in separating Thayer's from Herring Gull on one side, and from Kumlien's Iceland on the other.

The breeding ranges of Western Gull and Glaucous-winged Gull overlap in coastal Washington, and in the area of overlap, the *majority* of birds are hybrids. Like Glaucouswingeds, the hybrids are migratory, wintering south in decreasing numbers to southern California. As you might expect, when dealing not only with first-generation crosses but also with the entire gamut of backcrosses, variation in these birds can be extreme. "Typical" hybrids resemble Thayer's Gulls in many ways, adding still another source of potential confusion.

Thayer's is a four-year gull, as are all the gulls with which it is likely to be confused; that is, it becomes adult on attaining its fourth-winter plumage (after it is a little more than three years old). For reasons outlined in chapter 14, birders are most likely to encounter Thayer's Gulls in either firstwinter or adult plumages. Therefore, this account will focus mainly on these two plumages of Thayer's and on how they differ from the parallel plumages of similar species and hybrids.

Field Marks — Thayer's Gull Complex (All Ages)

On standing birds the overall size and proportions as well as the shapes of the bill and head (Fig. 44) are important clues.

Overall body size: On average, Thayer's Gulls are intermediate in size between Herring Gulls and California Gulls (*L. californicus*). This means that the vast majority of individuals should appear distinctly smaller than any nearby Western, Glaucous (*L. hyperboreus*), Great Black-backed (*L. marinus*), or Glaucous-winged gulls, as well as any hybrid combinations thereof.

Bill shape: The bill of Thayer's is relatively short (for a large gull) and of medium width, with a gently rounded culmen. This is distinctly different from the massive bills of most Glaucous-wingeds and Glaucous-winged × Western hybrids, which show prominent bulges at the gonydeal angle. It is also recognizably different (with practice) from the longer, pencil-shaped bill typical of Herring Gull. Iceland Gulls have very delicate bills that average even shorter and thinner than those of Thayer's.

Head shape: Thayer's Gull has a relatively small head with a somewhat rounded crown. Combined with the short bill, this imparts a delicate, dove-like look that is reminiscent of Mew Gull (*L. canus*). Herrings, Glaucous-wingeds, and Glaucous-winged × Western hybrids, with their larger bills, bigger heads, and flatter crowns, have a fiercer countenance. This distinction between Thayer's and Herring gulls is accentuated in birds older than one year because of the difference in eye color. The dark eyes of Thayer's enhance the gentle look, whereas the golden eyes of Herrings lend an even fiercer expression. Icelands closely approximate Thayer's in head shape, and the net impression of delicacy is even greater because of the smaller bill. Icelands also have a slightly different build, being on average shorter-legged, with a fuller look to the chest and wingtips that extend farther beyond the tail when at rest.

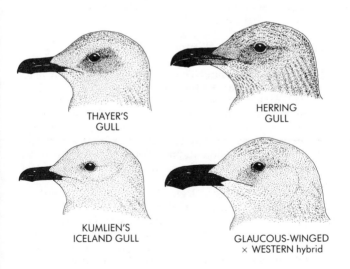

Fig. 44. Head and bill shapes of four similar gulls, as illustrated by birds in fresh first-winter plumage.

Problems with these shape characters: Having said all of this, I must now insert a strong caveat. I believe that our ideas regarding what a "classic" Thayer's Gull should look like (structurally) are based primarily on the appearance of *female* Thayer's. Females of most large gulls differ from males of their own species in being smaller-bodied, with smaller, more rounded heads and shorter, thinner bills. In some species the differences may not be appreciable in the field. *With Thayer's and Herrings, intersexual differences can be dramatic.* A female Thayer's may stand out amidst a flock of Herrings, but a male could more easily be passed by. More importantly, a smaller, shorter-billed female Herring Gull can closely approximate "the look" of a Thayer's and could readily be misidentified as such. (Similar mistakes could easily be made with a female Glaucous-winged × Western hybrid.) Indeed, measurements of bill length and width of some female Herrings are well within the ranges displayed by male Thayer's. Likewise, there is pronounced overlap of mensural characters between male Icelands and female Thayer's.

Keep in mind also that gulls in an advanced state of wear or actively molting the head feathers may appear longer-billed, because more of the culmen is exposed. Head shape for individuals in this condition is likely to be of little value.

Field Marks — First-Winter Birds

Bill color: All first-winter Thayer's Gulls have entirely black bills well into January. By February some will begin to exhibit some dull pinkish at the base of the bill, but this is typically limited in extent. First-winter Glaucous-wingeds, Westerns, and hybrids between the two will be entirely black-billed into late winter as well. By contrast, most first-winter Herrings display noticeable dull pink along the basal part of the bill early in winter. By late January, entirely black-billed Herrings are in the decided minority.

Bill color and pattern in Iceland Gull is trickier. Nominate birds often parallel the pattern of first-year Glaucous Gulls — that is, they have black-tipped bills that are extensively pink at the base — although somewhat darker-billed birds are perhaps more common. Kumlien's Icelands (the only Icelands likely to be seen on this continent) are typically darker-billed. Some may have entirely black bills like Thayer's. Others may show a mildly contrasting grayish or grayish green base to the bill. In North America, Icelands with sharply contrasting pink and black bills that appear to be first-year birds are likely to be second-winter *kumlieni* that have yet to attain their gray mantles.

Eye and leg color: First-winter Thayer's Gulls have dark eyes, as do all first-winter gulls with which they are likely to be confused. Those species that are pale-eyed as adults (e.g., Herring, Iceland) typically will not attain pale eyes before their second winter. Leg color of all ages of Thayer's Gull is pink, often being a shade or two brighter than in related species. This distinction is perhaps more apparent in adult birds and should be considered a minor clue at best.

Head and body plumage: First-winter Thayer's Gulls are quite variable in overall color but are typically a uniform buffy brown with a distinctly checkered appearance to the mantle and wing coverts. Many late-fall/early-winter birds are a darker, sootier brown, as are juveniles, which are rarely seen away from the breeding grounds. The undertail coverts are pale with contrasting brown bars. The rump and uppertail coverts are likewise strongly mottled or barred brown and white. Many individuals show a dark smudge through the eye or just anterior to it, a mark shared by some Herrings, but rarely by Icelands.

Herring Gulls are likewise variable in color and pattern, but in general tend toward a darker, "colder" gray-brown tone, with less checkering or spangling to the wings and mantle. First-year Herrings are also more likely to have contrastingly whiter head/neck regions, although some Thayer's also show this. First-winter Glaucous-wingeds average paler and more uniformly colored than Herrings, but again tend toward grayer tones with less-sharp patterning to the wings and mantle. Glaucous-winged × Western hybrids tend toward darker brown but overlap many of the darker Thayer's in color. Iceland Gulls are also sharply checkered above but are, on average, a much paler buff overall (more like first-winter Glaucous) than Thayer's. Again, individuals at the extremes for both species can overlap.

Tail pattern: The tail feathers of a first-winter Thayer's are solidly medium to dark brown, with limited pale mottling or barring on the outer two or three retrices. The amount of pigment in the tail feathers is variable from one individual to the next and usually matches closely the color of the wingtips. Whatever the shade of brown, the visual effect will remain that of a wide, darker tail band contrasting with a paler and mottled rump and uppertail coverts.

This effect should aid in distinguishing Thayer's from Iceland Gull, which typically has a very pale tail with fine barring on each feather in the manner of Glaucous Gull. Occasional darker Icelands with heavier tail barring may give the impression of having a distinct band due to convergence of the bars. Even when a band is present, however, it contains internal mottling and is pale in coloration.

Like Thayer's, Herring and Western also show a uniformly dark tail, although it is typically a darker blackish brown in color (again, the pigmentation in tail and wingtips generally matches). Glaucous-winged also has a wide, uniform tail band, but it is usually a shade or two paler than in Thayer's. Typical Glaucous-winged × Western hybrids approximate rather closely the usual tail pattern of Thayer's.

Wingtips: On standing birds, the color of the folded primaries at the wingtip is often an excellent clue to identity. In Thayer's Gulls the primaries are usually a medium brown that is darker than the rest of the wing. They are never black, as in most Herring, Western, and California gulls. The wingtip color of any given individual Thayer's can fall anywhere along a wide spectrum; the palest birds' wingtips are nearly concolor with the rest of the wing (similar to Glaucous-winged), whereas darker individuals may have chocolate-brown wingtips that at least approach the typical Herring Gull coloration. Most Thayer's also have cream-colored edges to the outer several primaries, which are revealed in the form of conspicuous pale crescents around the tip of each visible primary on the folded wing. Such pale crescents are seldom as conspicuous on Herrings or on Glaucous-winged × Western hybrids in mid- to late winter, but juveniles in fall or fresh-plumaged birds in early winter can have crescents every bit as bold. Likewise, worn Thayer's late in winter may lack noticeable crescents.

Consider, too, the color of the folded primaries compared to the color of the bunched tertials/secondaries. In most Herring Gulls the two feather groups will be nearly the same blackish color (marginally lighter on the tertials/secondaries). In Thayer's Gulls, on the other hand, the bunched tertials/secondaries are nearly always much lighter than the folded primaries. (Or, if concolor, both feather groups are light brown, well outside the normal Herring Gull range.) As expected in this difficult group, this character is subject to variation and is far from diagnostic, but it does seem fairly consistent.

As already mentioned, first-winter Glaucous-wingeds typically have wingtips concolor with (or even slightly paler than) the rest of the wing. Beware, however, of occasional Glaucous-wingeds with wingtips a shade darker than the rest of the wing, thus approaching the pale end of the Thayer's spectrum. Whether such individuals reflect individual variation or gene introgression from Western Gulls is problematic. Obvious Glaucous-winged × Western hybrids have wingtip coloration that matches that of many Thayer's Gulls.

Iceland Gulls also vary in wingtip color and pattern, although there is little consensus as to how much variation is possible within and between the two subspecies. In general, first-year Icelands' wingtips are distinctly paler (whiter) than the rest of the wing (as in first-year Glaucous). Most Kum-

ICELAND GULL THAYER'S GULL HERRING GULL

Fig. 45. Gulls in first-winter plumage, to compare patterns of wings and tail in Iceland, Thayer's, and Herring gulls. In overall darkness, Thayer's is intermediate between the other two; look for the exact pattern of the outer primaries, the appearance of the secondaries (pale, striped, or dark), and the presence or absence of contrast between the tail and uppertail coverts.

lien's will also show at least some gray in the outer webs of the outer several primaries, and many will have distinct dusky chevrons near the tips of these same feathers. Some individuals may appear to have entirely unmarked white wingtips. In general, *kumlieni* may average more pigment in the wingtips than *glaucoides*, but the range of variation is great enough that separating these subspecies in first-year plumage is probably impossible in the field.

Always remember that feather wear and bleaching can dramatically affect wing pattern and coloration, to the extent that extremely worn birds of *any* species can look white-winged or buffy-winged.

Flying birds: Wing pattern in flight is crucial to confirming the identification of a first-winter Thayer's Gull, and along with head/bill proportions it is one of the more striking clues (Fig. 45).

In examining the Thayer's wing pattern, we must first look at the individual feathers. The outer several primaries have the narrow outer webs darker brown than the rest of the wing. This darker color extends onto the inner webs only at the tip of each feather. The rest of the broad inner web of each primary is distinctly pale (whitish). At close range from above, this contrast of pale inner webs with dark outer webs imparts a striped look to the outer primaries of the spread wing. At greater distances, or when the bird is in rapid flight, the contrastingly colored webs cancel one another out, leaving the impression of uniformly light to medium brown primaries that are slightly darker at the tips.

The secondaries are similarly colored, with the outer webs dark and the inner ones entirely pale. Taken together, the pattern of the secondaries (as viewed from above) is one of a broad and distinct, but broken, dark bar across the trailing edge of the wing. This character is important in distinguishing Thayer's from Iceland Gull, which shows no such secondary bar. Icelands have uniformly pale upperwings that are, if anything, lighter on the primaries. Herring Gulls have both webs of each secondary dark and thus show a solid (not broken) blackish secondary bar. This bar on a Herring is made even more distinct by its contrast with the conspicuously pale inner primaries. These, in turn, contrast noticeably with the more extensively blackish outer primaries. Glaucous-wingeds have uniformly colored upperwings, with no discernible secondary bar. Glaucous-winged × Western hybrids closely match many Thayer's in upperwing pattern, having a secondary bar of medium contrast and outer primaries that are slightly darker brown than the rest of the wing. On average, they may be more extensively dark in the primaries than most Thayer's, but this is a tenuous distinction at best.

The underwing pattern of a first-winter Thayer's is entirely different from that of the upperwing. Because of feather arrangement in flight, the broader, pale inner webs of the flight feathers conceal the narrow dark outer webs, making these feathers appear whitish and somewhat translucent (an effect accentuated on strongly backlit birds). The dusky tips to the outer primaries form a very thin dusky trailing edge that can be seen at close range. The overall effect is quite dramatic and lends Thayer's Gull the look of one of the "white-winged" species (Glaucous, Iceland, or Glaucous-winged). This should eliminate confusion with such species as Herring, California, and Western gulls, all of which are extensively dark on the underside of the outer primaries. Glaucous-winged × Western hybrids, however, generally show a similar underwing pattern, with more dusky tips to the outer primaries. Their underwings often appear less frosty than those of the Thayer's, but this is a difference of degree and could be troublesome.

Summary of first-year distinctions: The following is a brief recap of the best characters for separating first-winter Thayer's Gull from each of its likely ID contenders.

Thayer's vs. Glaucous-winged: Usually straightforward. Most Glaucous-wingeds will be larger-bodied with bigger bills than most Thayer's. (Beware of small female Glaucous-wingeds, however.) Glaucous-wingeds have wingtips that are lighter than or concolor with the rest of the wing (rarely darker) and lack secondary bars. Thayer's always have secondary bars and wingtips at least marginally darker than the rest of the wing. Thayer's has a darker tail band and usually more sharply patterned upperparts.

Thayer's vs. Iceland: Can be extremely difficult. Icelands generally lack a strong tail band, and if present it is typically pale (nearly concolor with the rest of the upperparts) and mottled internally. Icelands also lack the secondary bar seen in Thayer's. The wingtips of Icelands are usually noticeably paler than the rest of the wing (not slightly darker as in Thayer's). Some Icelands will have a contrasting grayish base to the bill, whereas all Thayer's have entirely black bills. Iceland is generally paler/buffier in overall color.

Thayer's vs. Herring: Can be difficult. Comparisons of size, head shape, and bill length and shape are instructive but should always be backed up by careful analysis of other features, particularly wing pattern (upper and lower surfaces). Brown (rather than blackish) wingtips with conspicuous pale crescents are more suggestive of Thayer's, as are a uniformly buffier ground color to the entire body and more sharply patterned upperparts. Herrings often have conspicuously pinkish-based bills early in winter.

Thayer's vs. Glaucous-winged × Western: Can be extremely difficult. Most hybrids will be separable on the basis of their larger size and more massive bills, but these relative characters are most reliably applied by birders already experienced with Thayer's Gulls. Occasional smaller hybrids with more delicate bills (presumably females) can spark spirited debate among even veteran gull-watchers. Plumage differences from Thayer's are minor and subject to much variation; but on average, these hybrids are a darker, colder brown, with less checkering to the wings and mantle, duskier outer primaries in flight, and no conspicuous pale crescents on the folded wingtips.

Field Marks — Second-Year Birds

Plumage progression in Thayer's Gull is typical of four-year gulls in general. A partial molt (head and body feathers) in early spring (February to March) brings the bird into its first-summer plumage, and the subsequent complete molt beginning in late summer advances the bird into its second-winter plumage.

The first step in identifying a second-year Thayer's Gull is to recognize it as being a second-year gull in general. Among the large gulls this typically means acquisition of the gray mantle; retention of significant amounts of brown on the wing coverts and scapulars; increasing amounts of white to the head, neck, and underparts; an increasing pale base to the bill; acquisition of adult eye color; and retention of first-year patterns to the primaries, secondaries, and tail.

Thayer's Gull is no exception to this pattern. By its second winter it has acquired the gray mantle that it will wear as an adult. The scapulars may retain significant amounts of buffy brown, and the wing coverts will be wholly this color. In fresh plumage the scapulars and coverts will be brown-centered with pale fringes, creating a dappled look. The head, neck, and underparts are generally quite whitish but are usually washed or mottled irregularly with buff or gray-brown (this may take the form of a solid gray-buff wash on the belly). The brown tail is retained, with mottling still restricted to the outer two or three rectrices. The primaries are still brownish rather than black, and still tend to have prominent pale fringes (creating the pale crescents on the folded wing). Upper and underwing patterns are similar to those of first-year birds. By the second winter most will show at least some pinkish at the base of the bill, but this is variable in extent. Many birds may also retain some dark feathering around the eye. Second-year birds, like Thayer's of all ages, have dark eyes and pink legs and feet. The overall look recalls that of first-winter Mew Gull, a similarity that is more pronounced in small female Thayer's.

A careful study of overall size, head/bill proportions, and precise wing pattern should allow separation of second-year Thayer's from Glaucous-winged × Western hybrids of the same age. Size and proportions will also help eliminate most Glaucous-winged Gulls, as will the darker wingtips, the secondary bar, the darker tail band, the white underparts, and the presence (usually) of more pink at the bill base. Glaucous-wingeds in this stage are typically uniformly dingy gray-brown, with little or no patterning to the coverts and more completely black bills. Most Herrings and some Icelands will have conspicuously pale eyes by their second winter — a good close-range difference. Differences in size, head/bill proportions, wingtip coloration, and patterns of both wing surfaces that allow separation of first-year Thayer's from Herring still apply to second-year birds. Iceland Gulls can be slow to attain their gray mantles and may still resemble first-year birds in their second winter. Still, such individuals can often be aged by their sharply bicolored (pink-based, black-tipped) bills and pale eyes, a combination that should eliminate Thayer's from consideration. Be aware, however, that many Kumlien's Icelands will retain dark eyes through adulthood. Other features that separate first-year Thayer's from first-year Iceland (presence or absence of secondary bars, complete or mottled tail band, primaries darker or lighter than rest of wing) remain applicable in this stage.

Field Marks — Third-Year Birds

Third-year plumage is usually the least frequently seen plumage of any large gull. Again, plumage progression in Thayer's is typical of the large gulls; in Thayer's, third-winter plumage develops via a complete molt in early fall (at slightly more than two years of age).

Third-winter birds look essentially adult. They have a gray mantle and wings; white head, neck, and underparts; mostly white tail; and blackish primaries. Several features, however, set them apart from winter adults. The wing coverts often retain small amounts of brown. Likewise, the tail usually has some suggestion of a tail band — a complete narrow black subterminal band, or broken remnants, or, at the very least, irregular traces of dark gray. The primaries are less extensively black (and can still be somewhat brownish) and less sharply patterned than in adults, typically lacking the large white mirrors. Precise upperwing pattern is difficult to characterize and can vary tremendously from bird to bird. The bill, too, is highly variable and can range from nearly adult (greenish yellow with suggestion of a red spot at the gonys) to dull pinkish or yellow with a dark tip or subterminal band. The head and neck are often heavily streaked with gray-brown in winter, a condition common to many large gulls in adult winter plumage. Overall size, head/bill proportions, eye color, and wing patterns remain the critical features allowing separation of Thayer's from similar gulls.

Field Marks — Adults

Adult Thayer's Gulls in any plumage have yellow or greenish yellow bills with a red or red-orange spot at the gonys. Their legs are reddish pink and are often noticeably deeper in hue than the legs of Herring, Iceland, or Glaucous-winged × Western hybrids. Eye color is usually dark brown, accentuating the "gentle" look of the head. Some individuals have pale eyes heavily flecked with brown, but these appear solidly brown at any real distance. Adult Herrings always have bright yellow eyes, as do most adult Icelands. However, an unknown percentage of Kumlien's Icelands are dark-eyed as adults, and these individuals can readily be misidentified as Thayer's Gulls. Glaucous-winged × Western hybrids are usually dark-eyed, although some have pale eyes heavily flecked with brown.

In Thayer's the fleshy orbital ring surrounding the eye is reddish purple. This can be difficult to see in winter, but during the breeding season it is enlarged and more conspicuous. Iceland Gull also has a reddish purple orbital ring, but that of Herring is yellowish orange. Glaucous-winged × Western hybrids run the gamut on orbital ring color between yellow-orange (typical of Western Gulls) and reddish purple (typical of Glaucous-wingeds). But most birders will encounter these hybrids only during the nonbreeding season, when orbital ring color is difficult to see and therefore of little value.

Plumage: Adult Thayer's Gulls have white heads, necks, tails, and underparts, as do all the other gulls under discussion. In winter they are variably streaked, mottled, or washed with gray-brown on the head or neck (as are adults of most similar species). The gray mantle is a shade darker than on most Herring Gulls, and is therefore a couple of shades darker than on the average Iceland. Mantle color is equivalent to that of most Glaucous-winged × Western hybrids.

The wingtips of a standing adult Thayer's are sharply black with conspicuous large white "mirrors." The general impression of the wingtips on a standing Thayer's is similar to the pattern shown by a Herring, but the black area is less extensive and the mirrors are larger and more prominent. Wingtip pattern on standing Kumlien's Iceland is also quite similar, but the primaries of most *kumlieni* will range from charcoal gray to slate gray (with white mirrors) rather than being black. With wear these feathers may initially darken but will eventually fade to pale gray or brown.

On most adult Glaucous-winged Gulls, the primaries are the same light gray as the mantle (with white mirrors). On some the primaries are a shade or two darker, but they never approach black in color. Unhappily, as is the case with most other characters, the wingtip pattern of a standing Thayer's Gull is rather closely approximated by many Glaucous-winged × Western hybrids.

Flying birds: Although the wingtips of adult Thayer's and Herring gulls look very similar on standing birds, the similarities end when the birds take to the air. From above, Thayer's show much less black in the wingtip than one would expect from having seen the folded wing. The outer three primaries have lengthy black streaks on the outer webs, whereas the inner webs are largely white. On the fourth and fifth primaries from the outside, the black is reduced to large subterminal marks; and the sixth primary from the outside has a faint black subterminal bar (all six outer primaries have large white tips, this being a long white blaze on the outer-most primary). The overall effect is of a black-and-white-striped wingtip, with a lot of white on the tip of the outer-most primary. The remainder of the upperwing is gray, with a white trailing edge. As with other age classes, adult Thayer's Gulls appear essentially "white-winged" from below because the white inner primary webs conceal the black outer webs. The only black seen from below is the row of four or five subterminal marks, which form a narrow black trailing edge to the outer primaries. The remainder of the underwing is pale gray to white.

By contrast, Herring Gulls have extensively black wing-tips. Both webs of the outer several primaries are black, the white essentially being reduced to spots at the tips. The out-ermost primary has the largest white mark, and the next pri-mary in line has another white mirror in addition to the tip. The sum effect is very different from the striped or lined look seen in Thayer's Gull. Even more different is the appearance of the underwing. Because both webs of the outer primaries are black in Herring Gulls, the black shows through to the underside of the wing, essentially duplicating the pattern of the upper surface. This is so different from Thayer's that it provides immediate separation. However, it has been re-ported that a very few Herring Gulls (perhaps especially fe-

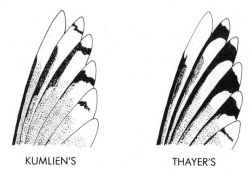

KUMLIEN'S   THAYER'S

Fig. 46. Typical wingtip patterns of adult Thayer's and Kum-lien's Iceland gulls in fresh plumage, as seen from upperside.

males from eastern Canada) have reduced black in the wing-tip.

Iceland Gulls of the nominate race *glaucoides* have entirely white wingtips (like Glaucous Gulls), and thus should be easy to distinguish from Thayer's. Unfortunately, most (if not all) Iceland Gulls likely to be seen in North America are of the race *kumlieni*, which approach Thayer's Gulls very closely in wing pattern (Fig. 46). The distribution of dark and white coloration on the outer several primaries is extremely similar, with Kumlien's showing: (1) less dark and more white; (2) a thin dark leading edge to the outermost primary; (3) outer webs and subterminal marks typically charcoal gray rather than black; and (4) one less primary with a dark subterminal mark. All of these differences are subtle and can be extremely difficult to assess on fast-flying birds. Further complicating matters is the possibility that the amount of pigment present in the mantle and wingtips of an Iceland Gull may be correlated with the amount of dark pigment in the eyes, which would make some darker *kumlieni* nearly impossible to separate from Thayer's in the field. In such cases one would have to rely upon subtle shape distinctions (Icelands being smaller with more delicate bills, shorter legs, and greater primary extension) and a careful, critical study of the precise wing pattern.

Adult Glaucous-winged × Western hybrids have highly variable wing patterns, but few will provide a very close match with Thayer's if examined critically. Wingtip patterns of standing hybrids may be inseparable from those of Thayer's, but in flight these birds typically show a more extensive area of black on the wingtip, with less of a striped or lined look to the outer primaries. The dark pigment on the primaries of hybrids can range from charcoal gray to jet black. From below, hybrids typically show little black in the wingtips (certainly less than adult Herrings or Westerns), and more closely approximate the usual Thayer's appearance. Still, taken together with size and head/bill proportions, careful study of the wing pattern on flying birds should allow separation of most adult hybrids.

Summary

You will have noted that the preceding account makes liberal use of such qualifiers as "generally," "typically," "most," and "on average." If I have managed to inject a sense of caution or have imparted a feeling that these gulls are confusingly variable, then I will have accomplished a major goal. The careful observer *can* readily identify most individual gulls, but only by using a combination of characters and by taking into account such factors as molt, feather wear, hybridization, sexual variation, geographic variation, and plain old individual variation. Occasional gulls will defy your best attempts at positive identification, and these are best left as instructive mysteries.

17

BRIEF NOTES ON OTHER GULLS

LESSER BLACK-BACKED GULL and similar forms: One of the big stories in North American birding during the 1970s and 1980s was the rapid rise in numbers of Lesser Black-backed Gulls, a European species, on this continent. In some areas it is no longer a surprise to see several in a day. So far, the majority detected here have been adults or near-adults, and the following discussion deals only with these older birds.

Most birders still use commendable caution in identifying these birds to species. But at times, there has been unwarranted speculation about the *sub*species, or race, involved.

The vast majority of Lesser Black-backeds (*Larus fuscus*) occurring in North America belong to the western European race *graellsii*. This form has a moderately dark gray back: darker than on North American Herring Gulls, but much paler than on Greater Black-backeds. But Europe has two other races. There is a northern Scandinavian race, *fuscus*, that is much darker above — as black as a Great Black-backed; and there is a southern Scandinavian race that is intermediate between the other two, called (appropriately) *intermedius*. Sightings of both of these have been claimed in North America. However, different races (of any bird) have different patterns of distribution. Simply because *graellsii* is occurring here regularly now, it does *not* necessarily follow that the other races should show up. Either of the other races would represent an exceptional rarity on this continent, and should be thoroughly documented.

Because of individual variation, and because the races intergrade to some extent, the identity of a bird of the race *intermedius* would be almost impossible to prove out of range by sight — or even by good photographs. Shades of gray are extremely difficult to capture accurately on film. Although it is worth noting if a Lesser Black-backed looks darker than normal, slapping the name *intermedius* on such a bird will not win you any respect.

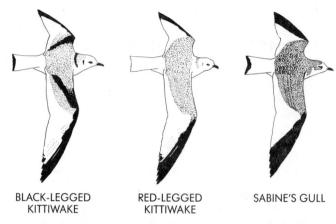

BLACK-LEGGED
KITTIWAKE

RED-LEGGED
KITTIWAKE

SABINE'S GULL

Fig. 47. Three gulls with similar patterns in their first autumn. The Black-legged and Red-legged kittiwakes shown are in first-winter plumage. The Sabine's Gull is in juvenal plumage; unlike most gulls, which molt into first-winter plumage early, Sabine's retains juvenal plumage during its first southward migration.

Typical examples of the race *fuscus* are scarce even as far west as Britain, so their occurrence in North America would be remarkable. Still, it would be worth trying to document a bird that appeared to be of this form. Aside from the deep black back, other useful points on a winter adult might include the precise pattern of the wingtip and the arrangement of dark streaking on the head and neck. Beware of the possibility of "runt" individuals of Great Black-backed Gull or hybrids between Great Black-backed and Herring. Such birds should have different leg color and heavier bills, and should lack the *long-winged* profile that the Lesser Black-backed shows when standing.

SABINE'S GULL and similar species: The wing pattern of Sabine's Gull at all ages is so striking that, in theory, it should be unmistakable. In practice, Black-legged Kittiwakes in first-winter plumage are often mistaken for Sabine's, at least temporarily (Fig. 47).

The black diagonal bar (carpal bar) on the inner part of the wing should separate the kittiwake from Sabine's, in which the back and inner wing coverts are evenly dark. However, harsh light conditions (a good possibility at sea) can heighten contrast so much that the kittiwake appears to have solidly tricolored wings. Adding to the problem, especially for inexperienced observers, the forked tail shape of Sabine's is often inconspicuous in the field, while the kittiwake's tail *pattern* can make it look strongly forked. Snap identifications of these birds may be wrong. The best tactic is to strive for a view of the precise wing pattern and back it up with bill shape and face pattern.

Even more similar to the Sabine's pattern is the first-winter Red-legged Kittiwake, a Bering Sea species that is very unlikely elsewhere in North America (although there are records for Oregon and Nevada). In first-winter plumage, this species lacks the black carpal bar, black tail band, and most of the dark hindneck collar of young Black-leggeds. (It also has a shorter bill and slightly shorter wings.) Thus the first-winter Red-legged can approach the look of winter *adult* Sabine's in several ways — something to consider when Sabine's is reported out of season.

18

THE MEDIUM-SIZED TERNS

ROSEATE TERN *Sterna dougallii*
COMMON TERN *Sterna hirundo*
ARCTIC TERN *Sterna paradisaea*
FORSTER'S TERN *Sterna forsteri*

The problem: Terns are so often seen at a distance — as flickering white shapes far out over the water, or as hunched forms on unapproachable sandbars — that birders may fall into the habit of leaving them unidentified or, worse, of making careless assumptions as to what they are likely to be. These four species are particularly susceptible to such glossing-over, because they are so similar in size, shape, and overall pattern.

Typical adults in the breeding season, as described in all the standard bird guides, can be identified by bill color. Unfortunately, not all are typical. Reliance on bill color alone, therefore, will automatically lead to error in a certain percentage of cases. To compound the problem, some of the better-known "back-up" field marks — such as darkness of the back, wingtips, and underparts and length of the legs and tail — are easily misinterpreted if they are not well understood. Variation with season and age creates part of the difficulty. With terns, even more than with most groups of birds, it is necessary to learn certain basics before relying too heavily on deceptively simple-seeming field marks.

Preliminary Points

Age variations: In these terns, juveniles and birds in their first winter look different from adults. They are pictured and discussed in a separate section, after the account of adults.

One-year-old and often two-year-old terns in summer also look different from adults. Realization of this fact was a long time coming, because the great majority of the terns that come north in spring are adults. It seemed logical to interpret this to mean that the previous year's fledglings were the current year's breeders. Indeed, when the normal immature summer plumages of Arctic Tern were first detected, they were described to science as two new species, *Sterna pikei* and *Sterna portlandica*. But what actually happens, we now understand, is that most immatures simply remain on the wintering grounds throughout their first full calendar year — and, depending on species, often the second as well. Those coming north with the adults are very few.

Some immatures in summer are similar to first-winter birds, although some or all of the flight feathers of the wings may be heavily worn and thus darker. This pattern has sometimes been called the *portlandica* plumage. Others, appearing more advanced, are more similar to adults but with "extra" dark markings — sometimes described as the *pikei* plumage — on the wings and white on the forehead. (See note below.) There has been some thought that these two types represented the typical one-year-old and two-year-old summer plumages, respectively, but some recent evidence suggests otherwise. Given the state of present knowledge, it usually will be unsafe for birders to try to guess the ages of summer immature terns. As for identifying them to species: they are not treated separately here, but with careful study all should be identifiable. In shape they are like adults (except that their tails are shorter), and in plumage they combine some features of adults with others reminiscent of juveniles of their species.

Understanding underwing pattern: Because of the way the wing feathers overlap, in looking at the underside of a tern's spread wing you can see the entire outermost long primary but only the tips and inner webs of the other primaries. The patterns of the tips of the individual primaries may seem like a minor point — but they create an overall pattern that is distinctive for each of these terns, and which can be seen from a surprisingly great distance. This is a very important field mark to study because it works for juveniles as well as adults.

Note: Another treatment uses the term "*portlandica* plumage" for all summer immatures. Dating from the era when these plumages were thought to be abnormal phases rather than part of the normal sequence, these terms are mentioned here merely for completeness and for historical interest.

It is, in fact, the only plumage character that can be used for all age groups at all seasons.

The *translucence* of the wings is another consideration. When birds are seen overhead against bright sunlight, some parts of their wings may allow light to pass through while other parts do not; the translucent sections appear to glow brightly, and the others appear as dark shadows. With terns, the pattern of this translucence is sometimes a helpful field mark.

Understanding upperwing pattern: The pattern of the upperside of the outer part of the wing — created by the relative shades of gray of each of the individual primary feathers — is an important field mark for adult terns.

The darkness of the upperside of a single primary in a tern's wing depends on two things: the darkness of the feather's ground color, and the amount of pale powdery "bloom" that covers it. Since this pale bloom is gradually worn away, the feather is palest when it first grows in and becomes steadily darker until the time of the next molt. (Tern primaries of the same age are not all of the same darkness, of course, because of differences among species in the darkness of the feather's base color and in its original amount of pale bloom.)

So, in general, tern primaries are darker when the feathers are older. This has a major effect on wing pattern because of the sequence of molt. Common Tern provides a good illustration of how this works. In the adult Common, the five inner primaries are replaced (in normal sequence, one by one beginning with the innermost) in late summer and early fall, before the southward migration. (Terns have 11 primaries, but the tiny outermost one is ignored here. Note also that there is individual variation in molt: in Common Tern, for example, the number of twice-molted inner primaries may vary from four to six, but five is the typical number.) Molt of the outer five primaries continues after arrival on the wintering grounds. In spring, before the birds migrate north, about five of the inner primaries are molted again. So during the summer, the inner primaries are significantly newer (and paler) than the outer ones. Furthermore, because primary molt always progresses outward on the wing, the last of the inner primaries replaced in spring (and thus the freshest) is next to the *oldest* of the retained outer primaries from the previous fall, so the contrast is especially noticeable: it shows up as a narrow dark *wedge* running in from the trailing edge of the wing. This is most obvious in fall migration, when the inners are brand-new and the outers are nearly a year old. In midwinter, when all the primaries are closer to the same age, no dark wedge is evident.

Roseate Tern has a molt schedule similar to that of Common Tern but replaces more of the inner primaries in spring, retaining only about three of the outermost old ones. Forster's Tern evidently has a molt like that of Common Tern, but its outer primaries are paler to begin with and do not darken as much with wear. Arctic Tern molts all its primaries just once per year, on the wintering grounds, so in summer it has the most uniform upperwing of these four terns.

Seasonal change: The first section under "Field Marks" below treats adults as they are seen in spring and early summer. Winter-plumaged adults differ in a number of ways: (1) Their bills become almost entirely black, with perhaps a little color at the base of the lower mandible; (2) some of the black on the head is replaced by white; (3) the underparts become entirely white (replacing pale gray in Arctic and Common, and the rosy flush in Roseate); and (4) in at least some terns, the tail feathers are molted both in spring and in fall, and the outermost tail feathers worn in winter are shorter and broader than those of summer. Also, there are minor changes in wing pattern brought about by the timing of the molt: in Common Tern, for example, the primaries look more uniform above in midwinter (when all are medium dark gray) than in midsummer (when the outer primaries are much darker than the inner ones).

The full winter plumages of adult Arctic and Roseate terns are quite unlikely to be seen in North America. In fall, however, some changes in their appearance may be evident. The Arctic Tern's bill may begin to darken by late summer; and Roseate Terns often lose their long outer tail feathers before they leave North America in fall, resulting in a major change in their flight silhouette.

Field Marks — Adults

Underwing pattern (Fig. 48): Arctic Tern has narrow, sharply defined blackish tips to the outer seven or eight primaries; the effect is of a sharp, narrow black trailing edge to most of the outer part of the wing. The primaries and secondaries of this species are almost entirely translucent, adding to its very

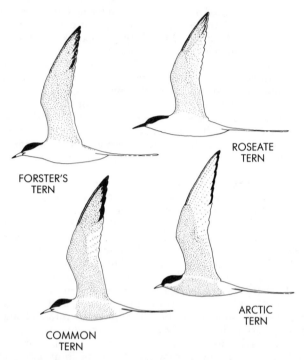

ROSEATE
TERN

FORSTER'S
TERN

ARCTIC
TERN

COMMON
TERN

Fig. 48. Underwing patterns, as seen on adult terns in summer. The most critical point to notice is the pattern of the trailing edge of the primaries. Unlike many other field marks, this trailing edge pattern on the underwing remains consistent for all ages and all seasons and provides an excellent distinction: Common and Forster's are similar, but the other two are quite different.

The amount and pattern of *translucence* of the wings, shown here as paler areas, can be a very good field mark when the birds are overhead against a bright sky. In Arctic Terns most of the flight feathers are translucent and glow bright white when backlit, while in Common Terns the area that admits light is limited to the inner primaries and outer secondaries. In Roseate Terns the whole trailing edge of the wing is brightly translucent, while the rest of the area of the flight feathers admits light in a diffuse way. Although the wings of Forster's are quite pale, they show little translucence even when they are brightly backlit.

white-winged look overhead. Common Tern has broader dark tips to the outer five or six primaries; the resulting dark trailing edge is broader than that of Arctic but not as long, and not quite so sharply demarcated. The Common Tern's wings show only a small area of translucence, or sometimes none, on the inner primaries. Forster's Tern duplicates the underwing pattern of Common but in slightly paler shades (medium gray instead of blackish gray); the difference is not usually apparent in the field. The wings of Forster's show little or no translucence. Roseate Tern has *no* dark tips to the primaries (except very narrowly on the outer one), so the trailing edge of the wing is entirely white, and this trailing edge can be conspicuously translucent.

Upperwing pattern (Fig. 49): Adult Arctic Tern in summer has uniformly pale gray upperwings. In the Common Tern the outer five or six primaries are noticeably darker than the inner five, and where these darker and paler gray areas meet, there is a dark *wedge* pointing in from the trailing edge of the wing; this becomes even more apparent in later summer and fall. Adult Forster's Tern in summer has pale silvery gray outer primaries, paler than the rest of the wing, especially early in the season (later on, they darken somewhat with wear). However, two-year-old Forster's in summer — which otherwise look much like adults — have much darker outer primaries, and can be confused with Common Tern. On adult Roseate Terns in summer, most of the wing is very pale, and about the outer three primaries are very dark. This dark leading edge of the outer wing looks very narrow in the field, but its degree of contrast is striking.

Tail pattern (Fig. 50): In adult Arctic Terns the tail is mostly white, but the narrow outer webs of the outer tail feathers are dark gray; these dark edges are not apparent at a distance, and the bird may look white-tailed when seen overhead. Common Tern has blackish outer webs on the outer tail feathers, which may show up a little more conspicuously than those of Arctic Tern and may be more apparent on birds overhead. In Forster's Tern the outer web of the outermost tail feather is *white*, the inner web of that feather is medium gray, and the rest of the tail is very pale gray. Tail pattern is one of the best confirming marks for separating Common and Forster's at close range, but at a distance in bright light either species may simply look white-tailed. The adult Roseate Tern really does have a pure white tail.

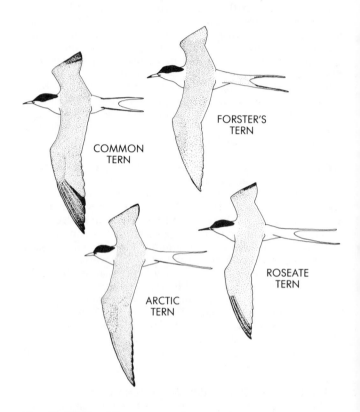

Fig. 49. Flight silhouettes and upperwing patterns of adult terns in summer. The extension of the tail behind the wings, compared to the extension of the head and bill in front of the wings, provides a clue for all species and is especially helpful for separating Common and Arctic. Note that the very long tail streamers of Roseate Tern are pure white, very thin, and sometimes inconspicuous, so that in the field the adults may sometimes look *short*-tailed. The pattern of the upperside of the primaries is distinctive for summer adults, but it is *not* reliable for immatures and must be used with caution for adults in winter plumage or in molt; see text for explanations of the complex seasonal variation in wing pattern.

Shape when perched: Standing terns provide a couple of clues that must be used with caution. One involves leg length. While Common and Roseate terns have about the same leg length, the legs of Arctic average distinctly shorter and those of Forster's average distinctly longer. The problem is that the illusion of leg length in the field is strongly affected by the way the bird is standing and by how much its belly feathers are fluffed out. For this reason, even when direct comparison to other terns is possible, leg length may not be a reliable mark.

The extension of the tail beyond the wingtips can be a useful mark on adults in summer, when their outermost tail feathers are complete and unbroken. On Common Tern, the tail never reaches beyond the wingtips. The tail extends noticeably past the wingtips on Arctic and Forster's, and especially so on Roseate, which has the combination of very long tail and relatively short wings. But if the tail feathers are missing, worn, or broken, this field mark will be unreliable.

Body plumage (Fig. 51): Arctic Tern in breeding plumage has the underparts medium gray, about the same shade as the

continued on p. 143

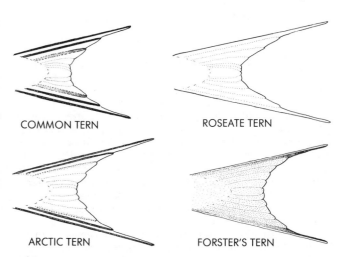

COMMON TERN

ROSEATE TERN

ARCTIC TERN

FORSTER'S TERN

Fig. 50. Tails of adult terns in summer, as seen from the upperside, to show shapes and patterns.

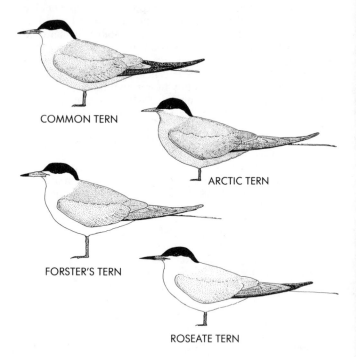

Fig. 51. Adult terns during the breeding season. In addition to bill shape and pattern, darkness of the underparts, tail length, and leg length (see text for these points), notice the wingtip pattern as it appears on these perched birds. On Arctic Terns the entire wingtip is relatively uniform (medium gray); on Forster's Terns it is also uniform, although slightly paler. On Roseate Terns, however, there is distinct contrast between the very dark outer three primaries and the much paler tone of the other primaries. Common Terns show the same kind of contrast, but here it is the outer five primaries that are dark, and we can just see the pale tone of the two innermost visible primaries (the rest of the primaries are hidden when the wing is folded).

Notice also the pattern formed by the lower edge of the black cap in front of the eye, and the amount of *white* that is left in this area between the gape of the bill and the cap. This amount of white is greatest in Forster's, smallest in Arctic, and intermediate in the other two species.

back. On some the face is a contrasting white stripe between the black cap and gray throat, but on others the throat is whitish also, reducing the contrast. Common Tern also has a gray breast in breeding plumage, and on some Commons the gray is as dark and extensive as on some Arctics. (Not treated here is the Siberian race of Common Tern, a regular stray to western Alaska, which is darker gray and has the bill and legs black in the breeding season.) Forster's Tern always has white underparts. Because it has a slightly paler back than Arctic or Common, and a slight grayish tinge to the rump and tail, adult Forster's in flight does not show much contrast between the rump and back (while Arctic and Common both show obvious contrast between the gray back and white rump). Roseate Tern has paler upperparts than the other three species; perched or flying, it may look white-backed, and adults never show apparent contrast between the back and rump. In breeding plumage, its breast is usually lightly washed with pink.

Flight silhouette and flight action: The combination of short bill, small head, and long tail gives Arctic Tern in flight the appearance of having its wings set far forward on its body. Its flight looks especially buoyant: the upstroke of the wings is quick, and the following downstroke is a slow, emphasized motion; the bird seems to float through the air. Common Tern has a larger head, longer bill, and shorter tail than Arctic, so in flight its wings appear to be set farther back on its body. Its action in flight looks less graceful than that of Arctic, with deep wingbeats that are emphasized equally on the upstroke and the downstroke. Forster's Tern is similar to Common in shape, but its bill and especially its tail are longer, and its wings may appear somewhat broader. Its wingbeats are usually shallower, slower, and more graceful than those of Common Tern. Roseate Tern has a long-looking head and long bill. Its outer tail feathers are also very long; but under some field conditions these narrow tail streamers may be very difficult to see, and at such times the bird actually looks "front-heavy." Roseate has relatively short wings and has the most distinctive flight of these four terns, with wingbeats that are shallow, fast, and stiff.

Bill shape and color: In all four species, males tend to have longer bills than females. But although there is overlap among the species, bill shape can be a helpful clue. Variation in bill color can cause confusion if it is not understood.

Arctic Tern has the shortest bill of these four, although many male Arctics are as long-billed as some female Commons. The Arctic's bill is deep red in summer, often with a slight dusky area near the tip of the upper mandible. Common Tern averages longer-billed than Arctic but shorter-billed than the other two species; its bill is variably red to orange-red at the base and black at the tip. Some Commons in summer lack the black tip on the bill, and since they also have gray underparts they are often misidentified as Arctics. Forster's Tern averages very slightly longer-billed than Common, but its bill is also usually somewhat *thicker* overall, and this is more likely to be noticed in the field. Its bill is variably orange to orange-red at the base. There is a tendency for the bill to be more red in Common, more orange in Forster's, but the great amount of individual variation makes this difference very unreliable. Roseate Tern averages about the same bill length as Forster's, but in the field its bill often gives the illusion of being longer, possibly because of the dark color. For most of the year the bill is black with a hint of red at the base, but for a brief period during the breeding season the bill becomes bright red for up to half its length.

All four species become black-billed in winter, and the bill may begin to darken by late summer, so bill color may not be a worthwhile field mark on fall migrants.

Voice: These terns all have a wide variety of calls, and the vocal differences between Common, Arctic, and Forster's are subtle. Birders who get to hear a lot of them, for instance those who live near mixed nesting colonies, can learn to tell them apart by voice; but written descriptions are unlikely to be helpful. However, one characteristic call of Roseate Tern, a musical *chivvyick*, is so different that it is easily recognized.

Special problems involving Forster's and Common: Forster's Tern seems to be misidentified as Common far more often than the reverse occurs. This is especially true in winter, when Common is largely absent from North America. Birders relying simply on the darkness of the primaries may be misled by first-winter Forster's, which are darker-winged than adults. The difference in head pattern (black scarf in Common, black eye patches separated by a white nape in Forster's) is nearly bridged by some Forster's that have gray napes in winter, even fairly dark gray. Young Forster's with dark napes and dark primaries can easily be miscalled. However, Common Tern is very scarce in North America after November; any reported later should be studied for tail pattern, bill shape, leg length, and precise head pattern. All Commons in winter (not just immatures) should show a dark carpal bar, which is lacking or faint on winter Forster's.

Another occasional problem involves two-year-old Forster's in summer, which can look just like adults but with darker primaries.

Field Marks — Juveniles and First-Winter Birds

When juvenile terns first become independent in summer, they can cause confusion for the birder. Their bills may be shorter than those of adults at first, and they also have shorter tails and shorter, more rounded wingtips, so their shapes look oddly unfamiliar to observers who know the adults. In these four species, juveniles show variegated wing patterns and dark markings on the back or scapulars. All have at least some brown or buff tones at first. From summer into fall the appearance of these birds changes gradually and continuously; the brown tones become less obvious, the head pattern becomes cleaner, and the bill grows to adult size. Therefore, among young birds of each species there is a lot of seasonal (and individual) variation; the notes below emphasize the points that tend to be more consistent and useful for separating the species. The illustrations show the birds as they would appear about September, when they would be far from the colonies and potentially most challenging for observers.

COMMON TERN: This species (Fig. 52) has the most variegated wing pattern of these four in juvenal/first-winter plumages, with a broad blackish *carpal bar* along the leading edge of the wing, *dark secondaries,* and paler coverts separating these two dark bands. Underwing pattern, with a broad blackish trailing edge on the outer primaries, is like that of the adult. The forehead has a strong wash of pale brown at first, but this is rapidly lost through wear, leaving the forehead whitish against a sooty half-cap that crosses the rear crown and nape. Barring or scaling on the lower back is apparent on fledglings, but wear soon makes this obscure. On recently fledged juveniles the bill is extensively pink at the base, but by the time of southward migration the bill is almost entirely black.

Fig. 52. Juvenile Common Tern, as it would appear about September of its first year.

Fig. 53. Juvenile Arctic Tern, as it would appear about September of its first year.

ARCTIC TERN: The carpal bar of juvenile Arctic (Fig. 53) is somewhat less striking than that of Common Tern, being narrower and not quite as dark. A more obvious difference is Arctic's *pale secondaries*, paler than the coverts, often looking *white* in flight. Underwing pattern, with a long, *narrow* *black trailing edge* on the primaries, is like that of the adult. The dark half-cap of Arctic is usually a deeper and more solid black than that of Common. The faint brown wash on the forehead and back, and the scaled effect on the lower back, are less apparent than on Common and are worn away more rapidly; at any given stage, Arctic tends to look more clean-cut than Common. Juvenile Arctic and Common both have dark outer edges to the tail, but on Arctic the tail is paler and the rump is whiter. The juvenile Arctic's bill usually looks all-black.

FORSTER'S TERN: The upperwing pattern of juvenile Forster's Terns (Fig. 54) is *more uniform* than in the other species, with only slightly darker secondaries and only a hint of a dark carpal bar. Underwing pattern, with a broad dark trailing edge on the outer primaries, is like that of the adult and thus similar to Common Tern. The darkness of the nape is quite variable, but even birds with a lot of dark gray across the nape show the outlines of the *black ear patches* that will be prominent later. Tinges of buff and brown on the face and upperparts are obvious on very young Forster's Terns, and although this color is rapidly worn away it may still be apparent on some fall migrants. Juvenile Forster's *lacks* dark outer edges to the tail, although the inside of the tail fork is dark. The black bill usually shows a pale area at the base.

Fig. 54. Juvenile Forster's Tern, as it would appear about September of its first year.

Fig. 55. Juvenile Roseate Tern, as it would appear about September of its first year.

ROSEATE TERN: The upperwing of juvenile Roseate (Fig. 55) has a dark carpal bar, nearly as prominent as on Common, but the Roseate's secondaries are white. The *white* trailing edge on the primaries, lacking any dark border, is an excellent field mark visible on both the upperside and the underside of the wing. At first the forehead is almost solidly dark, and even by autumn the head is still generally darker than in the other species. The back is also darker, with *barring* of black and brown that is especially heavy on the rear scapulars; this is most obvious on very young juveniles, but may still be quite apparent on fall migrants. Juvenile Roseate has a *longer and whiter tail* than the other three species. It also has an all-black bill, and noticeably *black legs*, unlike the reddish to brown legs of the juveniles of other species.

A Note on Hybrids

Unlike gulls, tern species very rarely hydridize. However, Common and Roseate terns have apparently interbred several times in the northeastern United States and in Britain. Birders should expect the hybrids to be intermediate between Common and Roseate in such matters as length and color of the bill, darkness of the back and wings, and length of the outermost tail feathers. The outermost tail feathers should usually be white, with a gray (not blackish) outer web; the underside of the wingtip could be quite variable, depending on the patterns of the individual primaries.

Apparent Common × Roseate hydrids have interbred successfully with each other and with parental types, and it may be impossible to identify the offspring of such pairings. However, birders should remember that even where large numbers of Commons and Roseates nest in the same colonies, hybrids make up only a tiny fraction of the population.

19

BRIEF NOTES ON OTHER TERNS

Imitation Sandwich Terns: The bill pattern of Sandwich Tern, black with a yellow tip, is well known. However, other species can also sometimes show a rough approximation of this pattern. I have seen several Forster's Terns in early fall with blackish bills that were paler at the tip; this may be some normal intermediate stage in their annual change from the mostly orange bill of summer to the all-black bill of winter. To identify a Sandwich Tern out of range, you should look at overall size, shape, and plumage pattern, not just bill pattern.

Sandwich Tern vs. Gull-billed Tern: With a little thought, these two are not hard to separate, but they can be a trap for the unwary. The pale bill tip of Sandwich can seem to vanish against a pale background, making the bill look shorter and thicker, more like that of Gull-billed. Juvenile Sandwich Terns add to the problem, since their bills are all-black and can be shorter at first. You can avoid confusion if you keep these possibilities in mind. In addition to the much *heavier* bill, Gull-billed also has a heavier body, broader wings, and (usually) shorter tail. Its slow, buoyant wingbeats are distinctive.

The Elegant Tern problem: Around the world there are several species of large terns with black crests and yellow to orange bills, and with white foreheads except in the breeding season. In North America our only usual representatives of this group are the Royal Tern and the Elegant Tern. Both are highly coastal, being virtually accidental even a few miles inland; Elegant is restricted to the southern Pacific Coast, while Royal is also found on the Atlantic and Gulf coasts. Nonetheless, both species have been documented as occurring hundreds of miles inland on very rare occasions.

Because either species is so rare away from salt water, these inland strays must be identified with great caution. If the tern is seen standing adjacent to some other species, relative size may be a clue and should be noted carefully. In breeding (alternate) plumage, Elegant tends to have a longer, shaggier crest than Royal and often has a pink "flush" on the feathers of the underparts. In the Elegant Tern's nonbreeding (basic) plumage, more of the black usually remains on the head, stretching forward to encircle the eye and extending forward as black streaks to the center of the crown. Royal in non-breeding plumage (which it wears for most of the year) becomes very white-headed, the eye usually (but not always) standing out as an isolated black spot on a white face. However, a Royal in molt can show a head pattern just like a typical winter Elegant.

The bill furnishes the best year-round distinction between the two species. It has been suggested that bill *color* could be a good mark — tending toward orange-red on Royal and orange-yellow on Elegant — but there is so much overlap that this would be worthless on a lone stray. Bill *shape* is a much better mark. The thinner bill of the Elegant looks exceptionally *long* in proportion to the rest of the bird. Whereas Royal Tern has a noticeable gonydeal angle on the lower mandible, giving the bill some heft and an overall straight look, Elegant usually appears to *lack* a clear gonydeal angle. This enhances the impression that the outer part of the lower mandible is very thin, and since there is no angle to serve as a balance to the curve of the upper mandible, the entire bill tip looks somewhat "drooped" on the Elegant.

These characters of shape are hard to describe convincingly, so if you find what appears to be either of these species out of range, you should make every effort to get photographs that show the shape of the bill and shape of the bird.

In a discussion of Elegant vs. Royal terns, the fly in the ointment is the existence of a bird called Cayenne Tern (*Sterna sandvicensis eurygnatha*), which is either a full species or a race of Sandwich Tern localized in the Caribbean and eastern South America. The Cayenne looks like a Sandwich Tern with a yellow bill, making it fairly similar to the Royal and Elegant terns. Cayenne Tern could be thought to resemble a small, pale-billed version of Royal or a slightly shorter-billed version of Elegant Tern.

Compared to Elegant, Cayenne Tern typically has a shorter, straighter-looking bill, and its bill is usually much duller yellow; its crest is also usually shorter. Cayenne and Elegant have each been reported convincingly in eastern North

America at least once. However, for the birder who finds one of these birds out of range, the best advice is: photograph it or forget it. Written descriptions just can't establish the record. Even if a description covered all the items separating Elegant from Cayenne, skeptics would rightly point out the problem of distinguishing either one from Lesser Crested Tern (*Sterna bengalensis*), which could conceivably stray across from northwest Africa.

A problem that is closer to home and more easily resolved involves the *juvenile* Royal Tern, which may have a smaller and yellower bill than the adult, and may mislead observers who are looking closely at terns for the first time. Fresh juveniles should be recognizable as such by the neat dark markings on the secondaries, tertials, scapulars, and tail. Bill shape and color should not be considered safe field marks for *any* juvenile terns.

20

THE SCREECH-OWLS

EASTERN SCREECH-OWL *Otus asio*
WESTERN SCREECH-OWL *Otus kennicottii*
WHISKERED SCREECH-OWL *Otus trichopsis*

The problem: Screech-owls present challenges to both the taxonomist and the field birder. Although all screech-owls are superficially very similar, they exhibit a great amount of geographical variation in size, color, and pattern. There is also individual variation — producing, in many areas, two or even three different color morphs of the same species.

With all this variation complicating the picture, scientists concluded only recently that the screech-owls of eastern and western North America were actually two distinct species. In the middle of the continent, where their ranges approach or overlap, the two species can pose identification problems for birders.

In the mountains of Arizona a third species, the Whiskered Screech-Owl, looks very similar to the Western Screech-Owl.

Preliminary Points

Use caution in dealing with variation: The section on field marks below treats the usual voice and appearance of each species, especially as they would apply in areas of overlap. However, *there are local exceptions* to many of the points presented here. If you think you have found one of these species out of normal range, or in an unexpected area, please read "Geographical Variation" on p. 158. The chances are that what you have discovered is not a vagrant but a local variant.

Field Marks — Screech-Owls

Voice: Each of the three species has two distinct types of common calls that are diagnostic for identification. Confusion over these has led to some reports of screech-owls giving the calls of both Eastern and Western. Since the birds also give a variety of other calls, it is best to concentrate on these two typical vocalizations for each species.

For a better understanding of these voice descriptions, listen to recordings or look at the diagrams provided here.

Fig. 56.

EASTERN SCREECH-OWL: A wail or whinny that starts on a rising note and then drops in pitch. Also a long, low trill on one pitch, lasting up to four seconds (Fig. 56).

Fig. 57.

WESTERN SCREECH-OWL: A series of notes on one pitch, more widely spaced at the beginning but speeding up at the end. Also a two-parted low trill with a short burst, a quick pause, and then a longer trill, all on one pitch (Fig. 57).

Fig. 58.

WHISKERED SCREECH-OWL: An even series of notes on one pitch, seeming to slow down slightly at the end. Also a series of long and short notes in a rhythmic pattern (sounding like Morse code), all on one pitch (Fig. 58).

Bill color: This is an excellent field mark, especially for silent adult screech-owls found perched in daylight, but one that must be used with care. In all three species, the *tip* of the upper mandible is usually pale. But the basal two-thirds of the upper mandible is generally *blackish* or dark gray in the adult Western Screech-Owl, dull *yellow-green* in the other two species.

One cautionary note is that juvenile Westerns are not quite as dark-billed as the adults at first. Their bills may look medium blue-gray at the base, and in bad light this color could be confused with the yellow-green of the other two species.

Pattern of underparts: The intricate markings of screech-owls reveal no obvious field marks, but the general patterns can be helpful (Fig. 59). The feathers of the underparts on all three species have a dark vertical stripe down the shaft of each feather, crossed by dark horizontal bars. On the Eastern, the dark crossbars are nearly as wide as the vertical stripes and are rather widely spaced. On the Western, the crossbars tend to be closer together and are mostly much narrower than the heavy black vertical stripes. The Whiskered has a pattern much like that of the Eastern, but often with a coarser or bolder look. (These descriptions apply to gray-morph birds; the markings are often less distinct in the red morph.)

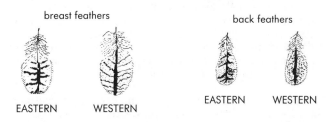

breast feathers   back feathers

EASTERN   WESTERN   EASTERN   WESTERN

Fig. 59. Screech-Owl feather patterns. The intricate markings of individual feathers combine to create different overall patterns on Eastern and Western screech-owls. The left two figures are sample breast feathers from Eastern (*left*) and Western (*right*); the right two figures are back feathers from Eastern (*left*) and Western (*right*).

Pattern of upperparts: Differences in back pattern among the three species are roughly parallel to the differences in their underparts, although the back feathers are darker and the pattern is harder to pick out. Western Screech-Owl has a back pattern dominated by the black vertical stripes, while Eastern and Whiskered have more obvious horizontal crossbars, the pattern of the Whiskered especially looking coarsely variegated or spotted.

Color morphs: The overall color of the birds will rarely be a field mark for separating Eastern and Western screech-owls. The Easterns on the southern Great Plains are mostly of the gray morph, but a small percentage of them are red or brown. In the southern part of its range, the Western occurs only in a gray morph; so any red or brown screech-owl found near the southern part of the contact zone is very likely to be an Eastern.

As far as is known, Whiskered Screech-Owls in the United States (found regularly only in Arizona) are all of the gray morph. The populations of Westerns with which they overlap in this country are all gray, also.

All screech-owls of the gray morph are at their purest gray when they are freshly molted, in fall; the feathers take on a slight brown tinge as they become worn, so the brown wash may be fairly noticeable by the following summer.

Size, proportions, and foot size: Eastern and Western screech-owls are the same size, although in both there is a trend from larger birds in the north to smaller birds in the south. Whiskered Screech-Owl averages smaller than the populations of Western with which it overlaps, but this difference is not apparent without direct comparison. However, the *feet* of the Whiskered are proportionately smaller than those of the other two species (Fig. 60), and a birder with some experience can perceive this difference in the field.

Ear tufts: There is a tendency for the ear tufts to be more conspicuous on Eastern, less so on Western, and even less so on Whiskered screech-owls. However, screech-owls can raise or flatten these feather tufts, so this average difference is never reliable as a field mark.

Other points: The Whiskered Screech-Owl gets its name for its long facial bristles, even longer than those of its relatives. However, this difference is difficult to judge even in the hand, and probably has no value as a field mark.

WESTERN   WHISKERED

Fig. 60. Western and Whiskered screech-owls; southern Arizona forms are shown for both. Compare size of the feet, darkness of the bill, and pattern of the underparts.

A character sometimes mentioned for separating Western and Whiskered involves the pattern of the inner web of the outermost primary, which is crossed by light bars in the Western but unmarked in the Whiskered. Unfortunately, this character is practically useless, even in the hand. The light bars on the Western are variable in their intensity; besides, many Whiskereds show at least a trace of light barring on these feathers, sometimes quite a noticeable amount.

Quick Summary

Be sure to refer to the text for further explanations.

EASTERN SCREECH-OWL: Voice, descending whinny and long, low trill; bill yellow-green; underparts with strong horizontal bars and vertical stripes; back with fine horizontal and vertical markings; red, brown, and gray morphs all possible in most areas.

WESTERN SCREECH-OWL: Voice, accelerating series and two-parted trill; bill usually black; underparts with strong vertical stripes; back with strong vertical stripes; no red or brown morph in most areas.

WHISKERED SCREECH-OWL: Voice, even series and "Morse code"; bill yellow-green; underparts with strong horizontal bars and vertical stripes; back with coarse horizontal and vertical markings; no red or brown morph. Feet proportionately small.

Geographic Variation

This is only a brief outline of those regional differences in appearance of screech-owls that may affect their field identification. Taxonomists have debated how many races should be formally recognized; much of the variation in screech-owls of the lowlands is *clinal* (showing gradual and continuous change from one area to another), so that subspecies are difficult to define. Birders who are interested in this debate, or in further details of screech-owl variation, should consult some of the papers listed in the Bibliography for some contrasting views.

EASTERN SCREECH-OWL: The most obvious geographical variation in this species involves the frequency of occurrence of the red and brown morphs. These color types are very uncommon toward the western limits of the species' range; they are also uncommon toward the north. The red morph becomes more common in parts of the southeast, where it outnumbers the gray morph in some areas. In Florida, the three color types (red, brown, and gray) are evidently about equally common. Size of the birds decreases toward the south. In addition, birds from the southern part of the range may give calls that are slightly shorter than those of northern birds.

The most distinctive race of Eastern is *O. a. mccallii*, found only in the Rio Grande Valley of southern and southwestern Texas. Currently it is regarded as a race of Eastern, but some have suggested that it might be a full species. There is apparently no red morph in *mccallii*, and its back is patterned like that of Western Screech-Owl; but in voice, pale bill, and pattern of underparts, it is more typical of the Eastern.

WESTERN SCREECH-OWL: A potential source of confusion involves some populations from the Pacific Northwest, which have pale bills (like the Eastern) and can occur in red or brown morphs. Those from adjacent areas, including the northern Great Basin region, sometimes occur in a brown morph, and even the gray-morph birds often show a wash of brown on the plumage. Voice and general plumage pattern, however, show that these birds are all indeed Western Screech-Owls.

Elsewhere, virtually all Westerns are gray. Toward the south they average smaller and paler, and some desert birds have a wash of pink in fresh plumage. There is a tendency for the southern birds to give slightly shorter calls than those farther north.

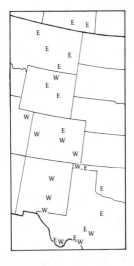

Fig. 61. The interface in screech-owl ranges. Because Eastern and Western screech-owls were considered one species for so long, the division between their ranges has not been fully worked out. This map shows a few summer localities reported for Eastern ("**E**") and Western ("**W**") through the center of the continent. Overlap between the two species has been found locally in central and southwestern Texas and may occur elsewhere as well.

21

HUMMINGBIRDS

The problem: It can be hard enough just to see these tiny, hyperactive creatures. But even given an excellent view, some hummingbirds remain very difficult to identify. In North America the adult males have distinctive patterns, but females and immatures of several species are superficially similar. Study of the finer points is complicated by the fact that within a species, plumages of immature females, immature males, and adult females are often more different from each other than they are from some plumages of *other* species — so a hummingbird that looks "obviously different" from the others in the neighborhood may simply represent a different age and sex class. Furthermore, males going from immaturity to adulthood can pass through confusing intermediate stages. And for a final complication, hybrids are not as rare among hummingbirds as they are among most bird families.

Preliminary Points

Hummingbirds challenge the observer's powers of perception. The fine details and subtle differences that separate them may be apparent only after a lot of comparative experience.

Of course it is harder to learn the hummers in an area where only one species occurs. Paradoxically, most Eastern birders do not know even their own Ruby-throated Hummingbird very well: they have never had to look closely to see what species it was. If you live in the East, try to learn the Ruby-throated as thoroughly as possible. Then, when you go west, you will recognize the Black-chinned as a very similar species, and you will have a basis for comparison for other hummers as well.

Birders should take every opportunity to spend time

watching well-attended hummingbird feeders, where a few hours can yield more good views than a month's worth of encounters "in the wild." Another big advantage to sitting and watching a feeder is that you see every bird at the same distance and in the same light conditions; it becomes much easier to judge minor differences in size and color.

So, looking closely at a hummingbird, notice these things:

Tone of underparts: Confusingly plain female hummers include four (Ruby-throated, Black-chinned, Costa's, Anna's) with no rufous in the tail and little or no obvious buff on the underparts, and four widespread species (Broad-tailed, Rufous, Allen's, Calliope) with at least some rufous in the tail and buff on the underparts. These two quartets of species receive detailed treatment below. When observing these or any other drab hummingbirds, be sure to note carefully the exact shading of color on the underparts.

Tail shape and pattern: In the museum, when ornithologists must identify a difficult hummingbird specimen, the precise shape and pattern of various tail feathers often provide the best evidence. Unfortunately, this level of detail is impossible to see in the field; but the general shape, color, and pattern of a hummer's tail can often be discerned, especially when the bird spreads its tail while hovering at a feeder. When a mystery hummingbird can be photographed, the most useful photos will usually be those that show the spread tail.

Bill shape: Length, thickness, and curvature of the bill are significant field marks for hummingbirds. However, recently fledged juveniles may be visibly shorter-billed than adults; their bills may not reach adult length until they are several weeks or even a few months old. In several species, males tend to be slightly shorter-billed than females.

Back color: The answer here is "green," of course, but differences among species in the precise shade of green can be helpful for experienced birders.

Juvenile hummingbirds have broad pale edgings to the back feathers, creating a pale scaled or scalloped effect until these edgings wear away. Adults in fresh plumage also have pale feather edgings, though not so broad or conspicuous as those of juveniles; but these are apparent only when the birds have recently molted, and most adult hummingbirds apparently molt on the wintering grounds, which are mostly south of the United States. (Two that are with us year round — Anna's and the nonmigratory race of Allen's — breed in winter and molt in summer, so adults of these two show pale back edgings in late summer and fall.)

Voice: Typical call notes are among the most important things to notice about any hummer. They are of little aid in separating the "impossible" species pairs (Ruby-throated vs. Black-chinned and Rufous vs. Allen's), but in most other cases they are extremely helpful. Notes given by foraging or perched birds are easiest to categorize. Most hummers also give a variety of squealing or chattering calls during aggressive encounters, but these are more difficult to learn (and to describe).

Actions: The characteristic feeding postures of some species may provide clues to identification; notice especially how the tail is held and how much it is moved while the bird is hovering. These points of posture apply only *on average* — that is, they are not diagnostic — and you may have to watch for a while to appreciate the differences among species.

Size: Although the species treated here show substantial size differences, these differences are very tricky to use unless you can study two or more species in direct comparison. Recently fledged juvenile hummingbirds can be smaller than adults.

Group I: Small Plain Species

ANNA'S HUMMINGBIRD *Calypte anna*
COSTA'S HUMMINGBIRD *Calypte costae*
BLACK-CHINNED HUMMINGBIRD *Archilochus alexandri*
RUBY-THROATED HUMMINGBIRD *Archilochus colubris*

Females and immatures of these four species are small to medium-sized hummingbirds lacking any rufous in the tail and usually lacking any obvious buff on the underparts. These four are likely to be confused only with each other, but see also Broad-tailed and Calliope hummingbirds (in Group II) and Lucifer Hummingbird (in "Other Hummingbird Problems" on p. 170).

Adult males: Given reasonable views, adult males of these four species are unlikely to be misidentified.

The adult male Ruby-throated is very superficially similar to the adult male Broad-tailed Hummingbird of the West: both have red throats and green upperparts. However, observers who are familiar with both are extremely unlikely to confuse the two. Ruby-throated tends to be slimmer, Broad-tailed is more chunky and has a larger tail. Ruby-throated has a black patch from the chin back to below the eye and looks darker-faced, with only a small white spot behind the eye; Broad-tailed usually has a diffuse pale area surrounding the eye. Ruby-throated is slightly more orange-red on the throat and golden-green on the back, while Broad-tailed tends toward rose-red on the throat and blue-green on the back. For most of the year (except briefly during molt) the wings of the adult male Broad-tailed make a shrill metallic trill.

ANNA'S HUMMINGBIRD — females, immatures: Anna's Hummingbird is slightly larger and more solidly built than the others in this group. Its tail usually looks less rounded than the others' and shows less black, more gray, in the outer tail feathers. When hovering, Anna's usually holds its tail in line with the axis of its body, with relatively little flipping or spreading of the tail. Its bill is similar in length to that of Costa's but may look slightly heavier; it tends to be shorter than that of Black-chinned (Fig. 62). The underparts are quite grayish, usually with an extensive wash of dull green on the sides. Adult females typically have some red spots on the throat, often concentrated in a patch on the center of the lower throat. The common call note of Anna's is a dry, loud *tzick* or *kipp*; in excitement, the bird may run several notes together into a rapid chatter.

Juvenile Anna's Hummingbirds (especially those not long out of the nest) can differ from adult females in confusing ways: they are smaller at first, their underparts may be paler, and they may lack the red on the throat and green on the sides. Voice may be the only sure way to identify some of these.

COSTA'S HUMMINGBIRD — females, immatures: This small hummingbird of the deserts often looks round-bodied or pot-bellied. The Costa's tail is *short* and visibly *rounded* (because the outer feathers are short, narrow, and round-tipped); when hovering, Costa's usually flips the tail up and down. When this hummingbird is perched, the wingtips ex-

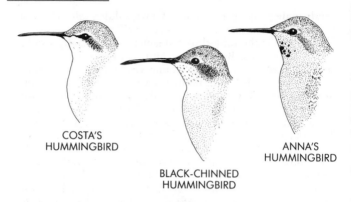

Fig. 62. Adult female hummingbirds of three relatively plain species: Costa's, Black-chinned, and Anna's. Note bill length, darkness of chest, pattern of face. Throat patterns can be quite variable, but the patterns shown here are typical for each species.

tend beyond the tip of the tail. Seen in profile, the bill looks notably thin (or flattened) and slightly decurved. In adult females and immature birds the back often has a pale or grayish look, and the underparts are nearly white, paler than in similar species. The throat is virtually unmarked white in adult females (occasionally with a few purple spots), but young males will show purple coming in on the throat, often starting near the back corners of the gorget. A dusky patch on the ear coverts is well defined (though not large), set off by the whitish throat and a pale line behind the eye. The call note of Costa's is a thin, hard *tik*; in excitement, the bird may run many notes together into a rapid ticking or twittering.

BLACK-CHINNED HUMMINGBIRD — females, immatures: Common over much of the West and almost identical to the Ruby-throated of the East, the Black-chinned Hummingbird makes a good basis for comparison with other plain hummingbirds. In body size it is smaller than Anna's and a little larger than Costa's. The outer tail feathers are longer and wider than in Costa's, for a less rounded tail shape, and the outermost feathers are bluntly pointed in most (more rounded in immature females); also, the tail usually looks more contrastingly patterned than in Anna's (Fig. 63). When hovering, the Black-chinned usually flips and spreads the tail

ANNA'S   COSTA'S   BLACK-CHINNED   BLACK-CHINNED
                               (adult female)   (half tail of
                                                immature female)

Fig. 63. Tail patterns of female hummingbirds, seen from upperside. On Anna's, note the reduced amount of black in the
outer tail feathers. On Costa's, the outer tail feathers are
round-tipped and shorter, creating a round-tailed appearance.
The adult female Black-chinned has a contrasting pattern,
and its outer tail feathers are bluntly pointed. On the immature female Black-chinned, the outer tail feathers are
more rounded at the tip, creating a tail shape somewhat more
like Costa's.

almost continuously. The bill averages longer than in Costa's
or Anna's and usually looks slightly decurved. The underparts are paler than in most Anna's, but somewhat grayer or
dingier than in Costa's. The throat varies from almost unmarked to lightly streaked (usually) to heavily marked with
dusky, but whatever markings may be present are spread
evenly over the entire throat. The dusky patch on the ear
coverts often spreads out more than on female and immature
Costa's, extending down into the throat somewhat and often
partly obscuring the pale line behind the eye. The common
call note, a descending *teew*, is very different from that of any
other western hummingbird.

Juveniles can be either darker or paler gray below than
adults, their bills may be shorter at first, and juvenile females
may look more round-tailed than adults; thus, some young
birds can look confusingly close to Costa's. Their voices,
however, are quite distinctive. Some immature males may
show black or purple feathers coming in on the throat.

**RUBY-THROATED HUMMINGBIRD — females, imma-
tures:** For all practical purposes, the Ruby-throated Hummingbird is identical to the Black-chinned except in adult
male plumage. There are some slight differences that may

help the observer to detect the possible presence of either species out of range, but such identifications can be no more than tentative unless the birds are mist-netted for examination in the hand.

The bill of Ruby-throated averages shorter than that of Black-chinned — but young birds average shorter-billed than adults, males average shorter-billed than females, and there is much overlap between the two species. In adult females, the forehead tends to be green in Ruby-throateds, more gray or brown in Black-chinneds, but this may not hold for younger birds. The voices of the two species are extremely similar. Some observers have suggested that, when hovering, Ruby-throateds may move the tail much less than Black-chinneds; this possibility merits further study.

Group II: The *Selasphorus* Complex

BROAD-TAILED HUMMINGBIRD *Selasphorus platycercus*
RUFOUS HUMMINGBIRD *Selasphorus rufus*
ALLEN'S HUMMINGBIRD *Selasphorus sasin*
CALLIOPE HUMMINGBIRD *Stellula calliope*

In this group, females and immatures show at least a trace of buff on the underparts and rufous in the tail. Adult males of Broad-tailed and Calliope are distinctive if seen well, and they receive no further attention here. Rufous and Allen's, however, are extraordinarily similar in all plumages; I shall treat them as a single unit for the most part (Rufous/Allen's Hummingbird) because most individuals cannot be separated in the field. This section is devoted mainly to separating Broad-tailed, Calliope, and Rufous/Allen's in female and immature plumages.

RUFOUS/ALLEN'S — females, immatures: Rufous/Allen's Hummingbird is the most widespread (and usually the most common) member of this complex. Its migrations are notably early. Northward migration (mostly along the Pacific Coast and through the westernmost deserts) is mainly from February to early April; southbound birds are already common throughout the West by early July. Because it is so numerous, and because it is sized between Broad-tailed and Calliope hummingbirds, it makes a good basis for comparison.

Plumage color and pattern of Rufous/Allen's varies with

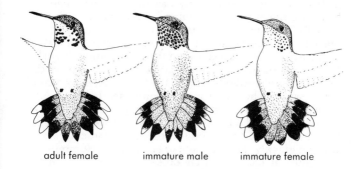

adult female   immature male   immature female

Fig. 64. Variation within Rufous Hummingbirds. The hordes of "female-plumaged" hummingbirds seen in late summer show a great amount of variation within species; much of this is owing to age and sex differences. Here, for example, are typical late-summer plumages of Rufous Hummingbirds: adult female, immature male, and immature female. Notice the striking differences in throat pattern and in shape and pattern of the tail feathers; shading of the underparts also differs somewhat.

sex and age (Fig. 64). Of the three categories considered here — adult females, immature males, and immature females — the immature males have the narrowest tail feathers and the greatest amount of rufous in the tail, while immature females have the broadest tail feathers and smallest amount of rufous. The central tail feathers of immature females often appear all-green in the field (because the limited rufous at the base may be hidden by the uppertail coverts). When hovering, Rufous/Allen's moves its tail very little and often holds the tail up almost horizontally; it shares this behavior with Broad-tailed and Calliope. A rusty wash on the sides, flanks, and undertail coverts is variable in darkness and extent but is usually more obvious and more contrasty than in Broad-tailed or Calliope. The throat may be lightly spotted with dusky (immature females), more heavily spotted with bronze and a little red (immature males), or blotched with red toward the center (adult females). The back and rump have variable amounts of rufous edging on the feathers. The call note of Rufous/Allen's is a musical *chip*.

BROAD-TAILED HUMMINGBIRD — females, immatures:
This is one bird that actually has an appropriate name. In body size the Broad-tailed Hummingbird is not much larger than Rufous/Allen's, but its tail is much larger, and with practice you can see this in the field. The outer tail feathers are conspicuously rufous toward the base. A smooth wash of buff on the sides, flanks, and undertail coverts is paler than in most Rufous/Allen's; in the field this may look washed out to white. The throat is very lightly spotted with dusky (young males may show some red feathers there). The back is a rich green or blue-green; juveniles may show rufous edgings to some back and rump feathers, but these apparently wear off quickly. The call note of Broad-tailed Hummingbird is a musical *chip* like that of Rufous/Allen's or slightly higher-pitched.

CALLIOPE HUMMINGBIRD — females, immatures: Small size alone is not enough for identifying this species — some Rufous/Allen's approach the Calliope Hummingbird in size. The very short bill and tail provide better clues (Fig. 65). The tail, especially, seems short and stubby even for the small size of the bird; it looks quite rounded when spread, and on

BROAD-TAILED   RUFOUS   CALLIOPE
HUMMINGBIRD   HUMMINGBIRD   HUMMINGBIRD

Fig. 65. Adult female hummingbirds, from left to right: Broad-tailed, Rufous (Allen's is extremely similar), Calliope. Tail shape, bill shape, and shading of the underparts are important marks. Throat pattern is variable, especially in Rufous and Allen's, and should be used with caution when identifying species.

the perched bird it does not extend as far as the tips of the folded wings. Rufous in the tail is usually limited to small areas on the edges of the outer tail feathers, near the base, and is not always visible in the field. The sides and flanks are pale buff, and this color often washes right across the center of the chest, not fading to white as on the larger *Selasphorus* hummingbirds. The throat is lightly and evenly spotted on both adult females and immatures. When hovering, the Calliope holds its tail very still and angled up to above horizontal. Its call note, not heard very often, is a very thin musical *chip*, like that of Rufous/Allen's but noticeably softer and higher-pitched.

Some immature female Rufous/Allen's Hummingbirds can be very similar to the female Calliope, so this species should be identified with caution, especially outside its normal range.

Separating Rufous and Allen's hummingbirds: Allen's Hummingbird comes very close to being totally unidentifiable in the field away from its breeding grounds.

A bird that looks like an adult male Rufous can be confidently identified, but a bird that looks like an adult male Allen's *might* also be a Rufous. Occasionally, a Rufous can develop the full adult gorget and tail pattern while retaining an almost entirely green back, thus looking like a classic Al-

RUFOUS

ALLEN'S

Fig. 66. Tails of adult male *Selasphorus* hummingbirds. Rufous Hummingbird and Allen's Hummingbird, as seen from upperside, to show width of outermost tail feathers and shape of the tips on the second-from-center pair of tail feathers.

len's. Because this variant of Rufous seems to be rare, it is probably safe to identify adult male Allen's by sight in areas where they are known to occur commonly. Anywhere else, it's important to confirm the identity of a suspected adult male Allen's by determining the shape of certain tail feathers (Fig. 66).

Female and immature Allen's are, in fact, indistinguishable from female and immature Rufous Hummingbirds under field conditions. The outer tail feathers tend to be narrower in Allen's, and the tail feathers next to the central pair tend to be more evenly shaped at the tip, but the differences among age and sex classes *within* each species (as shown for Rufous in Figure 64 above) far outweigh the differences *between* the two species. The amount of detail necessary for a specific identification is impossible to see in the field and questionable even in the best of stop-action photos.

Some Rufous/Allen's seen out of range have been identified specifically as immature male Rufous because they have had rufous feathers on the back — an identification based on the belief that the back is always green on Allen's. Unfortunately, this does not hold true, and immature males of both species can have rufous on the back.

Broad-tailed Hummingbirds out of season: The Broad-tailed is extraordinarily rare in North America in winter. Most reports of adult males wintering — or even present in late fall — probably refer to Anna's Hummingbirds (perhaps young males) with full red throats but without the red on the crown. Anna's can be recognized by its much grayer underparts and very different call.

Other Hummingbird Problems

WHITE-EARED HUMMINGBIRD: In Arizona, many reports of the rare White-eared Hummingbird are based on misidentified Broad-billed Hummingbirds. Female and immature Broad-billeds resemble White-eareds in having a white "ear" stripe and some red on the bill; many have some green on the sides (a mark often mentioned for White-eared). Young male Broad-billeds develop much of the adult male's blue-green color on the underparts before they lose the white ear stripe, which makes them even more likely to be mistaken for the White-eared.

Thus, birders who are not familiar with the Broad-billed

BROAD-BILLED
immature male

WHITE-EARED
adult female

Fig. 67. Immature male Broad-billed Hummingbird compared to adult female White-eared Hummingbird. Note bill length and throat pattern. Some immature female White-eareds show a less distinct facial pattern than the adult bird illustrated.

should be cautious about identifying White-eared Hummingbird. Notice the following points. *Face pattern:* The ear patch (below the white stripe) is virtually always *blackish* in White-eared, gray in the female or immature Broad-billed. In White-eared the crown is usually darker and duller than the back (Broad-billed has this effect occasionally), further emphasizing the white "ear" stripe. *Throat pattern:* In female/ immature White-eared, the throat has round dark spots on a whitish background; these spots are usually small and dusky near the base of the bill, large and green on the lower throat. Female/immature Broad-billeds may have limited spotting at the sides of the throat, but the center of the throat is distinctly smooth *gray;* when young males start to assume adult plumage, the throat color appears as large violet splotches, not rounded green spots. *Head and bill shape:* White-eared has a visibly *shorter bill* and usually seems to have a *larger head,* emphasizing the bill-length difference (Fig. 67). The species are roughly the same size, but Broad-billed appears more slender, White-eared more compact and chunky.

LUCIFER HUMMINGBIRD: Another problem in the Southwest, perhaps reported more often than it is actually seen, is the Lucifer Hummingbird. There are two major reasons for the confusion. (1) Birders may fail to notice the exact bill shapes of other hummingbirds until they start looking for the curved-billed Lucifer. Black-chinned and Costa's hummingbirds, common in some southwestern lowland areas, typically have slightly decurved bills. (2) Hummingbirds often carry a light dusting of pollen from contact with flowers; yellow pollen on the throat or upper breast can be reminiscent of the buffy underparts of the female Lucifer.

The adult male Lucifer should be easily recognized by the combination of field marks listed in standard bird guides as well as by the relatively *long* tail for the bird's size. Females can be more subtle. Like several other female hummingbirds, the female Lucifer has a pale stripe behind the eye, set off by a dusky patch on the ear coverts. On Lucifer this stripe tends to *broaden* toward the rear and usually connects with the pale throat, and a buff wash from the underparts usually extends up noticeably into this pale eyestripe. The Lucifer also usually looks heavier-billed than other small hummingbirds, and a close view will usually reveal some rufous at the base of the outer tail feathers; in females as in males, the tail looks somewhat long for the bird's size.

Hybrid hummingbirds: Hummingbird species hybridize far more often than members of most bird families (i.e., in hummingbirds hybridization is rare rather than extremely rare). Since it seems that any two species may interbreed where their ranges overlap, I make no attempt here to describe the known hybrid combinations. Birders encountering truly strange-looking hummers may be tempted to identify them as strays from the tropics, but the possibility of hybrid origin should be considered first. Some references on hybrid hummingbirds appear in the Bibliography.

22

THE YELLOW-BELLIED SAPSUCKER COMPLEX

YELLOW-BELLIED SAPSUCKER *Sphyrapicus varius*
RED-NAPED SAPSUCKER *Sphyrapicus nuchalis*
RED-BREASTED SAPSUCKER *Sphyrapicus ruber*

The problem: The taxonomy of this group was the subject of much debate in the past. Wherever the breeding ranges of any two of these forms come in contact, there is some interbreeding between them; but apparently most of the birds still tend to choose mates of their own kind. For years they were officially treated as forms of one species (because they frequently hybridize), but some experts argued that each form was a full species in its own right (because the interbreeding seemed to be limited, not purely random). The split of these three into full species did not gain acceptance until the 1980s.

The Red-breasted Sapsucker, of the Pacific coastal region, is very distinctive in the northern part of its range — having the entire head, as well as the breast, deep red. But in the southern race of Red-breasted (*S. r. daggetti*), the red of the head is invaded by a fair amount of white and black. Observers are sometimes confused by birds of this race, supposing them to represent some sort of hybrid.

The remaining two forms, the Red-naped Sapsucker (nesting in the Rocky Mountain and Great Basin ranges) and the Yellow-bellied Sapsucker (nesting farther north and east), are usually easy to separate. Comparing males with males and females with females, the Red-naped almost always has more red in the head pattern than does the Yellow-bellied. However, the color of the nape is not completely diagnostic for either species: Red-napeds (especially females) may lack red on the nape, and a few Yellow-bellieds do show a trace of red there. A rather surprising problem here is that the female Red-naped sometimes looks confusingly similar to the male Yellow-bellied Sapsucker.

The possibility of hybrids is another complication in identifying sapsuckers. Hybrids make up only a small fraction of the total population, but in some areas of the continent they do occur rather frequently. Their existence should always be taken into account — especially when you are identifying what seems to be one of the forms outside its normal range.

Finally, although juveniles of the three forms are distinctive enough, they can pose problems for birders simply because they are not treated separately in most bird guides.

Distribution

The approximate breeding ranges of the three species are mapped or described in most recent field guides. The northern and southern races of Red-breasted Sapsucker meet and intergrade in southern Oregon.

In migration and winter, the birds may turn up farther afield. The Yellow-bellied, the most migratory of the three, winters commonly in the eastern United States, sparsely but regularly in parts of the Southwest; it strays west to the California coast. The Red-naped winters at low elevations in the Southwest, from southern coastal California east at least to New Mexico and far western Texas. There have been a few claims of Red-napeds farther east, but proof of such records has been elusive. The northern race of Red-breasted winters mainly in coastal areas of its breeding range, while the southern race winters widely in California and rarely farther east.

Field Marks — Typical Adults

For simplicity's sake, this section illustrates and briefly describes only typical adults of each form. However, there is individual variation that affects identification in some cases; be sure to consult the subsequent sections before drawing any conclusions about an odd-looking bird.

YELLOW-BELLIED SAPSUCKER: Upper part of nape is crossed by a broad white stripe. Throat (entirely white in females, red in males) is surrounded by black "frame," including solidly black malar stripe. Back is more heavily marked with white than in the other forms, and the white is usually tinged with golden-buff (Fig. 68).

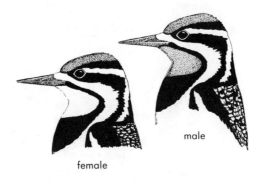

Fig. 68. Yellow-bellied Sapsuckers, typical adults.

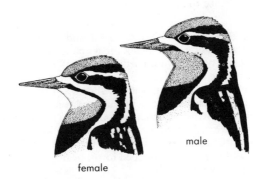

Fig. 69. Red-naped Sapsuckers, typical adults.

RED-NAPED SAPSUCKER: Stripe crossing upper nape is usually red, sometimes only partially red on white background. Throat of male is solidly red, and the red spreads out toward the sides to cover part of the black malar stripe, thus breaking the black "frame"; the red also usually spreads down onto the black chest area somewhat more than on Yellow-bellied. In typical female, chin and upper throat are white, lower throat is red, the throat patch being surrounded by a complete black "frame." Back has less white than in Yellow-bellied form; the white is generally arranged within two longitudinal bands (one down each side of back) and sometimes tinged with yellow (Fig. 69).

southern race   northern race

Fig. 70. Red-breasted Sapsucker. *Left,* southern race (*S. r. daggetti*). *Right,* northern race (*S. r. ruber*). In this species the sexes are similar, but females tend to show a little more white on the face than males in each race.

RED-BREASTED SAPSUCKER: Breast and head are mainly or entirely red, lacking the black breast patch and crown and nape markings of the two preceding forms (Fig. 70).

Southern race, *S. r. daggetti:* Head color tends toward orange-red or scarlet. This subspecies shows a little of the face pattern of more eastern birds: black lores, white spot behind eye, blackish mottling on cheeks, long white malar stripe; in females these marks may be more apparent, and the white spot behind the eye may be extended into a stripe. Back pattern much like that of Red-naped form, or may have slightly less white. Belly dull yellow.

Northern race, *S. r. ruber:* Head a deeper shade of red, normally with only a small amount of black on the lores and white at beginning of malar area. Back with less white than in other forms, the markings arranged within two narrow stripes, and usually tinged strongly with yellow. The red area tends to stretch farther down the breast than in the southern race *daggetti,* the belly is a deeper yellow, and the two colors contrast abruptly where they meet.

Variation in Adults and Resulting Identification Problems

YELLOW-BELLIED SAPSUCKER: Females may have a reduced amount of red on the crown, and on some birds the red is completely absent, so that the crown is entirely black.

Rarely, females have a few red feathers in the throat (visible only at close range). These are interesting variants but should create no real identification problems. More troublesome is the fact that occasional Yellow-bellieds, mostly males, have some red feathers in the white nape stripe. Therefore, any supposed "Red-naped Sapsucker" east of the Rockies should be studied carefully, with special attention to the throat and back patterns.

RED-NAPED SAPSUCKER: Males should always be distinctive, although the red on the nape can be reduced on some (even reduced to the point of being absent). The red on the nape is on the tips of the feathers, so worn birds (as in midsummer) can show less red here than birds in fresh plumage.

Females can pose two kinds of problems. (1) They are more likely than males to have reduced red on the nape, sometimes to the degree that the nape can look white in the field, especially in midsummer (but such birds should still be identifiable by the red lower throat). (2) On some the red of the throat is more extensive, occasionally leaving only a few white feathers on the chin, but such birds may still have a complete black malar line, all of which can suggest the throat pattern of the *male* Yellow-bellied. It seems very unlikely that any one bird could combine these two variations — showing both a greatly reduced amount of red on the nape and a greatly increased amount of red on the throat — but if one did, it could look very similar to the male of the Yellow-bellied Sapsucker.

YELLOW-BELLIED SAPSUCKER × RED-NAPED SAP-SUCKER: This hybrid should be intermediate in appearance between the two parental types. It may not be possible to identify this hybrid combination in the field with complete certainty: the parental forms are similar enough that a bird which seems intermediate could be just an extreme variant of one form or the other.

RED-BREASTED SAPSUCKER (northern race — S. r. ruber) × either RED-NAPED or YELLOW-BELLIED SAPSUCKER: These hybrids (Fig. 71) can look quite similar to the Red-breasted's southern race (*daggetti*). The best distinction is chest pattern: the hybrids should always show a lot of black there; *daggetti* may have some black flecking showing through its red breast, but it apparently never has a well-defined black chest patch.

Fig. 71. A hybrid, with a Red-breasted Sapsucker of the northern race (*S. r. ruber*) as one parent, and either a Red-naped or a Yellow-bellied Sapsucker as the other parent. Hybrids of this combination are sometimes mistaken for the southern race of Red-breasted (*S. r. daggetti*), but the hybrids usually show a substantial amount of black on the chest (unlike *daggetti*).

One more hybrid: At least twice, Red-naped Sapsucker has hybridized with Williamson's Sapsucker. Obviously, you are not likely to see this hybrid type (and just as obviously, I'm not going to describe it!). Field identification of such a hybrid could be tricky. Females would probably have extensive brown, perhaps resembling a molting juvenile Yellow-bellied; even with a male, one would have to take into account the possibility of a melanistic Red-naped.

Field Marks — Juveniles

Juveniles of these sapsuckers differ from adults in being much browner, especially on the head and breast, where brown replaces the black and red and at least partly obscures the white pattern. Lacking the major field marks that we use for adults, we must identify juveniles by other means.

It is important to note the timing of the postjuvenal molt, in which young birds lose the brown and develop the adult pattern. In the Red-breasted and Red-naped sapsuckers, this molt happens early. They begin to show some of the red pattern by late August or early September, at the very latest; by the time the first migrants begin to move, in mid- to late September, they have basically the same head patterns as adults (although the young Red-napeds may retain a lot of brown on the breast during the fall). By contrast, the Yellow-bellied goes through this molt much later or more slowly. Immature Yellow-bellieds continue to have much brown about the head throughout the fall and early winter, and sometimes even as late as March. So any "obvious imma-ture" seen after September is pretty certainly a Yellow-bellied Sapsucker.

The remaining question — how to identify the species of true juveniles in summer — will not be a problem in most areas, since they are most unlikely to be seen outside the breeding range of their own form; but it may be of critical importance where the breeding ranges of two species come in contact. The descriptions below will identify most typical juveniles. There is variation, of course, and extreme variants would be impossible to separate from hybrids in the field.

RED-BREASTED SAPSUCKER: Head dark dusky brown, looking more uniformly dark than in the other forms (but still with some indication of a light malar line, and often a light spot behind the eye). Breast dark brown, almost uni-formly so; other forms show more dark-and-light scalloping on breast. Begins to show a suffusion of red on head and breast at a very early age.

RED-NAPED SAPSUCKER: Head medium brown, with whitish stripes (partially obscured) reflecting adult's head pattern. Crown uniform dark brown, sometimes with faint, inconspicuous paler spots; often a reddish suffusion on fore-head; when molt of crown feathers begins, red appears first on forehead and then progresses evenly toward rear of crown. Red on nape develops rather early. Breast more distinctively scalloped than in juvenile Red-breasted Sapsucker but often less so than in juvenile Yellow-bellied.

YELLOW-BELLIED SAPSUCKER: Head medium brown, with rather broad whitish stripes reflecting adult's head pat-tern. Crown medium brown, heavily marked with small bright spots of buffy or whitish (rarely, a juvenile Yellow-bellied may have a uniformly dark brown crown like that of juvenile Red-naped). When molt of crown feathers begins (later than in other forms), red feathers appear in a random scattering on all parts of crown, but the brightly spotted ef-fect may remain obvious well into winter. Breast usually dis-tinctly marked with dark brown scalloping on buffy back-ground. Back is more strongly patterned than in the other forms, heavily spotted and barred with rich buff on black.

23

THE WOOD-PEWEES

WESTERN WOOD-PEWEE *Contopus sordidulus*
EASTERN WOOD-PEWEE *Contopus virens*

The problem: Identification of the two wood-pewees is not an everyday problem over most of North America, because their normal ranges barely overlap. However, it can create major difficulties on the western Great Plains, where either species can be expected in migration; and active birders everywhere are vexed by the question of how to detect long-distance vagrants.

Unfortunately, the known visible differences between the two are comparative, subtle, and subject to variation. On current knowledge it is probably impossible to distinguish them with certainty in the field by sight alone. Their songs are very distinctive, but other vocalizations may not be, and wood-pewees rarely give their full songs away from their breeding areas.

Plumage Differences

Adults in spring: In spring there are *average* differences between the species that may be readily appreciated by traveling birders who get to see both on their breeding grounds. The birds would be worthy of close study: there may yet be undiscovered field marks, beyond these simply comparative ones, that would prove reliable for identification.

In fresh spring plumage the Eastern Wood-Pewee tends to be slightly paler and greener on the upperparts, the Western tends to be slightly darker and browner (but either can be an intermediate gray tone). The same kind of difference is somewhat more apparent on the wide gray breastband: in the Eastern it tends to be paler, greener, narrower, and more nearly interrupted in the center; in the Western it tends to be darker (especially toward the sides), dingier, browner, and more nearly continuous across the breast. The Eastern often has a slightly stronger wash of pale greenish yellow on the lower underparts. The throat is often a cleaner white in Eastern, often a more brownish white in Western (but either species can show either extreme). The underside of the bend of the wing is usually whitish in Easterns, usually medium gray in Westerns; this coloration spills over slightly onto the leading edge of the wing and is sometimes visible near the bend of the wing on perched birds. In either species the lower mandible may be almost all dark or almost all pale; but typically it is nearly all dull pale yellow in Easterns (with a small dusky area at the tip), while in Westerns the dusky area usually covers at least the distal half of the lower mandible.

Adults from midsummer on: The discussion of differences above applies only to typical adults from spring into early summer. By midsummer, with fading and wear on the plumage, wood-pewees become increasingly drab. The wings gradually become dull and brownish, and the pale edgings to the tertials and coverts wear away. In this condition the differences between the species are, to say the least, obscure; and because they do not molt again until they reach the wintering grounds, they continue to look more and more drab until their autumn departure from North America.

Juveniles: As midsummer approaches and adult wood-pewees become increasingly worn, full-grown independent juveniles appear on the scene; they can be recognized (with a close study) by their very fresh plumage. The clues are especially apparent on the wings. The tertials have wide white edges (much as on fresh spring adults); the greater and median coverts have sharply contrasted pale tips, forming distinct *wing bars* that usually are noticeably *buffy*. (Spring adults also have wing bars, but they are a little less distinct and are grayish white, not buffy.) Juveniles also tend to be darker than adults of their own species at the sides of the breast and on the upperparts.

Comparing the species, the slight average differences noted for spring adults also apply to juveniles: Easterns tend to be paler and greener, Westerns darker and browner. Juveniles of both species usually have much duskiness on the lower mandible, and although it may be more extensive on Westerns, this is too variable to be of much aid in identification. Most suggestive for field use is a difference in wing pattern: in juvenile Easterns the two wing bars are about the same color, usually buffy; in juvenile Westerns the upper (anterior) wing bar is usually duller and grayer than the lower one, and often narrower and less conspicuous. Even considering this difference, however, it is probably not safe to identify the two without direct in-the-hand comparisons.

Voice

The full song of each species is very distinctive.

The Eastern Wood-Pewee's song (Fig. 72) consists of pure whistles, rich, full-toned, and slightly plaintive in quality; the changes in pitch are strongly emphasized, almost exaggerated.

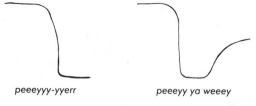

peeeyyy-yyerr   *peeeyy ya weeey*

Fig. 72.

dree, di-deep   *pzzeeyeer*

Fig. 73.

The first part of the Western Wood-Pewee's song (Fig. 73) has a thin, liquid, whistled quality; the second part is harsh and burry, a single downward-slurred note. The second part is often given alone, especially at mid-day and during spring migration.

As different as these songs are, wood-pewees have sometimes been misidentified by voice as "the other species." This is possible because oversimplified interpretations of the songs can lead to the idea that a wood-pewee giving clear notes must be an Eastern, while one with buzzy or harsh calls must be a Western.

Actually, either species may give buzzy or dry trilled calls in aggressive interactions. Juveniles of either species may give calls that are harsher or hoarser than any calls of adults. Juvenile Eastern Wood-Pewees, giving hoarse calls and looking darker than adults, may sometimes be misidentified as Westerns. Also, both species give a variety of clear whistled notes. Most calls given by Western Wood-Pewees, in fact, are liquid whistles without a trace of any harsh or burry quality. These calls have led to many false reports of Eastern Wood-Pewees in the West.

One result of all this variability in voice is that it can be difficult to *prove,* by a mere description, that you have heard the full song of either species outside its normal range. Singing vagrant wood-pewees should be tape-recorded if at all possible.

Comparison to Other Species

Empidonax **flycatchers:** Most species of *Empidonax* have prominent eye-rings, automatically ruling out confusion with the wood-pewees. However, the eye-rings may be faint or absent on Willow Flycatcher (*E. traillii*) and sometimes on Alder Flycatcher (*E. alnorum*). Since Willow Flycatcher often lacks eye-rings and may have less distinct wing bars than other *Empidonax,* it is the one most likely to be mistaken for a wood-pewee.

Compared to the wood-pewees, Willow Flycatcher is smaller and more compact; it lacks the long-winged proportions (its wingtips hardly extend beyond the base of the tail, while in the wood-pewees the wings extend one-third to one-half the way to the tail's tip). The Willow Flycatcher also tends to have a slightly shorter bill than do the wood-pewees, with a less noticeable hook at the tip of the upper mandible.

The larger *Contopus* species: Olive-sided Flycatcher (*Contopus borealis*) is similar to wood-pewees in shape but has much more strongly patterned underparts, the sides of the "vest" typically showing noticeable mottling and streaking. The Greater Pewee, formerly called Coues' Flycatcher (*C. pertinax*), is more uniformly gray below than even the drabbest Western Wood-Pewees; it has a proportionately larger bill, with a bright pinkish orange lower mandible.

24

THE EMPIDONAX FLYCATCHERS

LEAST FLYCATCHER *Empidonax minimus*
HAMMOND'S FLYCATCHER *Empidonax hammondii*
DUSKY FLYCATCHER *Empidonax oberholseri*
GRAY FLYCATCHER *Empidonax wrightii*
BUFF-BREASTED FLYCATCHER *Empidonax fulvifrons*
WESTERN FLYCATCHER COMPLEX (formerly *E. difficilis*)
  PACIFIC-SLOPE FLYCATCHER *Empidonax difficilis*
  CORDILLERAN FLYCATCHER *Empidonax occidentalis*
YELLOW-BELLIED FLYCATCHER *Empidonax flaviventris*
ACADIAN FLYCATCHER *Empidonax virescens*
ALDER FLYCATCHER *Empidonax alnorum*
WILLOW FLYCATCHER *Empidonax traillii*

The problem: The flycatchers of the genus *Empidonax* represent a classic problem group for birders. They are all extremely similar in appearance: little gray birds (tinged with olive, brown, or yellow) with wing bars and eye-rings. Their specific characters are so subtle that there is often more variation *within* a species than there is *between* any two species in the genus. Even museum specimens are often difficult to name. Until recently, it was flatly assumed that sight identification of the "Empids" in the field was impossible. On the breeding grounds, each species has a distinctive song. However, because of imprecise voice descriptions, even the songs have been confused at times.

Preliminary Points I: How to Learn the *Empidonax* Flycatchers

These birds have the potential for causing extreme confusion for the birder. The very *worst* approach to learning the *Empidonax* is to try to identify nonsinging birds on migration. Even if you convince yourself of the identity of various birds, you will never *know* whether you are correct, and all of your impressions and comparisons may turn out to be false.

The basic rule is this: your knowledge of field recognition of *Empidonax* flycatchers must develop through study of *known-identity birds.* The best approach is to find a singing Empid in spring or early summer (most parts of North America have at least one or two breeding species), carefully identify it by song, and then study it thoroughly. Run it through the entire list of "what to look at" below, with special attention to aspects of the bird's shape. Study the shape of the bill as it appears from different angles. Listen closely to any call notes. Study the color and pattern of the plumage, and try to note how it changes as the bird moves from shade to sunlight.

If you can become thoroughly familiar with even one species of *Empidonax,* by careful study of individuals that you *know* are identified correctly, you will have a basis of comparison for beginning to learn the others.

Preliminary Points II: What to Look at on *Empidonax*

Once you have found an Empid and identified it by its song, these are things to study in order to become familiar with the subtle characteristics of that species.

Bill shape: The exact shape of the bill (as viewed from directly above or below) is not the easiest thing to see, but it is among the most important. There are two basic groups: those in which the bill is relatively narrow and the sides are

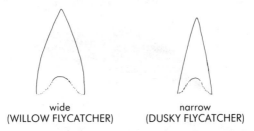

wide
(WILLOW FLYCATCHER)

narrow
(DUSKY FLYCATCHER)

Fig. 74. The two basic in bill types in *Empidonax* flycatchers. Outlines as viewed from directly below. The wide bill tends to have convex edges, while the edges are straighter on the narrow bill.

straight, and those in which the base of the bill is broader and the sides appear slightly convex (Fig. 74). (Least and Buff-breasted flycatchers are somewhat intermediate between these two groups.) Within these categories, species vary in the actual length and width of the bill. As you gain practice, bill shape can become one of the most helpful characters.

Pattern of lower mandible: While studying bill shape from below, take a good look at the pattern: whether the lower mandible is entirely pale or has a dark tip, how extensive the dark tip is, if present, and whether it contrasts sharply or blends smoothly into the pale base.

Shape of wingtip: More variable than bill shape, but often providing a useful clue, is the *primary extension*. This is defined as the distance that the primaries extend beyond the ends of the tertials and secondaries on the folded wing (Fig. 75).

Overall proportions: Difficult to quantify, but often helpful for experienced birders, are some aspects of the bird's shape. These include the usual shape of the head (smoothly rounded vs. slightly crested, although this will vary as the head feathers are raised and lowered); size of the head, relative to the bird's body; length of the tail, especially as related to the length of the wingtips; and overall bulk of the bird.

Plumage characters: In looking at any of these field marks involving color or pattern, it is essential to keep in mind the effects of molt and wear on the plumage. Empids tend to look "cleanest" and most "colorful" when they are in fresh plum-

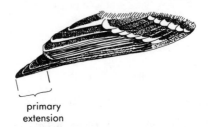

primary
extension

Fig. 75. The term "primary extension" refers to the distance that the longest primaries extend beyond the tertials and secondaries on the folded wing of *Empidonax* flycatchers.

age (having recently completed a molt). As the plumage gradually becomes more worn during the following months, several changes occur. Areas of the upperparts that were greenish, brownish, or blue-gray in fresh plumage tend to fade toward a plainer (and often slightly paler) gray. Yellow areas on the underparts tend to fade to whitish. The wings may become slightly paler, and wing bars that were buffy or yellow in fresh plumage fade toward white. The wing bars and the pale tertial edgings also become narrower, as the edges of these feathers are worn away. In general, most Empid species in worn plumage look even more similar to each other.

An Empid that is in the midst of an active molt may look odd in a variety of ways. Its plumage may look "patchy," with unexpected breaks in the wing bars or eye-ring. Its tail tip may look uneven. The length of the primary extension may be an unreliable character for a bird in molt.

The species accounts that follow will describe the timing of molt and the resulting seasonal changes in appearance of each species. Always take into account this potential for seasonal change. A good rule is this: if you can't see an Empid well enough to tell whether the plumage is in fresh or worn condition, there is no point in contemplating the *color* of the plumage.

Throat color. The exact color of the throat (white, gray, pale yellow, grayish yellow) is often very important. The degree to which the throat contrasts with the face can be significant.

Color of upperparts. This is tricky, but it is worth noting if you can study a fresh-plumaged Empid in good light (open shade is best — bright sunlight tends to wash out colors). The general tone of the back can vary from green to brown to gray, and it may or may not contrast with the color of the head.

Eye-ring. Not all Empids have identical eye-rings. The eye-ring can be faint or lacking on Willow, Alder, and Acadian flycatchers. The shape of the eye-ring can differ: typically it is *not* quite of even thickness all the way around, being slightly thinner across the top of the eye and slightly broader behind the eye; this effect is exaggerated in some species, including Western Flycatcher, which often has the eye-ring lengthened to a point behind the eye. The degree of contrast between the eye-ring and the face is worth noting.

Wing-bar color and contrast. The color of the wing bars is sometimes a useful mark. They tend to be buffy in fresh plumage in all species, fading to whitish as they become worn, but in some species (e.g., Acadian) the buff tones are more obvious and persistent. The *contrast* in the wings is also worth noting. In some eastern species (Least, Yellow-bellied, and Acadian) the wings tend to be very blackish, so the pale wing bars and tertial edgings show strong contrast. In the western species, the wings are generally not as dark, so the contrast is less obvious.

Voice: Obviously important, and not just the songs; call notes are often of critical importance in identification. Five of the North American species have call notes that sound like *whit*, basically identical under field conditions, but the call notes of the other six are quite different. Some of the species pairs that are most similar visually (Willow/Alder, Hammond's/Dusky, Western/Yellow-bellied) can be separated rather easily by call notes.

Preliminary Points III: What *Not* to Look at on *Empidonax*

The heading above is partly in jest, of course, because there is nothing you should *avoid* looking at on a problem bird. But the following points — although some may catch your attention and others have sometimes been suggested as major field marks — seem to have little value in identification.

Yellow belly: All Empids have yellow bellies, especially when they are in fresh plumage. The brightness of the yellow varies more with age and season than it does according to species. The brightness of this yellow may provide a clue as to the freshness of the plumage, but only in this very indirect way does it have a bearing on the specific identification.

Pale lores: All Empids have a pale area on the lores. There is a slight tendency for this spot to be more obvious on some species than on others, but at best it is only a very minor supporting field mark.

Pale outer webs: On most Empids, the outermost tail feather on each side has the outermost web paler than the rest of the tail. The degree of contrast can sometimes be a useful character in the museum, where lighting is controlled and many specimens are available for comparison, and it has been mentioned in some references on *Empidonax*. But in the field, the effects of lighting make this character completely unusable.

Wing and tail action: All Empids flick the tail and wings at least occasionally while perched. Some tend to do this more often than others, and these general tendencies are noted in the species accounts below, but such vague trends *cannot* be used as field marks; at most, they are no more than very minor supporting characters. The one exception is the distinctive tail-dipping behavior of the Gray Flycatcher.

Preliminary Points IV: A Large Dose of Caution

Certainty of sight identifications: If you reach the stage at which you feel you can name every Empid you see in the field, you are probably deluding yourself. From my own perspective, I can say that I have studied these birds closely for years and have examined thousands of museum specimens and thousands of live individuals in the field — and I believe I can confidently name about 80 percent of the Empids I see, with strong hunches on another 10 to 15 percent. These percentages go up or down a little depending on region and season, but I don't expect the confidence factor will ever approach 100 percent (and if it did, I still wouldn't be able to *prove* many of my identifications).

Finding an Empid outside its normal range: Records of *Empidonax* out of range should *never* be accepted on the basis of sightings alone, regardless of how many or how skilled the observers. Thus, if you have the mixed fortune of finding an Empid that is truly rare in your area, you should think carefully about how to document the occurrence.

Tape recordings of the song would be ideal, but vagrants do not often sing. Photographs taken in the field rarely show enough detail for certain identification (although when Greg Lasley found the first Hammond's Flycatcher for eastern Texas, he took more than *sixty* close-up photos and was able to convince even the skeptics!). Generally, with a nonsinging vagrant Empid, your only chance of confirming the record would be to have the bird mist-netted for careful measurement and photography in the hand.

Field Marks — *Empidonax* Flycatchers

LEAST FLYCATCHER: The Least Flycatcher (*E. minimus*) is the most common migrant Empid throughout much of east-

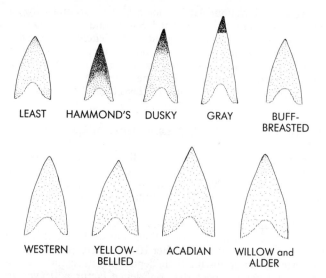

LEAST   HAMMOND'S   DUSKY   GRAY   BUFF-
BREASTED

WESTERN   YELLOW-   ACADIAN   WILLOW and
BELLIED   ALDER

Fig. 76. Bills of *Empidonax* flycatchers, as seen from below, to compare outlines as well as patterns of lower mandibles. Typical shapes and patterns are shown here, but all species vary somewhat.

ern North America and is found locally in the Northwest as well.

Size and shape: As the name implies, this is a small species. Its head is rather round looking and sometimes appears proportionately large. The primary extension is variable but usually looks short.

Bill shape and color: Least is intermediate in bill width between the "wide" and "narrow" types, and is also short-billed, so it looks smaller-billed than the other eastern species. The lower mandible is mostly or entirely orange-yellow, sometimes with an ill-defined dusky tip.

Voice: Song, a sharp, snappy *che-beck*, the second syllable sounding a little higher-pitched and more emphatic. The song may be repeated many times at intervals of less than one second. Call, a thin, dry *whit* or *pit*.

Plumage color: Least Flycatchers are a fairly uniform brownish gray on the upperparts, usually somewhat darker brown on the forehead and washed with olive on the back. The throat is whitish or off-white (not bright white), contrasting with the darker face and with the gray-brown wash crossing the chest. The white eye-ring is usually of fairly even thickness, well defined and conspicuous. Contrast on the wings is usually obvious, with blackish ground color setting off white wing bars and tertial edgings.

Molt and seasonal variation: Adult Least Flycatchers appear very worn by late summer, drab above and very pale below, with narrow wing bars. The adults migrate south early (they are mostly gone from North America by early September) and undergo their complete annual molt after arriving on their wintering grounds. Most Least Flycatchers seen during fall migration will be immatures, similar to adults but with buff wing bars and buffy white tertial edgings.

Least Flycatchers also have a spring molt that involves much of the body plumage and often some wing feathers, especially on first-year birds. This molt is generally completed on the wintering grounds, before the birds start northward; but some spring migrants are still in the latter stages of the molt and may have a generally disheveled appearance about the head, perhaps with a less conspicuous eye-ring than usual.

Behavior: Least Flycatcher tends to be active, often changing perches. It usually does a lot of flicking of the tail and wings, jerking the tail strongly upward and often flicking the wings at the same time.

Comparisons to Other Species: For birders in the East, Least Flycatcher will often be the most common Empid, and it serves as a good point of comparison. Of the other eastern species, only Willow has a similar *whit* call note. Compared to Willow, Alder, and Acadian, the typical Least may be recognized by its smaller size, smaller bill (both shorter and slightly narrower proportionately), generally shorter primary extension, and more conspicuous eye-ring.

Yellow-bellied Flycatcher (p. 202) is similar to Least in size and shape but usually differs in its much stronger yellow and green tones. On some worn Yellow-bellieds in late summer and fall, however, these colors may be much reduced; the birds may even look grayish white below. Yellow-bellied has a proportionately larger bill (slightly longer and broader) than Least, and its voice is different. Some noncalling, heavily worn birds of these two species in late summer may not be safely identifiable.

In the West, Dusky and Hammond's flycatchers can be similar to Least. Dusky (p. 194) has a similar *whit* call note, and it can be very similar to Least in plumage, especially in fall when both are in variably worn condition. Dusky's bill is as long as or longer than that of Least, but narrower, and often has a more extensive dusky area at the tip of the lower mandible. Dusky also tends to have a slightly grayer throat and longer tail, and less contrast in the wings.

Hammond's Flycatcher (p. 192) is a small bird like Least, but its bill is even smaller, being short and thin with the lower mandible usually at least half dark. Hammond's has a *long* primary extension, whereas that of Least is usually moderate to short. In addition, the throat of Hammond's is usually distinctly gray, not whitish, its chest is often a darker olive-gray, and its upperparts often show more contrast between the gray head and olive back. Because Hammond's molts before its southward migration, color differences are most pronounced in fall, when the plumage of Hammond's is in fresh condition.

HAMMOND'S FLYCATCHER: This western species has often been confused with Dusky Flycatcher in the past. Their breeding ranges overlap extensively, but the Hammond's Flycatcher (*E. hammondii*) is generally found farther north or at higher elevations.

Size and shape: Hammond's is a small Empid that tends to look short-tailed, short-billed, and large-headed. Typically the primary extension is noticeably long. Although the tail is actually about medium length (relative to the bird's size), the long wingtips make Hammond's seem short-tailed.

Bill shape and color: The bill of Hammond's is straight-sided, narrow, and short, the smallest bill (in proportion to overall size) of any Empid. The lower mandible is usually at least one-half to two-thirds dark, fading to dull dusky yellow or pinkish yellow at the base. Many Hammond's look entirely dark-billed in the field, and some (young birds?) can be more extensively pale on the lower mandible.

Voice: Song, slightly variable in pattern, but made up of three basic elements. First is a dry rapid *chi-pit* or *tse-brrk,* sharply two-syllabled. When this element of the Hammond's song is given by itself (as may happen often on the breeding grounds, especially later in the season), it can strongly suggest the *chebek* of Least Flycatcher. The second element is a low-pitched, rough *brrrk*. The third element is similar, but rises in pitch: *grrip!* The usual sequence of the song is *chi-pit . . . brrrk . . . grrip! . . .* but sometimes elements are repeated, left out, or given in a different order. The call heard most frequently at all seasons is a sharp *peep* or *peek*, similar to the call of a Pygmy Nuthatch or the single note of a Long-billed Dowitcher.

The songs of Hammond's and Dusky flycatchers have often been confused, partly because they have been poorly described. Here are some differences to listen for (it will help if you study good recordings). The first element of Hammond's song is more sharply two-syllabled; the second element of Hammond's is lower-pitched and rougher than any song element of Dusky; the third part of Hammond's (the ascending note) is somewhat like the second element of Dusky's song, but sounds lower-pitched and shorter; and the song of Hammond's rarely or never includes a note like the high-pitched clear *pweet* in the song of Dusky (although Hammond's does give an isolated *call note* that is clear and high-pitched).

Plumage color: Hammond's is relatively dark, and in fresh plumage it is relatively "colorful" for an *Empidonax*. The back is a fairly dark olive-gray, and although this color extends up onto the nape, the *face* is more gray and less olive, looking *blue-gray* in fresh plumage. The white eye-ring is conspicuous, well defined, and thicker behind the eye. No sharp contrast separates the face from the throat, which always looks gray. The breast is olive-gray or brownish gray, usually dark, especially toward the sides. The belly is pale to fairly bright lemon-yellow. Often the dark color of the breast extends down the sides and flanks, creating a "vested" look. The dusky gray wings have wing bars and tertial edges that look quite buffy in fresh plumage (fall and winter), fading toward dull white in spring and summer.

Molt and seasonal variation: Adults go through a complete molt in late summer, from late June or July to late August or September, *before* they leave the breeding grounds. Juveniles have a partial molt, replacing the body plumage, which is also completed before their southward migration. Thus all

Hammond's Flycatchers are in very fresh plumage during fall migration, with buffy wing bars, fairly bright yellow on the belly and dark olive-gray on the chest, and contrast between the gray head and olive back.

In late winter, before they begin their spring migration, Hammond's go through a partial molt involving only body plumage. This molt is more extensive in some individuals than in others, so some spring Hammond's are in visibly fresher plumage than others.

Behavior: Hammond's tends to be active, flicking the tail frequently and often flicking the wings at the same time. This species has a distinctive call note; but, more than most Empids, it may remain frustratingly silent for long periods.

Comparisons to Other Species: The similarity between Hammond's and Dusky flycatchers is notorious. Their songs are distinctive, but it requires careful concentration to hear and learn the differences; see under "Voice" above. Their call notes are also diagnostic, as the sharp *peep* of Hammond's is unlike the *whit* of Dusky.

Visually they are more challenging. There are structural clues that can be helpful for observers who are very familiar with these birds: the Dusky Flycatcher's bill averages longer, with a less extensive dusky area at the tip, and the Dusky has a slightly longer tail, emphasized by the fact that its primary extension is much shorter than that of the Hammond's.

Plumage color is very helpful for separating these two *in early fall*. Because Hammond's molts *before* migrating south, it is in fresh plumage at that season. Dusky molts *after* migrating south, so early fall Duskies look fairly pale and somewhat worn (juveniles) or very worn and drab (adults). In spring and summer, Hammond's and Dusky are extremely similar in plumage color, although there is a slight tendency for Hammond's to be darker on the face and chest.

DUSKY FLYCATCHER: This western species (*E. oberholseri*) is intermediate between Hammond's and Gray flycatchers in several ways.

Size and shape: Dusky Flycatcher is a medium-sized Empid with a medium-length narrow bill and a medium-long tail. The primary extension is short for the size of the bird, contributing to the impression that the bird is longer-tailed than Hammond's.

Bill shape and color: The bill of Dusky Flycatcher is straight-sided, narrow, and of medium length (averaging between those of the short-billed Hammond's and the long-billed Gray). The lower mandible is usually extensively pale at the base, fading gradually toward the dark tip.

Voice: Song, variable in pattern, but with three basic elements: (1) a short, medium-pitched *chrip*, sounding vaguely two-syllabled; (2) a rough note, *ggrrreep*, starting on a low pitch and slurring sharply upwards; (3) a clear, high-pitched *pweet*. The usual song sequence is *chrip . . . ggrrreep . . . pweet* or *chrip . . . ggrrreep . . . chrip . . . pweet*. Song elements may be left out or repeated out of sequence. See the voice description under Hammond's Flycatcher (p. 192) for a comparison of the songs of these two species, which have often been confused. Call, a dry *pit* or *whit*. The female's call is very slightly lower than the male's, and you can discern the difference when both members of a pair are calling on the breeding grounds. At this season, males also sometimes give a plaintive *dew, dew-hic*, especially in the late morning and the evening.

Plumage color: Dusky Flycatcher is drab for much of the year. The throat is pale gray (but can look whitish in bright light). The back is washed with olive but shows little apparent contrast to the gray head, and the wing bars do not contrast strongly. Although the eye-ring is white and well-defined, it is not always conspicuous, because the head is not very dark. A pale area on the lores is often more pronounced on Dusky than on other Empids.

Molt and seasonal variation: Dusky Flycatcher molts in fall after arriving on the wintering grounds — a complete molt in adults, a partial one (mostly body plumage) in juveniles. During fall migration, adults are worn and drab, mostly gray above and whitish below, with narrow whitish wing bars. Juveniles at that season are slightly more colorful, with more buff on the wing bars, yellow on the belly, and olive on the back, but these colors are fading rapidly as late summer turns to fall.

In early winter (when only a few remain north of the Mexican border), the freshly molted Duskies are in their most "colorful" plumage of the year, with fairly bright pale yellow on the belly, olive on the back, olive-gray on the chest, and pale buff wing bars. These colors are present but less pronounced on spring migrants (most of which have undergone another partial molt in late winter). The colors gradually fade during late spring and summer.

Behavior: Dusky tends to be slightly less active than Hammond's. It occasionally flicks the tail while perched, but does not seem to flick the wings at the same time quite as often as Hammond's or Least flycatchers. This tendency is so variable that it should not be used as a field mark.

Choice of nest sites is a fairly consistent difference between Dusky (which usually builds its nest less than 12 feet off the ground) and Hammond's (which usually nests more than 12 feet up, often much higher). Hammond's also tends to sing and forage in spots surrounded by dense vegetation, while Dusky may be found in more open situations at times.

Comparisons to Other Species: In the hand, Dusky Flycatcher can be quite similar to Gray Flycatcher; they are less likely to be confused in the field because of the Gray's tail-dipping behavior (see p. 197). The most similar species to the Dusky is Hammond's (p. 192), and the Least Flycatcher (p. 189) can also be similar; see discussions under those species.

Dusky's lack of distinctive characters makes it subject to confusion with various other Empids. Willow Flycatcher can be superficially similar, but Willow has a wider bill, usually with the lower mandible entirely pale, and usually has a whiter throat.

GRAY FLYCATCHER: This pale Empid (*E. wrightii*) breeds mostly in the Great Basin region of the West. Behavior, shape, and coloration make the Gray Flycatcher one of our most distinctive members of the genus.

Size and shape: Gray Flycatcher is noticeably long-billed and long-tailed. The long bill often makes the head look proportionately small, and the crown is usually smoothly rounded. The primary extension is fairly short for the size of the bird. Young birds in late summer can be visibly shorter-billed and shorter-tailed than adults — a potential source of confusion.

Bill shape and color: Of the species with narrow, straight-sided bills, this one is on average the longest-billed (although some Grays can overlap in bill shape with the longest-billed Duskies). The lower mandible is pale pink with a small, sharply defined black area at the tip.

Voice: Song, a simple, uneven repetition of two elements. Given most frequently is an emphatic two-syllabled note with a low-pitched chirping sound, *chuwip*. A higher-pitched, weaker *teeah* is tossed in at irregular intervals. Call, a dry *pit* or *whit*, similar to Dusky's call but perhaps not as thin. The female Gray's call is very slightly lower than the male's.

Plumage color: Gray Flycatcher generally looks paler than any other Empid (except the very different Buff-breasted). The upperparts and face are medium gray, with a faint olive wash on the back but not on the head. Although the white eye-ring is well defined, it may not contrast noticeably because the head is not very dark. The throat is very pale gray — sometimes nearly white — but there is no sharp separation in color between the throat and the sides of the head. The breast is pale to medium gray, usually with a slight olive tinge. The belly is a very pale yellow and may look white in the field. The dusky gray wings have dull whitish wing bars and tertial edges. The tail is very dark gray with a white outer web on the outermost pair of tail feathers.

Molt and seasonal variation: Adults go through a complete molt in fall, after arriving on the wintering grounds. Juveniles have a partial molt, mostly involving body plumage, which may begin in late summer near breeding areas but is mostly completed after fall migration. Thus all Gray Flycatchers are in fresh plumage in early winter.

During the summer, as the plumage becomes more worn, adult Grays become slightly paler and plainer: the shades of yellow below and olive on the back and chest fade even further, and the wing bars and tertial edges become narrow and inconspicuous.

Behavior: The tail dipping of Gray Flycatcher is the most distinctive behavioral trait of any Empid. This movement begins with a rapid, very slight upward twitch of the tail, followed by a slower, emphasized downward swing, after which the tail is raised to its original position, the whole action recalling a phoebe rather than any other *Empidonax*. Some other species may sometimes flick the tail down-up instead of up-down, but these are still tail flicks almost too rapid for the eye to follow.

This species is relatively inactive, often dipping the tail but only infrequently flicking the wings. When foraging the Gray tends to perch low and often flies down to take insects on or near the ground. (Many other Empids will do this at times, especially in cold weather when insects are relatively inactive.)

Comparisons to Other Species: The Gray Flycatcher is unlikely to be mistaken for other types, although the Dusky Flycatcher (p. 194) is similar in the hand.

BUFF-BREASTED FLYCATCHER: The Buff-breasted Flycatcher (*E. fulvifrons*), our smallest and most distinctively colored Empid, is found very locally near the Mexican border.

Size and shape: This tiny bird has a rather short tail that may appear deeply notched. The primary extension is fairly long for the bird's small size. Usually the Buff-breasted's crown looks smoothly rounded, but it may be slightly peaked toward the rear.

Bill shape and color: The bill is fairly short, and intermediate in shape between the wide-billed and narrow-billed categories. The lower mandible is entirely pale (yellow or pinkish yellow).

Voice: Song, a rather musical *chee-bit,* with the second note lower than the first, often followed by a few soft notes or a short trill. Sometimes the second syllable is sharper and higher-pitched than the first: *chee-beet!* Call, a short dry *pit* or *pt.*

Plumage color: The Buff-breasted Flycatcher is a pale and brownish Empid. Its head is pale enough that it does not contrast strongly with the eye-ring, which is whitish and often pointed at the rear edge; the only strong "pattern" on the face is the contrast of the dark eye. The throat is white, the breast is washed with pale buff, and the belly is buffy white to yellowish white. The wings are noticeably darker than the dusty brown back, but not blackish like those of the eastern Empids, and the whitish wing bars and tertial edgings are not sharply contrasted. The tail shows conspicuously white outer webs to the outer tail feathers.

Molt and seasonal variation: Adult Buff-breasteds may become very worn and drab by midsummer, to the extent that the buff wash on the breast virtually disappears. They then undergo a complete molt on the breeding grounds in late summer, so very fresh-plumaged birds may be seen in late August or early September, just before they leave the United States.

Behavior: This is a fairly active bird of open pine woods, usually singing from high perches but foraging at all levels, including close to the ground. The Buff-breasted usually pumps its tail several times just after alighting, but otherwise it does not show much tail motion or wing flicking.

Comparisons to Other Species: The Buff-breasted Flycatcher is unlikely to be confused with any other Empid. The only potential problem involves worn midsummer birds with little or no color on the breast, but these should be recognizable by their very small size and overall pale brown look.

WESTERN FLYCATCHER COMPLEX (formerly *E. difficilis*)
PACIFIC-SLOPE FLYCATCHER *(Empidonax difficilis)*
CORDILLERAN FLYCATCHER *(Empidonax occidentalis)*

Birds of the Western Flycatcher group are common in humid forests on the Pacific Coast and in the mountains of the West.

As this book was nearing completion, the American Ornithologists' Union Check-list Committee reached the conclusion that the "Western Flycatcher" is actually a complex of at least two very similar species. The two now recognized are the Pacific-slope Flycatcher, which breeds from southeastern Alaska to Baja California, and the Cordilleran Flycatcher, which breeds from southern Alberta south to Mexico and west through the isolated mountain ranges of the Great Basin states. The Cordilleran Flycatcher reaches its western limits in Oregon (west to Crater Lake) and California (west to the Siskiyou Mountains, but it is replaced by the coastal form in the Mount Shasta region). As a migrant, the Pacific-slope occurs well east of its breeding range; in the lowlands of the Southwest, for example, it is actually a more common migrant than the Cordilleran Flycatcher.

With this taxonomic move, the Western Flycatcher finally lives up to its name of "*difficilis*" — now, it really is difficult! On present knowledge, the *only* way to separate the Pacific-slope and Cordilleran species in the field is by the call notes of the males. Females are now totally indistinguishable under field conditions, as far as we know. For this reason, the name

"Western Flycatcher" is going to continue to be very useful for field observers, and it will be understood to apply to this complex of forms. In this chapter I continue to refer to all of these birds as Western Flycatchers except in the very few instances where there are differences between the forms. And I strongly urge that birders keep that name in use rather than adopting some awkward combination term like "Pacific-slope/Cordilleran flycatcher sp." or, even worse, making guesses as to which species is being seen.

Size and shape: The Western is a small Empid, with interior birds averaging slightly larger than coastal birds. Its primary extension (see p. 186) is usually rather short. It may appear slightly long-tailed for its size, and it usually shows a slight peak at the rear of the crown.

Bill shape and color: The bill of Western Flycatcher is wide and the lower mandible is entirely yellow-orange to pinkish; this color is usually fairly bright and conspicuous in the field.

Voice: Song, variable, but always very high-pitched and thin, usually a repetition of three parts; for example: *tseweep . . . pttsik . . . tsip . . . tseweep . . . pttsik . . . tsip. . . .* No other western *Empidonax* song is so high-pitched and squeaky. The common call note of the males is the best distinction between the Pacific-slope and Cordilleran forms of Western Flycatcher. Pacific-slope males give a single, slurred, sharply ascending note: *peweat!* or *pseeyeap!* Cordilleran males give this call at about the same range of pitch but make it strongly two-syllabled, with the second note higher: *pit-peet!* The common call note of females (of both forms) is a very thin, high-pitched *tseet.*

Plumage color: The Western Flycatcher is the only western Empid with yellow (dull pale yellow or grayish yellow) on the *throat,* and it also has strong olive-green tones on the back (generally washed with brown). The breast is washed with dull brownish olive. The eye-ring is conspicuous, white or yellowish white, and usually has a distinctive shape: narrowed or even broken across the top of the eye, broadened (often to a point) behind the eye, for a teardrop or almond-shaped effect. The wings are dusky, not blackish, and the wing bars usually look dull white.

There is virtually no difference in color between the Pacific-slope and Cordilleran flycatcher species. However, those nesting on the Channel Islands off southern California (currently classified as a race of Pacific-slope Flycatcher, although they could be split off later) tend to be slightly duller: grayer above and paler below.

Molt and seasonal variation: Fresh-plumaged juveniles in midsummer have noticeably buff wing bars. Adults at that season are becoming worn, and by late summer they may be very pale below — some show virtually no yellow on the throat in early fall. Western Flycatchers molt after arriving on their wintering grounds (a complete molt in adults, a partial but variable one in juveniles). Their spring molt is usually not very extensive; it occurs in late winter just before the birds migrate north.

Behavior: Western Flycatcher is usually an active Empid, flicking the tail frequently while perched and often flicking the wings at the same time. It is not shy or elusive inside the forest, but it rarely spends much time in open habitats; even in migration, it tends to occur in heavily shaded spots.

Comparisons to Other Species: Its strong green and yellow tones will usually separate the Western from the other species in its normal range. But in late summer and fall, some Westerns have no visible yellow on the throat. To recognize such individuals it is important to note the wide bill with pale lower mandible, appearance of the eye-ring, call notes, and other points.

Much more difficult is the separation of Western and Yellow-bellied flycatchers. Their normal ranges barely overlap (see below); but if one or the other occurred well out of range, proving its identity would be a challenge. Call notes provide the only clear-cut distinction. The two species' overall colors differ slightly; Yellow-bellied has stronger green tones, while Western tends toward duller green above and more buffy or brownish yellow below. Yellow-bellied tends to have blacker wings, setting off the wing bars and tertial edgings in sharper contrast. The eye-ring tends to be more teardrop-shaped in Western and of more even thickness in Yellow-bellied, but this is highly variable. Finally, Western tends to be slightly longer-tailed, and to have slightly more of a peak on the crown (Yellow-bellied tends to look more round-headed). It should be emphasized that all these points are subtle, variable, and almost impossible to detect without direct comparison. Sight records of either species out of range would be impossible to prove without excellent tape recordings and photos.

In winter in the Southwest, inexperienced birders sometimes misidentify Hammond's or Dusky flycatchers as Westerns because those species have conspicuous yellow on the belly at that season. However, the lack of yellow on the *throat* on these fresh-plumaged winter birds should rule out confusion.

YELLOW-BELLIED FLYCATCHER: The Yellow-bellied (*E. flaviventris*) is a small Empid of humid coniferous forests. It is most common in eastern Canada.

Size and shape: This small Empid often appears rather large-headed and short-tailed. Its crown usually looks smoothly rounded, not crested or peaked. Its wings have a fairly short to medium-length primary extension.

Bill shape and color: The Yellow-bellied's bill is rather large for the size of the bird, looking broad at the base and with slightly convex outer edges. The lower mandible is entirely orange-yellow.

Voice: Song, a rather hoarse *che-bunk*, without strong emphasis on either syllable; the second note seems to drop in pitch. This is a softer vocalization than the snappy *che-beck* of the Least Flycatcher, in which the second note sounds accented and higher-pitched. Call, variable, but often a rising, two-syllabled, whistled *per-weee*, somewhat like one call of the Eastern Wood-Pewee. This may be shortened to a rising *preee*, a *peer* on one pitch, or a sharp, descending *pyew*. Some of these may be similar to notes of Acadian Flycatcher, but all of Yellow-bellied's calls have a more musical quality.

Plumage color: This species tends to be very green above and yellow below. Despite the name (after all, most Empids have yellow bellies), the yellow *throat* (actually dull grayish yellow) is its most distinctive character among the eastern species. Yellow-bellied usually shows a strong greenish olive wash on the sides of the breast. The eye-ring is usually conspicuous but narrow, and of nearly even thickness all the way around. The wings are quite black, contrasting with the green back and setting off the wing bars and tertial edgings in strong contrast.

Molt and seasonal variation: Yellow-bellied Flycatchers have a complete molt in late winter, before they start northward, so they are in uniformly fresh plumage during spring migration. During late spring and summer their colors fade; the yellow tones may be obscure on some late-summer and fall birds, and they may appear nearly grayish white below. Juveniles go through a molt of the body plumage before they leave the breeding grounds, so that they appear fairly fresh during fall migration, but adults look drab and pale at that season since most of their fall molt is completed after their arrival on the wintering grounds.

Behavior: Yellow-bellied Flycatcher is usually found in the interior of dense woods, even in migration, so it is often difficult to observe. It tends to be active, doing much flicking of the wings and tail.

Comparisons to Other Species: See notes under Western Flycatcher (p. 199). In late summer and fall, the Yellow-bellied may be confused with the Acadian Flycatcher (p. 203), which is also very green-backed and can have a conspicuous yellow wash on the underparts (including the throat). Acadians with yellow throats may also be seen in early spring (before the arrival of Yellow-bellied, which is typically a late migrant).

The two species differ in structure: Acadian is a larger bird, with a larger bill (although Yellow-bellied is also large-billed for its size). The Acadian's primary extension is usually conspicuously longer, and Acadian also has a longer and broader tail. When Acadian does have yellow on the throat it is usually a clear pale yellow, slightly different from the grayish yellow tones of Yellow-bellied.

ACADIAN FLYCATCHER: The Acadian (*E. virescens*) is the characteristic Empid of the southeastern United States, barely extending north into extreme southeastern Canada.

Size and shape: This is a large Empid with a large bill and long wings. Its primary extension averages longer than that of any other species in the genus, and the tail often looks wide.

Bill shape and color: Acadian has the largest bill of any Empid, on average: long and broad (especially broad at the base), with slightly convex outer edges. The lower mandible is almost always entirely pinkish yellow.

Voice: Song, an explosive and loud *peet-sah* or *peet-sup*, usually accented on the first syllable, sometimes with equal accent on both syllables. Call, a loud but flat *peek!*, similar to the first note of the song.

Plumage color: Acadian could be characterized as very green above and very pale below. Uniformly greenish olive from the crown to the rump, it fades into a slightly paler and brighter green in the malar area of the face; because this area is so pale, it does not contrast strongly with the white throat. The underparts show a faint olive breast band and a faint yellowish wash on the belly. The wings show strong contrast, with very blackish ground color setting off the buffy wing bars and tertial edgings. The eye-ring is usually very narrow and rather sharply defined, but it can be faint on some individuals.

Molt and seasonal variation: The description above applies to spring Acadians. By midsummer, adults usually look very whitish below, and their wing bars have usually become whitish and very narrow. Unlike other eastern Empids, adult Acadians will go through a complete molt in late summer before they leave the breeding grounds; they will be in fresh plumage (with buff wing bars and yellow wash on the underparts) in fall migration, but they rapidly depart from North America as soon as their molt is completed.

Juveniles are very distinctive; bright green above with conspicuous buff tips to many feathers on the crown, nape, and wing coverts, forming a scaled effect. Their underparts are washed with yellow, and they have rich buff wing bars. These birds go through a partial molt before they migrate, losing the distinctive buff-scaled effect on the back; in fall migration they are still likely to have a yellow wash on the underparts, often including the throat.

Behavior: Acadian usually gives an impression of lethargy, doing very little flicking of the wings or tail except when excited. It often perches with the wings drooped somewhat.

Comparisons to Other Species: See under Yellow-bellied Flycatcher (p. 202). Acadian is very similar in structure to Alder and Willow flycatchers; it can be especially close to the "classic" Alder, which has strong green tones above. Acadian usually has a longer primary extension. Its face is paler than that of Willow or Alder, usually contrasting much less with the white throat, and on Acadian the lower part of the face (in the malar region) usually is washed with a fairly bright pale green. Acadian's call, a loud flat *peek*, is very different from the *whit* of Willow Flycatcher, and recognizably different from the *kep* of Alder Flycatcher.

ALDER FLYCATCHER: Until the 1970s, the Alder (*E. alnorum*) and the Willow Flycatcher (*E. traillii*) were regarded as one species called "Traill's Flycatcher." Visually the two are almost identical, but their voices are distinctive. Although their breeding ranges overlap in many areas, Alder is the more northerly of the two.

Size and shape: The Alder is a large Empid with a fairly heavy bill and long primary extension. The tail is of only moderate length, but it often looks broad.

Bill shape and color: This is another species in which the bill is wide and may seem to have slightly convex edges. The lower mandible is usually entirely yellowish pink but sometimes has a small dusky area at the tip.

Voice: Song, harsh and burry, often described as a three-syllabled *fee-bee-oh*, but actually sounds like a two-syllabled *rrree-beep*; a faint third syllable, as in *rrree-beea*, may or may not be audible. The song is strongly accented on the *second* syllable, which sounds both louder and higher-pitched than the first. At times the song is shortened to an ascending *rrreep!* Call, a rather flat *peep* or *kep*, reminiscent of a distant *Picoides* woodpecker or the *kip* note of the Western Kingbird, and distinctly different from the call of the Willow Flycatcher.

Plumage color: The most consistent plumage character of Alder (and Willow) is the white throat, contrasting noticeably with the face and usually with the breastband (but a very few Alder/Willow flycatchers have the throat washed with yellow). In fresh plumage, Alder tends to be strongly washed with olive on the upperparts and has clear gray tones on the face. Its eye-ring varies from conspicuous (but narrow) to virtually absent. Although the wings are quite dark, the contrast in the wing pattern is lessened by the fact that the wing bars and tertial edgings are often somewhat dull.

Molt and seasonal variation: These birds are in fresh plumage during spring migration. By the time of fall migration, adult Alders (and Willows) are in worn plumage. Their wing bars, and their eye-rings (if any), may be much reduced by wear, and their upperparts are quite drab. Juveniles are somewhat fresher at that season, with buffier wing bars, more yellow on the belly, and slightly more color on the upperparts, but these colors are fading very rapidly on these young birds. Both adults and juveniles molt after arriving on their wintering grounds. They may undergo another (partial) molt in late winter, but if so, it is completed before they start northward.

Behavior: Alder (and Willow) Flycatchers tend to be relatively sedate, doing little flicking of the wings or tail except immediately after landing on a perch.

Comparisons to Other Species: See under Acadian Flycatcher (above). The most similar species by far is Willow Flycatcher, discussed in detail below.

WILLOW FLYCATCHER: The Willow (*E. traillii*) is the southerly representative of the "Traill's Flycatcher" complex, widespread in the United States and in extreme southern Canada, and overlapping broadly with the Alder Flycatcher in many areas. Because it is virtually identical to the Alder Flycatcher, it is described here only in a comparative sense.

Voice: Song, harsh and burry — a rough *fitz-bew* or *fritz-be-yew*. Like the song of the Alder Flycatcher, this may sound vaguely three-syllabled. However, Willow Flycatcher puts the accent on the *first* syllable, and the second syllable seems to drop slightly in pitch; in Alder Flycatcher's song, as mentioned above, the *second* syllable is emphasized and seems to sound higher-pitched. At times the song of Willow is shortened to a strong *rrrip!*, dangerously similar to the *rreep!* of Alder. Call, a thick *whit!*, very different from Alder's call note. It is easier to hear the difference than to describe it — but the *whit* of Willow gives the illusion of a slight rising inflection, and seems to have the hardest or most emphasized sound at the end, while the *kep* of Alder is emphasized or accented at the beginning, and may seem to drop slightly in pitch.

Comparisons to Other Species: On present knowledge, Willow and Alder flycatchers *cannot* be separated by sight alone, not even in the hand. However, there are some tendencies toward plumage differences between the two. If you happen to be looking at very typical individuals that are identifying themselves by song or call, you may notice some of the following points.

Alder tends to be slightly darker above than Willow, with stronger olive tones, and with the crown and face often darker than the back. The eye-ring is variable in both species, but it is narrow at best, and may be faint or lacking. Willow is more likely to lack the eye-ring altogether, and Alder is more likely to have a conspicuous eye-ring, but the two species overlap completely in this character. There is a slight tendency for the wing bars to be whiter and more contrasty on Alder than on Willow; Willow Flycatchers in western North America seem especially likely to have less contrasty wing bars.

Capsule Descriptions of All Ten Species

The brief reminders in this table are not intended to provide a shortcut to naming the *Empidonax*. Many of the pointers listed here will be difficult or impossible to understand unless you have read this chapter's introductory material and species accounts.

Species	Song	Call	Bill Shape (see Fig. 74)	Lower Mandible (see Fig. 76)
Least Flycatcher *E. minimus*	*che-BEK*	*whit*	intermediate	pale, often with faint dusky tip
Hammond's Flycatcher *E. hammondii* Molts earlier in fall than Dusky Flycatcher.	low-pitched, rough; *chipit . . . brrk . . . grrrip*	*peep*	narrow and short	about one-half dark
Dusky Flycatcher *E. oberholseri*	*chrip . . . grrreep . . . pweet*	*whit*	narrow and of intermediate length	pale, fading into dark tip
Gray Flycatcher *E. wrightii* Long-tailed; distinctive tail-dipping habit.	irregular; *chuwip . . . teeah . . . chuwip*	*whit*	narrow and long	pale with contrasting dark tip
Buff-breasted Flycatcher *E. fulvifrons* Breast washed with buff; small, distinctive; very local in Southwest.	*CHEE-bit*	*whit, pit,* or *pt*	small	pale

Primary Extension (see Fig. 75)	Throat	Back	Eye-ring	Wing Bars
moderate to short	off-white	washed with brown to olive	conspicuous	sharp contrast
long	gray	olive-gray	conspicuous on dark face	only moderate contrast
fairly short	pale gray	olive-gray	fairly conspicuous	only moderate contrast
fairly short	grayish white	gray with faint olive wash	no strong contrast	no strong contrast
fairly long	whitish	brownish		

Species	Song	Call	Bill Shape (see Fig. 74)	Lower Mandible (see Fig. 76)
Western Flycatcher complex:	high-pitched, variable;	males, ascending *tseeyeap*	wide	pale
Pacific-slope Flycatcher *E. difficilis* and **Cordilleran Flycatcher** *E. occidentalis*	*pttsik . . . tsip . . . tseweep,* repeated	(Pacific-slope) or *pit-peet* (Cordilleran); females, high, thin *tseet*		
Yellow-bellied Flycatcher *E. flaviventris*	*che-bunk*	variable; *perwee* or *pree* or *pyew*	wide	pale
Acadian Flycatcher *E. virescens*	*PEET-sah*	loud, flat *peek*	wide and long	pale
Alder Flycatcher *E. alnorum*	*rree-BEEA*	*kep*	wide	pale
Willow Flycatcher *E. traillii* Visually not separable from Alder Flycatcher.	*FITZ-bew*	*whit*	wide	pale

Primary Extension (see Fig. 75)	Throat	Back	Eye-ring	Wing Bars
usually rather short	yellow	olive-green	elongated toward back	only moderate contrast
fairly short	yellow	very green	narrow and even	strong contrast
quite long	white or sometimes yellow	strongly green	well defined	usually buff and contrasty
long	white	olive-gray to olive brown	variable	only moderate contrast
long	white	olive-brown	often indistinct	not sharply contrasting

Other Similar Flycatchers

Wood-pewees (see chapter 23), unlike most *Empidonax*, have no eye-rings and relatively indistinct wing bars. However, the same is true for many Willow Flycatchers, especially in the West. But Willow Flycatchers can be separated from wood-pewees by their wider bills, whiter throats, and shorter wings; on wood-pewees, the wings appear to extend at least one-third of the way down the length of the tail.

Visitors to the Southwest often expect the Northern Beardless-Tyrannulet (*Camptostoma imberbe*) to look very different from other flycatchers. As a result, the plain immature of the Verdin (*Auriparus flaviceps*) is often mistaken for the Beardless, while the real Beardless is sometimes passed off as an *Empidonax*. However, *bill shapes* differ (Fig. 77): the bill is short and conical in the Verdin, wide and flat in *Empidonax*; that of the Beardless is narrow and stubby, a little like a tiny edition of a vireo's bill. The Beardless has a *narrow dark line from bill to eye*, and although it rarely looks pointy-crested, it usually has a *bushy-headed* look. The immature Verdin has a very plain gray face with no markings at all, and its head looks smoothly rounded.

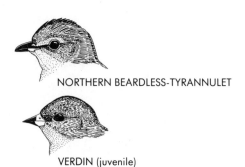

NORTHERN BEARDLESS-TYRANNULET

VERDIN (juvenile)

Fig. 77. Northern Beardless-Tyrannulet and juvenile Verdin. The tyrannulet is sometimes confused with the *Empidonax* flycatchers, and the juvenile Verdin is sometimes confused with the tyrannulet. Note bill shapes and face patterns.

25

THE CHICKADEES

BLACK-CAPPED CHICKADEE *Parus atricapillus*
CAROLINA CHICKADEE *Parus carolinensis*

The problem: The Black-capped Chickadee and the Carolina Chickadee, extremely similar in appearance, replace each other abruptly north and south of a line through the eastern United States. Their identification poses a serious challenge for birders near the contact zone. Although their songs are distinctive, some confusion has resulted from vague descriptions of the differences. To further complicate the picture, the two species hybridize in some areas.

Preliminary Points

Distribution: In the lowlands, the dividing line between the breeding ranges of these two species runs through central New Jersey, southern Pennsylvania, central Ohio, northern Indiana, central Illinois and Missouri, and southern Kansas, where the Carolina Chickadee reaches its western limit. In the Appalachians, the Black-capped replaces the Carolina well south into West Virginia, and evidently some Black-cappeds breed at high elevations as far south as North Carolina.

During the breeding season there is very little overlap between the species. In fact, just the opposite may occur: in some areas in summer there appears to be a narrow gap where *neither* species nests regularly. This hiatus, where it exists, is largely erased in winter, as Black-cappeds spread southward to overlap somewhat with Carolinas.

Exact details of distribution remain to be clarified in many areas. Even in well-studied regions some wandering may occur, so range is never totally dependable for identification near the contact zone.

Reliability of field identifications: If you are in an area where one of these species is expected, and you hear the typical song and see the field marks described below, there is no reason not to trust your field identification. But because hybrids are possible (or even likely in some areas), chickadees that look or sound odd should not be "stretched" to fit one species or the other. For the same reason, if you find what seems to be a typical individual well outside its normal range, your field identification of it is not likely to be accepted. Try to tape-record the bird's voice, and if possible have the bird mist-netted for measurement and photography in the hand.

Field Marks — Black-capped Chickadee vs. Carolina Chickadee

Edgings of greater coverts: "More white in the wings" is often quoted as a field mark for Black-capped, but this character has been widely misinterpreted to apply to the edgings of the secondaries (which are pale in both species). The critical area is on the greater coverts (Fig. 78). In the Black-capped the greater coverts have broad white outer edges, contrasting with the dark gray inner webs of these feathers and with the dark gray centers of the tertials. These edgings are most obvious on fresh-plumaged winter birds, but they remain apparent into the spring; on worn birds in summer, they can be obscure. (On juveniles in summer, these edgings may be buffy rather than white.) In Carolina Chickadee the greater coverts have gray outer edges, hardly paler than the inner webs; thus they look uniformly medium gray, often contrasting with the paler edgings of the secondaries. The difference is easy to see, with practice (but note that chickadees have very fluffy plumage, and the wing coverts are sometimes hidden by the body feathers on fluffed-out birds in winter).

Lower edge of bib: In Carolina Chickadee, the division between the black throat patch and the white breast forms a relatively neat, even line. In Black-capped, this division tends to be more uneven, with some white feather-edgings in the lower part of the black area, and some clouded or partly obscured black underlying the upper edge of the white.

Edgings of flight feathers: The outer edges of the primaries, secondaries, tertials, and tail feathers have pale edgings in both species. These are most obvious on the secondaries,

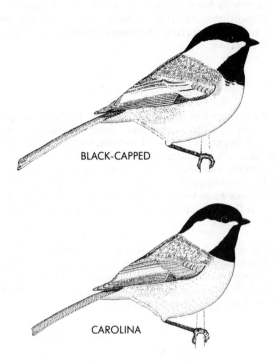

Fig. 78. Adult chickadees in fresh plumage. *Above*, Black-capped Chickadee. *Below*, Carolina Chickadee. Notice especially the pattern of the greater coverts, and the appearance of the lower edge of the bib. The differences in size and in proportionate tail length may be noticeable when the two species are seen together.

where (on birds in fresh plumage) the broad edgings appear to run together in a solid patch. These edgings tend to be white in Black-capped, pale gray in Carolina Chickadee. But variations in lighting make this a difficult mark to use, even on typical birds, and there is some overlap between the species in this character.

Size and shape: The Black-capped averages slightly larger and proportionately longer-tailed than the Carolina Chickadee.

Some observers have suggested that the Black-capped also looks proportionately larger-headed. Size and shape could provide minor supporting characters when the two species are seen together.

Voice

Calls: As expected in highly social birds, both species give a wide variety of calls, which have been extensively studied (see the Bibliography). Most of the notes given by the Black-capped have close counterparts in the Carolina's repertoire. Identifying the two species on the basis of most of these calls would be possible only for a specialist. The familiar *chick-a-dee-dee* notes tend to be faster and higher-pitched as given by the Carolina Chickadee, but they are somewhat variable in both species.

Song: The songs of these two species — the whistled *fee-bee* of the Black-capped and the corresponding notes of the Carolina — often provide the best distinction. However, over-simplified descriptions of the differences can be misleading. Figure 79 diagrams the typical songs.

fee-beee
BLACK-CAPPED

see-bee-see-bay
CAROLINA

Fig. 79.

Notice that in Carolina Chickadee the first and third notes are much higher-pitched. This may be more significant than the mere number of notes in the song; either species may sometimes give a three-noted variation, as shown in Figure 80.

Many other variations are possible. For each species, however, the "typical" song shown above is by far the most frequent; probably nearly all nonhybrid males use the typical song at least part of the time.

fee-bee-eee
BLACK-CAPPED

see-bee-bee
CAROLINA

Fig. 80.

In areas where the two species come into contact, some individuals have odd songs not typical of either species — and some have been heard to give the songs of both species. Such birds are likely to be hybrids, but it has been suggested that males of one species may learn the song of the other so as to defend the territory against all possible chickadee intruders. Obviously, a bird near the contact zone that sings both songs or "funny" songs cannot be safely identified in the field.

Other Chickadees

GRAY-HEADED CHICKADEE *Parus cinctus**
BOREAL CHICKADEE *Parus hudsonicus*
MEXICAN CHICKADEE *Parus sclateri*
MOUNTAIN CHICKADEE *Parus gambeli*
CHESTNUT-BACKED CHICKADEE *Parus rufescens*

The problem: Like other birds, Black-capped Chickadees may rarely occur in a leucistic (paler than normal) plumage. On one occasion, such a Black-capped was misidentified as a Gray-headed Chickadee by many observers. Discussion of this problem has to involve also some treatment of Boreal

---

* **Note:** The name "Siberian Tit" has been used for this species in recent checklists issued by the American Ornithologists' Union and the American Birding Association. This was supposed to conform with British usage — even though the species never occurs in Britain! The name seems unlikely to gain permanent acceptance among North American observers.

Chickadee, the species with which the Gray-headed is most likely to be confused.

To round out the chapter, I mention identification problems that occasionally crop up with the other three chickadee species in North America.

GRAY-HEADED CHICKADEE and BOREAL CHICKADEE:
This table compares some important characters of these two species to each other and to Black-capped Chickadee:

	Black-capped	**Boreal**	**Gray-headed**
Greater coverts	contrastingly edged with white	gray; no contrast	contrastingly edged with white
White on face	extensive; reaches back to nape	limited; blends into grayish on sides of neck	extensive; reaches back to nape
Contrast between cap and back	strong	very little	very little
Shape			proportionately longer-tailed
Voice		hoarser than Black-capped	hoarser than Boreal

Many birders have tried to use crown color to separate Gray-headed and Boreal chickadees, but the difference is not striking: it is "brownish gray" in Gray-headed and "grayish brown" in Boreal. Flank color is another tricky point. On fresh-plumaged birds in winter, the Boreal definitely has darker and browner flanks, but this can be less apparent on worn-plumaged birds in summer. A major source of confusion is provided by juvenile Boreal Chickadees, which may have grayer crowns, paler flanks, and hoarser calls than adults; no doubt these juveniles have been responsible for many reports of Gray-headeds.

Therefore, identification of Gray-headed Chickadee should always be backed up by reference to the greater coverts and the amount of white on the face. In these characters the Gray-headed is more similar to Black-capped Chickadee; this added to the problem on the occasion when a leucistic Black-capped, with a gray crown, turned up at a feeder in Alberta. On this individual the gray crown still contrasted sharply against an even paler gray back, and other minor characters also pointed to its true identity. However, abnormalities like leucism can vary in their effects; any supposed Gray-headed Chickadee outside its normal range should be identified with great caution.

MEXICAN CHICKADEE: The Mexican Chickadee is not usually an identification problem as it does not overlap in range with any other chickadee species. Occasional reports of sightings out of range (e.g., from the Santa Catalina Mountains of Arizona) undoubtedly refer to Mountain Chickadees in worn plumage; such birds may lack the white supercilium and may be quite gray on the sides, but they do not duplicate the very extensive black bib that covers most of the upper breast in Mexican Chickadee.

MOUNTAIN CHICKADEE: The famous field mark of the Mountain Chickadee, the white supercilium, is created by white tips on black feathers; so when the bird is in very worn plumage (mid- to late summer), the white stripe may be diminished or lacking. In such condition this species can be confused with either Black-capped or Mexican chickadees.

On the other side of the coin, Black-cappeds may rarely show traces of a white supercilium. Such an aberrant bird might be mistaken for a Mountain Chickadee — but the latter species has a much hoarser *chick-a-dee* call and a noticeably longer bill than the Black-capped.

CHESTNUT-BACKED CHICKADEE: Visiting birders may be momentarily confused by the birds found on the California coast south of San Francisco Bay. In this race of Chestnut-backed Chickadee (*P. r. barlowi*) the sides and flanks are dusky gray. Most bird guides mention and illustrate only the more northern populations, in which the sides and flanks are chestnut like the back.

26

BENDIRE'S THRASHER

BENDIRE'S THRASHER *Toxostoma bendirei*
CURVE-BILLED THRASHER *Toxostoma curvirostre*
SAGE THRASHER *Oreoscoptes montanus*

The problem: Observers looking for Bendire's Thrasher in some parts of the Southwest may run afoul of the Curve-billed Thrasher — which can be very similar, and which is frequently more common and much more conspicuous. Adults of the two species have different bill shapes, but this can be difficult to judge without prior experience; eye color and tail color, sometimes suggested as field marks, are too variable to be diagnostic. Breast pattern can be a useful character, but it varies with season and geography. A further complication is that juveniles of both species are superficially much like adult Bendire's.

Smaller, shorter-billed, and more distinctly marked, the Sage Thrasher would never be mistaken for the Curve-billed; but there can be some confusion between Sage and Bendire's thrashers at some seasons, especially when Sage is in worn plumage.

Field Marks — Bendire's vs. Curve-billed

Bill color: The Curve-billed Thrasher has an all-black bill; Bendire's has a *pale base to the lower mandible*. This is a reliable mark at all seasons, but it can be hard to see at a distance. The overall bill color of Bendire's tends to be paler than that of Curve-billed, dark gray rather than black, so the pale basal area does not contrast sharply.

Bill shape: This can be difficult to judge without previous experience. On Bendire's, although the upper mandible appears curved, the lower mandible is virtually straight; on

Curve-billed, appropriately, the upper and lower mandibles are both curved. In addition to being longer, the bill of Curve-billed tends to look *heavier* (thicker toward the base). Bill shape may be a less reliable mark for immatures: even after they molt out of juvenile plumage, young Curve-billeds may not have developed the full adult bill length. Even a few adults of either species may seem to have intermediate bill shapes.

Breast pattern: Geographic variation in Curve-billed Thrasher makes breast pattern a complicated field mark to describe. In simplest terms, the spots on the underparts tend to be larger and more rounded on Curve-billed, while on Bendire's they tend to be smaller, more sharply defined, and shaped like little arrowheads pointing up toward the bill. But this simplified version will sometimes lead to error.

In both species, breast pattern is most obvious when the birds are in fresh plumage: mostly late fall and winter (Fig. 81). In Curve-billed Thrasher, breast pattern is also more obvious in the eastern parts of its North American range (from about the Arizona–New Mexico border east), where the ground color of the breast is much lighter, making the spots stand out more clearly.

So taking into account the entire underparts, and remembering that the *visibility* of the pattern varies, it is true that Curve-billed tends to have larger and rounder spots overall, especially toward the sides of the breast. Many Curve-billeds also have a few small, dark "arrowhead" spots (like those of Bendire's) at the center of the upper breast, just below the throat; most also have a few more spots like this — often the most sharply defined spots of all — at the center of the *lower* breast or upper belly, lower than all the roundish spots, for a pattern never seen in Bendire's. On Bendire's, the spots are smallest and darkest at the base of the throat, and become larger and paler toward the lower breast (especially at the center, less so toward the sides), but they retain their arrowhead shape.

Eye color: Typically the iris is orange in adult Curve-billeds, yellow in Bendire's. But there is much individual variation. Probably Bendire's never matches the deep orange eye of some Curve-billeds, but its eye may tend toward orange-yellow; conversely, some adult Curve-billeds (plus many immatures) have plain yellow eyes.

Voice: The sharp *whit-wheet!* call of the Curve-billed Thrasher is one of the best-known bird sounds in the Southwest. Curve-billed has several other calls, including a snappy, rattling *pitpitpitpit* (which may remind easterners of one Wood Thrush call) and a harsh *tchuck.* Bendire's tends to be a much quieter bird, occasionally giving a low *chuk* or *chgk.* The songs of the two species are quite different: Curve-billed delivers a typical thrasher performance, with abrupt phrasing

CURVE-BILLED
THRASHER

BENDIRE'S
THRASHER

SAGE
THRASHER

Fig. 81. Adult thrashers in fresh plumage (as seen in late fall or early winter). Compare bill shapes, head shapes, and pattern of the underparts. Keep in mind that by midsummer, the markings on the breast will be much less distinct than they are in fresh plumage.

and interspersed guttural notes, while Bendire's has a sweet-voiced continuous warble without the start-and-stop quality of most of its congeners.

Size and shape: Birders experienced with both species may notice that Curve-billed is larger and somewhat heavier-bodied than Bendire's, and that Curve-billed tends to look larger-headed proportionately.

Habitat: Habitat preferences furnish a minor clue in identification. There are many places where the two species are found together, mostly areas of open desert with a rich variety of plants (including cholla cactus, the favored nest site for Curve-billed and often for Bendire's). Curve-billed is more likely than Bendire's to live in suburban areas, and Bendire's also avoids areas of dense vegetation. On the other hand, Bendire's is found in some places where Curve-billed is absent, such as open grassland with scattered yuccas, and around hedgerows in agricultural country.

Field Marks — Juvenile Bendire's and Curve-billed

Depending on location, juveniles of these thrashers may be seen any time from early spring to late summer. With a close view, they can be recognized as juveniles by their pale rufous wing bars and tertial edgings, narrow rufous tips to the tail feathers, rufous wash on the rump and uppertail coverts, and short, thin, dark streaks on the upper breast. The body feathers (as on many juvenile birds) are more "loose" or "filmy" than those of adults, but the wings and tail appear quite fresh at first, whereas adults at this season will be in moderately worn plumage.

The danger here is that juvenile Curve-billeds may be mistaken for Bendire's. Not only do they have fine, short streaks on the breast instead of large round spots, but they also may have relatively short, straight bills and less orange (more yellow) eyes. The important thing is to recognize these birds *as juveniles* (by the characteristics noted above). Beyond that point, identifying them to species can be extremely difficult, unless a bird happens to give the typical Curve-billed call. Even the color of the base to the lower mandible can be an unreliable clue on young birds, because juveniles may retain traces of the pale, fleshy "flanges" at the corners of the mouth so often seen on nestlings.

Notes on Sage Thrasher

In fresh plumage (as in late fall and winter), Sage Thrasher is unlikely to be misidentified. Compared to all other western thrashers, it is much more distinctly marked — with extensive dark streaking on the underparts, well-defined white wing bars and tail corners, and fine dark streaking on the crown and back. Problems arise, however, when birders encounter Sage Thrashers in very worn plumage, mostly in midsummer. At this season the white wing bars may be worn away, the white tail corners may be obscure, the fine dark streaks on the upperparts have long since disappeared, and the streaks on the breast may have faded substantially. Birds in such worn condition may seem to have most of the field marks of Bendire's Thrasher.

Observers familiar with both species will notice the much shorter bill of Sage Thrasher. The best plumage character is the pattern of the underparts. Although Sage may have small "arrowhead" marks on the upper breast (like those of Bendire's), these become larger, equally distinct marks extending down to the belly and lengthening into streaks on the sides and flanks, a pattern that Bendire's never duplicates. Overall plumage tone tends to be buffy brown on Bendire's, while Sage is more grayish brown above and off-white below.

27

THE PHILADELPHIA VIREO COMPLEX

WARBLING VIREO *Vireo gilvus*
PHILADELPHIA VIREO *Vireo philadelphicus*

The problem: At most times and places in North America, the Philadelphia Vireo is less common than the birds that it resembles. Because of this, it may be overlooked; conversely, other species may be "turned into" Philadelphia Vireos by overly optimistic birders. The main contender for identification is the Warbling Vireo, especially in fall, when it may have bright yellow tones. Another potential source of confusion is the Tennessee Warbler: fall birds, and even adult females in spring, can be unexpectedly similar to this small vireo.

Preliminary Points

Variation: The trademark color of the Philadelphia Vireo, the yellow on the underparts, can be surprisingly variable. Some individuals, especially autumn birds, wear a fairly bright, deep yellow over the entire underparts. But on many autumn birds and most spring birds the yellow is much lighter, often a peculiar creamy yellow tone, sometimes very pale. The range of different shades worn by Philadelphia Vireos can be confusing to observers who have not seen many individuals.

Although the variation in Philadelphia Vireo all seems to be seasonal and individual, not geographical, Warbling Vireos are divided into several geographical races. Differences among these are mostly minor, but Warbling Vireos from the Pacific Coast tend to be smaller, darker-crowned, and perhaps more colorful than those from some other areas, and therefore slightly more like Philadelphia Vireo. Warbling Vireos also may vary seasonally, with some autumn birds showing a lot of yellow on the underparts.

Field Marks — Philadelphia vs. Warbling Vireos

Color and pattern of underparts: Brightness of yellow is not diagnostic for Philadelphia Vireo: especially in autumn, some Warblings have richer yellow on the underparts than some Philadelphias. But the distribution of the color is different. On Warbling Vireo, the strongest yellow tones are generally on the *flanks*, with slightly paler yellow extending onto the undertail coverts and up along the sides. Some Warblings even have a yellow wash across the center of the breast, but this is of a paler and duller shade than the yellow on the flanks.

On Philadelphia Vireo, the intensity of yellow on the underparts is quite variable, but the area to study is the center of the lower throat and center of the upper breast: this area should be as bright as, or brighter than, any other region of the underparts. If the underparts are strongly colored, the center of the lower throat will be among the richest yellow areas (not fading toward whitish, as in the brightest Warblings). If the underparts are quite pale, there will still be yellow concentrated in this area (although it may be paler toward the *sides* of the throat and breast, so a good view is necessary).

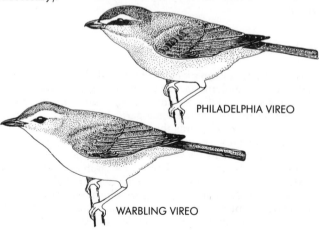

PHILADELPHIA VIREO

WARBLING VIREO

Fig. 82. Philadelphia Vireo and Warbling Vireo, to compare shape (especially head shape and tail length), face pattern (especially the appearance of the eyestripe and the form of the supercilium), and distribution of color on the underparts.

Face pattern: The dark lores of Philadelphia Vireo are emphasized in all field guides. However, most Warbling Vireos have at least a small dusky area before the eye; this is fairly noticeable on some, and observers must resist the temptation to turn these into Philadelphias. Conversely, on some fall Philadelphias (perhaps younger birds) the dark lores are not so well defined. The area *behind* the eye is worth noting too: on Philadelphia there is often a sharply defined, broad postocular stripe (not quite as dark as the lores), while Warbling often has a much less noticeable stripe there. The shape of the *supercilium* ("eyebrow") also affects the overall face pattern. On Philadelphia Vireo, the whitish supercilium narrows immediately behind the eye and then fades out only a little farther back, while the supercilium of Warbling Vireo often looks widened or arched above and behind the eye, creating a "surprised" or "wide-eyed" expression.

Shape: Birders who have the opportunity to see lots of individuals of these two vireos may find shape differences helpful in separating them (Fig. 82). The Philadelphia Vireo usually appears to have a more rounded head, while the Warbling Vireo usually looks more flat-crowned; this often creates the illusion that the Philadelphia has a proportionately larger head and shorter bill. (Actually, the Philadelphia is only very slightly shorter-billed on average, with much overlap between the species.) Philadelphia Vireo also tends to be shorter-tailed than Warbling Vireo (by as much as 10 percent). This difference in tail length is difficult to see in the field, but it contributes to the illusion that the Philadelphia is the more "stubby" or "chunky" of the two species.

Field Marks — Philadelphia Vireo vs. Tennessee Warbler

The similarity between these two unrelated species can be surprisingly close. Many Tennessee Warblers (especially in fall) share the general color of the Philadelphia Vireo, including the creamy yellow shade on the breast. Tennessee Warblers also have notably dark lores. In a quick view, if the general color and pattern are seen but other things are missed, even an experienced birder may be misled.

With a better view, *bill shape* will immediately separate the two (Fig. 83). The Tennessee Warbler's bill is thinner and tapered to a fine point, creating the illusion that it is propor-

PHILADELPHIA VIREO   TENNESSEE WARBLER

Fig. 83. Philadelphia Vireo and Tennessee Warbler. Their general colors can be quite similar, and both have dark lores, but note the differences in bill shape and in the pattern behind the eye.

tionately longer. Adding to the different shape is the slimmer body and slightly *shorter tail* of the Tennessee Warbler. The *postocular stripe* (behind the eye) is usually much narrower and less sharply defined on the warbler than on the vireo. *Back color* can be helpful: Tennessee Warbler has the center of the back bright grass-green at all seasons, brighter than the olive-green back of the vireo. The undertail coverts are almost always white on the Tennessee Warbler, but usually (though not always) washed with yellow on the Philadelphia Vireo.

28

TIPS FOR IDENTIFYING FALL WARBLERS

The apt phrase "confusing fall warblers," coined by Roger Tory Peterson years ago, serves to conjure up disturbing images for the birder. The array of drab warbler plumages seen in fall cannot compare to the bright patterns of spring males. But fall warblers can be made far less confusing by recognition of a few basics. Many birders even regard fall warblers as fun, a challenge renewed for a brief period each autumn.

One encouraging fact is that all our warblers are in fresh plumage in fall migration. All warblers molt in late summer, before they leave the breeding grounds. Young birds that have just fledged are in their juvenal plumage (which is often confusingly dull and streaky) only briefly, for a few weeks after they leave the nest, and then they molt their head and body plumage before they migrate south. Adults go through a complete molt immediately after nesting and before migration. Fall warblers may be drab, but at least those drab feathers are fresh — we do not have to struggle to see markings on worn or faded plumage at that season.

Another reason for optimism is that adults of many species look virtually the same all year. This is true of Hooded, Wilson's, Blue-winged, Golden-winged, Black-throated Blue, Black-throated Green, Kentucky, Yellow-throated, Prothonotary, American Redstart, and several other warblers. In some species, such as Nashville and Canada warblers and Northern Parula, the summer and winter plumages of adults show only slight differences. Those species in which the adults look completely different in fall — such as Blackpoll and Bay-breasted warblers — are the exceptions.

The autumn migration of warblers begins earlier in the season than many birders realize. Over most of North America, some adult warblers are already on the move by late July. In many species, the adults migrate southward earlier than the young birds, and many adults have left North America by the end of August. By mid-September, a high percentage of the migrant warblers seen on this continent are likely to be young birds. This can easily lead to some false impressions: for example, a birder who sees two dozen American Redstarts in late September without finding a single adult male among them might reach the mistaken conclusion that these birds molt out of their bright plumage in fall. Actually, the distinctive adults simply tend to pull out early. So it is during the later stages of migration that the fall warblers are at their most confusing.

The distinctness of immature warblers in fall varies with the species. For virtually all of them, however, these first-autumn birds are quite similar *in overall pattern* to autumn adults. The differences are mostly matters of degree: the markings are present but less distinct, the colors are sometimes less bright. Immature males are often similar to adult females, while immature females are often the plainest of fall warblers. But even with the drabbest of them, a close look will usually reveal a shadow of the adult pattern; so the birder who can identify female warblers in spring should be able to figure out most fall warblers. In fact, careful study of warblers in spring is one of the best ways to prepare for recognizing them in fall.

Here are some pointers on specific things to watch for when faced with one or more confusing warblers during fall migration.

Consider shapes: Warblers come in a variety of shapes; the differences are subtle, but with practice they are very useful in identification. (In the following three chapters, notice how often shape is mentioned even for very similar species.) Bill shape and tail length are two obvious variables. Overall head and body shape, wing length, and length of the undertail coverts are worth noting. Behavior adds to the impressions of shape. For example, several species frequently wag their tails up and down; Connecticut Warbler walks on the ground with a methodical gait, emphasizing its heavy shape; redstarts often fan their tails and droop their wings; Chestnut-sided Warbler often holds its tail up above the level of its back.

Look at wing pattern: Of course no area of a warbler's plumage pattern should be ignored completely, but some aspects are more useful than others for rapidly narrowing down the choices. Wing pattern (Fig. 84) is one of the first things to notice. With only a few exceptions, the general wing pattern for a given species of warbler will be the same at all seasons,

Fig. 84. Sample wing patterns of warblers. With a quick but clear view of a mystery warbler in fall, a good thing to notice first (almost as important as face pattern) is wing pattern. Here are examples of (**a**) strongly contrasted wing bars and tertial edgings on a black wing, (**b**) wing bars and tertial edgings well defined but not sharply contrasting, (**c**) feathers with dark centers and pale edgings, and (**d**) "unpatterned" wings. Even in the last example, as on any "unpatterned" bird, the arrangement of the wing feathers imposes a hint of pattern. These are only representative patterns; several others also occur.

for both sexes, and for all ages past the juvenile stage. Wing pattern is also often a relatively easy thing to see in a quick view.

Look at face pattern: For someone who knows the spring males of warblers like Prairie, Magnolia, or Blackburnian, the drabness of some first-autumn females can be shocking. Plain as these fall birds may seem, however, their *faces* almost always show at least a subtle indication of the typical pattern. Look closely at the face of an unknown dull warbler, and you are likely to find that you know it after all.

Listen for call notes: Some birders can recognize practically every species of warbler by its chip note. This is probably not possible for everyone, because it takes a very sharp ear and a major amount of study. But anyone can learn to separate the loud, hard *check* of Yellow-rumped Warbler from the soft *zip* of Cape May Warbler, or the musical *chip* of Yellow Warbler from the light *tsit* of Orange-crowned Warbler, and these things can be very useful for clinching the identity of a warbler seen imperfectly.

Be cautious in using tail pattern: Nearly all of the many species of *Dendroica* warblers (and several from other genera) have conspicuous white spots in the outer tail feathers, visible from below when the tail is folded or from either angle when the tail is spread. The shape and size of these spots are distinctive for many birds, and the resulting tail patterns (when the birds spread their tails in short flights) are often useful for recognizing some warblers. Note, however, that for many species there is variation in the amount of white in the tail, adult males having the most and immature females having the least.

Know the patterns of occurrence: Knowing what to expect is a major advantage. Fall passage of Yellow Warblers peaks early, while Orange-crowned Warblers (which can be similar to dull female Yellows) come through later. On the Atlantic seaboard in fall, Blackpoll and Cape May warblers are often very common in trees near the coast but less common inland; Palm Warblers are most numerous out at the beach itself, on the ground around thickets behind the dunes; Pine Warblers tend to stick closely to (you guessed it) pines. Knowing these tendencies can help you make quick educated guesses when necessary. When you catch a good "wave" and there are confusing fall warblers flitting everywhere, you'll be able to decide which ones to pursue for a careful identification and which ones to pass up.

29

THE BLACKPOLL TRIO

PINE WARBLER *Dendroica pinus*
BAY-BREASTED WARBLER *Dendroica castanea*
BLACKPOLL WARBLER *Dendroica striata*

The problem: Although the spring males of these three warbler species are utterly different, birds in fall plumage have
caused many headaches for birders. Especially similar are the
fall Blackpoll and Bay-breasted warblers, with their olive upperparts, yellowish underparts, strong wing bars, and finely
streaked backs. Their best-known field marks (pale legs and
white undertail coverts in Blackpoll, dark legs and buff undertail coverts in Bay-breasted) can cause difficulties: many
Blackpolls actually have dark legs, and the difference between white and very pale buff on the undertail coverts of
some birds can be debatable even with good views.

Pine Warbler differs notably from the other two in having
an unstreaked back. But this is not always enough for identification, because the back streaks on Blackpolls and Bay-
breasteds are sometimes very faint. Immature Blackpolls
with dark legs, white undertail coverts, and very faintly
streaked backs probably account for some reports of Pine
Warblers out of range.

Preliminary Points

Fall plumages: The birds considered here, those to be seen
during fall migration, belong to two plumage classes.

1. *Adult winter plumage.* Adults go through a complete
molt in late summer on the breeding grounds. By the time
they begin to migrate south, they are in fresh winter plumage.

2. *First-winter plumage.* These warblers wear juvenal
plumage only briefly; although the flight feathers are re-

tained for a full year, the juvenal head and body feathers start to be replaced by first-winter plumage shortly after the young birds become independent. By the time they begin to migrate south, they are in fresh first-winter plumage. Since juvenal plumage is seen only on the breeding grounds (and often with easily identified adults in attendance), it is ignored in the following discussions of field marks. Differences between adult winter and first-winter plumages are mentioned only when they affect identification.

What to look for first: With this group, an approach that begins with too much reliance on one field mark is likely to lead you astray some of the time. It is better to start by quickly taking in impressions that will suggest which species a bird is; then you can check a series of specific points to confirm or disprove your first impression.

The most effective things to look for in your first glance are:

1. *Back streaks.* If you don't see streaks at first it doesn't necessarily mean the bird is a Pine Warbler, because the streaks are faint on some Blackpolls and Bay-breasteds; but if you do see streaks, you can immediately rule out Pine and concentrate on separating the other two.

2. *Overall color.* The color and pattern of the breast and the color of the upperparts will usually suggest the correct identification.

3. *Face pattern.* Although this is a "soft" criterion and never to be relied upon, the face patterns of the three species are usually different (and usually easy to see).

4. *Flank color.* Most fall Bay-breasteds have at least a trace of reddish brown on the flanks; on many the color is strong enough to be apparent at first glance, immediately identifying the bird (although apparent lack of this color does not necessarily mean the bird is *not* a Bay-breasted, of course).

5. *Leg color.* If the legs are bright pale yellow or pinkish, the bird is almost certainly a Blackpoll Warbler; if the legs appear dark, it could be any of the three species.

Field Marks — Fall Migrants

Back pattern: The back is *streaked* in Blackpoll and Bay-breasted, *unstreaked* in Pine Warbler. The streaks of the first two are usually apparent, but sometimes (especially in first-winter birds) they are very faint, so you may need a superb view to be sure that a particular bird's back is actually un-streaked. In well-streaked individuals of Bay-breasted the streaks tend to be more broken up into "chains" or series of short streaks, while in Blackpoll the streaks tend to be more long and continuous; this distinction is rarely obvious in the field, however.

Breast color and pattern: The fall Blackpoll tends to be fairly bright pale greenish yellow on the breast, while the Bay-breasted tends toward dull pale buffy yellow. There is also a tendency for the breast to be lightly streaked in Blackpoll, unstreaked in Bay-breasted, but this is only a generalization. Actually, most Bay-breasteds have a couple of faint streaks at the side of the breast; and on a few Blackpolls (probably first-winter birds) the breast has no visible streaks. Both species often have a dusky olive wash at the side of the breast, near the bend of the wing.

Breast color in fall Pine Warblers varies from bright yellow to dull pale brownish gray. Rather coarse streaks at the sides of the breast are evident on the brightest yellow-breasted individuals, and obscure or absent on the dullest birds.

Color of upperparts: Bay-breasted tends to be brighter above than Blackpoll. In particular, the unmarked *pale lime-green nape* of Bay-breasted Warbler is often conspicuous. The upperparts of Pine Warbler vary from fairly bright olive-green to dull grayish or brownish, with the apparent brightness corresponding approximately to the brightness of the throat and breast color.

Face pattern: Not really diagnostic, but often an excellent clue. Blackpoll usually has a well-defined *dark eyestripe*, setting off a conspicuous pale supercilium. Bay-breasted has a hint of the same pattern but usually with much less contrast, so that the face looks rather *pale and plain*. Pine usually has a distinctive pattern with a pale supercilium, dark lores, the beginnings of a dark moustachial stripe leading into the lower edge of a solid dark patch on the ear coverts, a pale crescent below the eye, and some pale area curving up from the throat onto the side of the neck, behind the dark ear coverts.

Flank color: Nearly all fall Bay-breasteds have at least a hint of reddish brown or chestnut on the flanks; on probably more than 70 percent of fall birds this color is sufficiently developed to be visible in the field. In its faintest manifestation, however, this trace of color may be hard to distinguish from the faint dusky streaks that often extend down onto the flanks of a Blackpoll. Note also that many fall Pine Warblers have a strong wash of dull dusky brown on the flanks.

Undertail coverts: As a generalization, these are pale buff in Bay-breasted, white in Blackpoll and Pine warblers. Actually, although this color is apparent on some individuals (with the undertail coverts either bright white or strongly buff), on others it is a difficult field mark. The buff on Bay-breasted is often so pale as to appear white in the field; worse, the undertail coverts may rarely be washed with yellow in Blackpoll or with pale brown in Pine Warbler.

Pattern of lower underparts: On many Blackpoll Warblers there is a noticeable *contrast* between the white of the undertail coverts and lower belly and the yellowish of the flanks and central belly; this is sometimes easier to see than the exact shade of the undertail coverts. Bay-breasteds rarely show any such contrast, the undertail coverts and belly being all of about the same shade. Pine Warbler is variable in this character; most yellow-breasted individuals do show some contrast, but the yellow tends to end higher up on the belly than in Blackpoll Warbler.

Leg color: The legs are dark (brown to black) in Bay-breasted and Pine warblers, and in many first-winter Blackpoll Warblers as well. Most adult Blackpolls have pale legs, varying from yellow to pink, which can be obvious in the field and are probably diagnostic for this species (although bright-legged adults will usually have obvious plumage characters also). It has been claimed that some Bay-breasted and Pine warblers may have pale legs; anyone who sees such a bird should try to document it in some way.

On most Blackpolls, including dark-legged immatures, the *soles of the toes are yellow;* this sometimes can be discerned in the field, with a close view. Pine Warblers may also have yellow soles, but in Bay-breasted they are apparently always dark.

Tertial edgings: In Pine Warbler, the outer edges of the tertials are always *dull* — medium gray or brownish gray, not showing any definite contrast to the centers of these feathers. In Blackpoll and Bay-breasted warblers the tertial edgings are

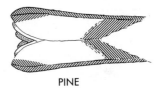 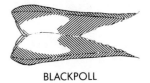

PINE   BLACKPOLL

Fig. 85. Tail patterns, as seen from below. *Left,* Pine Warbler. *Right,* Blackpoll Warbler (Bay-breasted is similar).

white, and usually show a fairly sharp line of contrast against the blackish feather centers.

Tail pattern: The white spots in the outer rectrices, visible only from beneath when the tail is folded, are roughly the same in Blackpoll and Bay-breasted warblers. Pine Warbler usually has *larger white tail spots,* extending farther up the shafts of the feathers toward the base of the tail (Fig. 85). (However, if the outermost pair of rectrices is missing, through molt or accident, the smaller white spots on the next pair of rectrices inward will be visible.) This mark must be used with caution: on some birds the white or pale undertail coverts may be long enough to reach (and appear to blend with) the white tail spots, making it impossible to tell just how long these spots are.

Shape: Bay-breasted and Blackpoll warblers are very similar in shape, but Bay-breasted tends to look a little bulkier and thicker-necked. Pine Warbler is heavier overall than the other two, with a noticeably larger bill. These differences are hardly diagnostic, but they can contribute to the first-impression identification for observers who get to see a lot of these birds.

Comparison of Pine Warbler to Other Species

The combination of strong wing pattern and finely streaked olive upperparts should separate Blackpoll and Bay-breasted from all other fall warblers. However, Pine Warbler may be
continued on p. 239

Fig. 86. Fall Plumages of Warblers

Blackpoll Warbler: *Top right,* well-marked adult; *lower right,* obscurely marked immature. Most fall birds are between the two extremes shown.

- Back streaked (sometimes very faintly)
- Breast greenish yellow, softly streaked (streaks sometimes obscure)
- Usually with distinct dark eyestripe and pale supercilium
- Legs and feet pale or dark (soles of toes yellow)
- Tertials usually with distinct white edges
- White undertail coverts contrast with yellow flanks

Bay-breasted Warbler: *Top left,* typical immature (fall adults similar).

- Back streaked (sometimes very faintly)
- Breast dull buffy yellow, practically unstreaked
- Most have a chestnut wash on flanks (may be faint or absent)
- Face usually looks rather plain and pale
- Upperparts brighter than in Blackpoll; conspicuous lime-green nape
- Undertail coverts buff (but can be very pale, almost white)
- Legs and feet (including soles of toes) virtually always dark

Pine Warbler: *Lower left,* generalized autumn bird.

- Back unstreaked
- Face pattern with noticeable ear patch
- Extensively white belly and undertail coverts
- Tertial edgings dull, showing little contrast
- Legs dark, toes or soles sometimes pale
- Breast and upperparts variable in color (see text)

confused with other species that show wing bars and plain backs.

The immature Prairie Warbler can be remarkably similar in pattern to some Pine Warblers: it can have virtually the same face pattern, and both species in fall can show wing bars that are well defined but not sharply contrasted against the rest of the wing. However, Prairie Warbler is smaller, slimmer, and more active than Pine Warbler, usually "wagging" its tail noticeably; it also tends to forage lower, although this is not a consistent difference. The yellow on the underparts is also usually smoother and more extensive in Prairie Warbler, reaching back nearly onto the undertail coverts.

Claimed sightings of dull-plumaged Pine Warblers in the Southwest would have to rule out possible confusion with female or immature Olive Warblers, which also have unmarked gray backs, strong wing bars, large bills, and dull yellow markings around the foreparts. The dullest Olive Warblers should show the following characters to distinguish them from Pine Warblers:

- *Yellow* edgings to the secondaries, unless badly worn (gray in Pine Warbler)
- Noticeable yellow or buff region on side of neck — as bright as, or brighter than, any other part of head/body plumage
- Dark gray line or patch behind eye, not broadening to a solid dark ear patch as in Pine Warbler
- Yellow wash on crown

30

THE WATERTHRUSHES

NORTHERN WATERTHRUSH *Seiurus noveboracensis*
LOUISIANA WATERTHRUSH *Seiurus motacilla*

The problem: The two waterthrushes are very different from most other warblers but very similar to each other. They are often identified by the general color of the supercilium (eyebrow stripe) and underparts: white in Louisianas, yellowish in Northerns. However, many Northerns (especially those nesting in Alaska and western Canada) are quite whitish below, and these birds are sometimes misidentified as Louisiana Waterthrushes.

Field Marks — Louisiana Waterthrush vs. Northern Waterthrush

Flank color: The ground color of the underparts is variable in both species. Louisianas are always mostly white below, but on the flanks there is a contrasting patch of color: pale pinkish buff, tawny, or dull cinnamon. On some individuals this is faint and can be seen only with an excellent view of the bird; but the odd *color,* and the way it *contrasts* with the adjacent white, add up to a diagnostic field mark for Louisiana Waterthrush. The same color is present on the Louisiana's undertail coverts, but it is more difficult to see there under field conditions. On Northern Waterthrushes the underparts vary from buff to yellow to white, but if the flanks are buff the remainder of the underparts are also. There may be rare Northerns with whitish underparts and some contrasting color on the flanks, but if so the flanks are likely to be pale yellow without any buff, pinkish, or cinnamon tones.

Supercilium: In both waterthrushes the fore part of the supercilium (between the eye and the bill) is dull and indistinct in color, but the appearance of the rear part of the supercilium can be a clue. In Northerns, this section varies from yellow to buff to white, and it tends to taper toward a narrow point rearward. In Louisianas, not only is this section clear white, it also tends to *broaden* toward the rear, which makes it quite conspicuous.

Throat pattern and color: The throat is spotted in Northerns and often immaculate in Louisianas. However, many Louisianas show a few spots here; and some even have more throat spotting than some sparsely marked Northerns. The ground color of the throat is always bright white in Louisianas, and varies from yellow to buff to white in Northerns.

Facial contrast: In the Louisiana, the combination of the broad white end of the supercilium and the bright white throat creates a first impression of a striking face pattern. Northerns rarely approach this degree of facial contrast (Fig. 87).

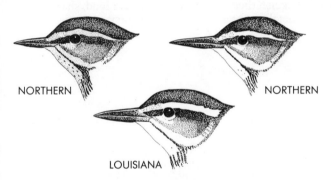

Fig. 87. Face patterns of waterthrushes. *Upper left,* "typical" Northern Waterthrush, easily identified by its small bill, noticeable throat spotting, and strong yellow or buff cast to the throat and supercilium. *Upper right,* a potentially confusing Northern Waterthrush with a longer bill, reduced throat spotting, and whitish throat and supercilium. *Bottom,* a typical Louisiana Waterthrush; notice the heavy bill and the broad white rear section of the supercilium. Some individuals have smaller bills and more extensive throat spotting than the one shown. The flanks should always be checked for the distinctive patch of cinnamon-buff in this species.

Bill size: The Louisiana has a fairly long heavy bill, often appearing disproportionately large for the size of the bird. The Northern, at the eastern end of its range, has a substantially smaller bill. However, farther west the Northern tends to be longer-billed (some birds have bills even longer than most Louisianas); and since these long-billed populations may also average whiter below, they can be particularly tricky for the observer. Even the longest bills of Northerns are usually not as heavy (i.e., not as thick, seen in profile) as those of many Louisianas, but this is a subtle difference.

Some minor supporting characters: The streaks on the underparts of the Northern are usually blackish and sharply defined, while those of the Louisiana tend to be slightly paler and more diffuse; but they overlap in this character, so it is helpful only in identifying typical individuals. In Louisianas the cinnamon-buff color of the flanks may also show up at the sides of the neck and chest, and the small pale crescent below the eye may be whiter and more conspicuous than in Northerns. Birders who hear both species regularly may learn to distinguish their chip notes: both have loud, sharp, somewhat metallic notes, that of the Louisiana being slightly "richer" in tone quality.

31

NOTES ON OTHER WARBLERS

Tennessee Warbler vs. Orange-crowned Warbler: These two *Vermivora* species are not extremely difficult to separate, but Tennessee is rare in the West and Orange-crowned is often scarce in the East, so birders may lack comparative experience with the two.

The best-known field mark is that the *undertail coverts* are yellow on Orange-crowned, white on Tennessee. But on an occasional Tennessee, the yellow of the underparts may wash back onto the undertail coverts (and Orange-crowneds are sometimes very pale there), so other marks may be needed for confirmation. *Back color* differs: Tennessee is consistently a richer, brighter grass-green or moss-green on the upper back and scapulars, while Orange-crowned is a duller, more olive-green there (but both species are equally bright on the rump). Tennessee has a significantly *shorter tail* than Orange-crowned, for a total silhouette that is noticeably different. The *longer supercilium* on Tennessee is usually apparent, extending farther back on the face than that of Orange-crowned. Tennessee also usually (not always) has more white edging in the tail than Orange-crowned (although still less than in most of the *Dendroica* warblers).

Orange-crowned Warbler as a surrogate rarity in winter: One of the more numerous and widespread wintering warblers in North America (although far less common than the Yellow-rumped), the Orange-crowned lacks obvious markings and is variable in color. As a result, it is sometimes mistaken for other (and rarer) warblers in winter, perhaps especially on Christmas Bird Counts.

Some winter Orange-crowneds are very bright yellow below, and their lack of obvious markings may bring to mind a Yellow Warbler. But Orange-crowned has at least a faint indication of a dark line through the eye, while Yellow's face either is totally blank or has a suggestion of a pale eye-ring.

Yellow Warbler also has a rich, musical *chip* for a call note, unlike the thin, hard *tsit* of Orange-crowned Warbler.

Some winter Orange-crowneds show a very conspicuous (albeit broken) pale eye-ring, gray head, and yellow underparts. They may be misidentified as Nashville Warblers or as one of the *Oporornis* warblers (like MacGillivray's or Connecticut). However, Nashville has a complete eye-ring and no trace of a dark eyestripe, and its underparts (including the throat) are a clear pale yellow. The *Oporornis* are chunky, heavy-bodied warblers with notably *long* undertail coverts, extending much of the way down the tail; their legs are usually pinkish (not gray to black as in Orange-crowned). Nashville Warbler and the species of *Oporornis* all have louder, harder call notes than Orange-crowned.

A good rule of thumb, when you suspect that you've found any of these rare and relatively unpatterned warblers in winter, is to ask yourself: Why isn't this bird an Orange-crowned Warbler?

Drab Northern Parulas: The adult male Northern Parula in spring is unmistakable, but some first-autumn females can be extremely drab. However, in addition to very small size (this is one of our smallest warblers), this species has a diagnostic character: the *bicolored bill*, with a yellow or pinkish lower mandible contrasting against the black upper mandible. No similar warbler, aside from the closely related Tropical Parula, shares this mark.

Myrtle vs. Audubon's warblers: Because these two forms interbreed in a narrow zone in southwestern Alberta, they were officially combined in 1973 into one species, called Yellowrumped Warbler. Although both forms are still illustrated in most bird guides, recent books have given little guidance on how to tell them apart. But they are still worth identifying. The true birder is interested in all kinds of birds, not just "countable" or "listable" ones . . . and there is a possibility that these two may be re-split into two full species again someday. In the meantime, it is still commendable to call them "Audubon's Warbler" and "Myrtle Warbler" (not just "Yellow-rumped") whenever they can be separated.

Unfortunately, *throat color* can sometimes be tricky. Bright yellow and bright white are sure signs of Audubon's and Myrtle, respectively, but many winter birds of either have pale buff or off-white throats. However, on Myrtle the pale throat extends to the side of the neck, setting off the back edge of a dark ear patch; on Audubon's, the pale throat area is usually smaller and more restricted, not spreading to the sides of the neck. The *dark ear patch* almost always contrasts more on Myrtle: it is darker, set off more sharply against the throat and side of the neck, and often outlined above by a *pale eyestripe*. Audubon's typically looks much more *plain-faced*, with no obvious dark ear patch and no more than a faint pale stripe behind the eye.

The breast pattern on winter birds tends more toward narrow streaks on a whitish background on Myrtle, while Audubon's shows more of an overall clouded gray-brown in this area. However, there is a lot of individual variation in this, so it is no more than a minor field mark. Audubon's also tends to have more white in the tail than Myrtle Warbler, but this varies with sex and age in both forms, adult males having the most white and immature females having the least. For many birders, *call notes* will provide a good clue: Myrtle gives a louder, harder *check*, while Audubon's delivers a softer *chep*.

32

IDENTIFYING SPARROWS: THE GENERIC APPROACH

For many birders, it seems that *all* sparrows are difficult to name. There are various reasons for this, often including the secretive nature of the birds themselves, but magnifying all other problems is the fact that the "field-marks approach" works very poorly on sparrows.

Here is a typical encounter between a beginner (myself, a few years ago) and a sparrow. The sparrow sets off the encounter by flying up onto a fence wire. Fighting off a sense of panic, the birder tries to focus on field marks. Does the bird have a streaked or plain breast? Streaked; okay. Is there or is there not a pale central stripe on the crown? Can't see that at this angle. What about a central breast spot? And wing bars; do those pale lines qualify as wing bars? At this point the bird drops back into the grass. The observer has noted only *one* definite field mark: the streaked breast; that would rule out some species, except that even most plain-breasted sparrows have streaks in juvenal plumage.

On the other hand, an experienced birder will often know what a sparrow is after a split-second glimpse — narrowing down the choice, if not to species, at least to a group of two or three related forms. Can practiced eyes really tabulate field marks so fast? Not likely; the expert is probably using a different system entirely, one that begins not with field marks but with the characteristic shape and behavior of each group of sparrows.

Consider, for example, a comparison between the typical eastern forms of Savannah Sparrow and Song Sparrow. They are quite similar in *plumage pattern*, but their *shapes* are so different that the practiced birder will never confuse them. The major groups of North American sparrows are listed and described in the illustrated synopsis here (Figs. 88–97). When you see the sparrows you know in the field, think of them as members of these groups, and try to see how shape, habitat, and behavior help to make them distinctive.

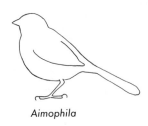

Aimophila

Fig. 88. *Aimophila*. Bachman's, Botteri's, Cassin's, Rufous-winged, and Rufous-crowned sparrows. Medium-sized to large sparrows, heavy-bodied and rather flat-crowned, with long tails that are usually rounded at the tip. Inhabit dense vegetation near the ground; often shy and difficult to observe. Some are found in pairs all year, but never in flocks. A variety of call notes, but some species tend to be silent.

Spizella

Fig. 89. *Spizella*. American Tree, Chipping, Clay-colored, Brewer's, Field, and Black-chinned sparrows. Small sparrows with rounded heads, small bills, and medium-long tails that are usually notched at the tip. Generally found in wooded or brushy areas, not open grass or marshes. In migration and winter usually in small flocks; often feed on the ground, but also seen high in trees, and likely to perch conspicuously in the open. Most call notes are thin and lisping.

VESPER SPARROW

Fig. 90. Vesper Sparrow. A medium-large sparrow with a medium-length, square-tipped tail, the outer tail feathers noticeably white. Inhabits fields, including dry fields and brushy areas. In winter often found in small, loose flocks; not particularly secretive, often perching in the open. Call note a loud *hsip*.

LARK SPARROW

Fig. 91. Lark Sparrow. A rather large sparrow; tail rather long, with a broad rounded tip and conspicuous white outer edges and corners. Inhabits brushy country near areas of bare ground; often perches conspicuously in the open. Often in small, loose flocks in winter. May fly rather high, giving a sharp, metallic call note.

Amphispiza

Fig. 92. *Amphispiza*. Black-throated, Sage, and Five-striped sparrows. Rather large sparrows with distinctive patterns, living on or near the ground in desert country. Often in pairs or family groups, but never in large flocks. Five-striped is often secretive but the other two are not. Call notes mostly light and tinkling or metallic.

SAVANNAH SPARROW

Fig. 93. Savannah Sparrow. A small, short-tailed sparrow, similar to *Ammodramus* (next) but not usually so chunky, large-headed, flat-crowned, or large-billed as the field-inhabiting members of that genus. Inhabits fields and marshes. Not particularly secretive. Often in loose flocks in winter. Thin, lisping call notes; often calls when flushed.

Ammodramus

Fig. 94. *Ammodramus*. Baird's, Grasshopper, Henslow's, Le Conte's, Sharp-tailed, and Seaside sparrows. Chunky, short-tailed birds with flat foreheads; the first three species listed above look large-headed and large-billed, while the latter three have proportionately smaller heads and thinner bills. Inhabit fields, wet meadows, and marshes, tending to be secretive, not perching freely in the open except when singing. Never found in flocks. Most call notes are thin and lisping; usually silent when flushed.

FOX SPARROW

Fig. 95. Fox Sparrow. A large sparrow; rather chunky, with a medium-long tail. Bill shape varies regionally: some races have a large bill with a swollen lower mandible. Usually on the ground in woods or brush, foraging by scratching with its feet among dead leaves. Often mixes with other sparrows in winter, but seldom forms flocks of its own kind. Call notes sharp and distinctive.

Melospiza

Fig. 96. *Melospiza*. Song, Lincoln's, and Swamp sparrows. Robust, medium-large sparrows, with longish tails that are rounded at the tip. Usually found low in dense vegetation, and can be secretive. Never in large flocks: usually solitary, or in pairs at the most. Call notes are loud and distinctive.

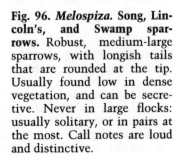

Zonotrichia

Fig. 97. _Zonotrichia_. White-throated, Golden-crowned, White-crowned, and Harris's sparrows. Medium-large to large sparrows, with tail fairly long and square-tipped, crown slightly peaked, bill not disproportionately large. In winter found in brushy areas, almost always in flocks; feed on the ground but often perch conspicuously in the open when disturbed. Call notes sharp and distinctive.

Some Pitfalls of Sparrow Identification

Median crown stripes: In several cases among the sparrows, the presence or absence of a pale stripe down the center of the crown is a significant field mark. But there is a potential hazard here: some sparrows with crowns that are either solidly colored or evenly patterned with fine streaks may show a short, pale median stripe on the forehead, just above the base of the upper mandible. Viewed from some angles, this could be interpreted as a median crown stripe.

Central breast spots: The central spot on the breast is an often-quoted field mark for the Song Sparrow, American Tree Sparrow, and some others, but it is not an infallible mark. The streaks may or may not seem to coalesce into a central spot on any of the streak-breasted sparrows. On plain-breasted species, any ruffling of the feathers can expose their darker basal areas, briefly creating the impression of a dark spot.

Breast streaking: Bird guides often separate sparrows into broad categories by noting whether they have streaked or plain underparts, but it can be misleading to use this as an absolute field mark. In almost all sparrows, the juveniles have finely streaked breasts, and some species (for example, Chipping Sparrow) retain these streaks for some time after they are independent. Even adults of some plain-breasted species can show a vaguely streaked or mottled effect in this area. Conversely, summer adults of some streaked-breasted sparrows can be in such worn plumage that they appear un-streaked.

Other sparrow-like birds: It is worth remembering that a con-fusing little thick-billed brown bird does not have to be one of our sparrows. There are some other common candidates, like Pine Siskins, winter-plumaged longspurs, and female-plumaged *Carpodacus* finches. Although they are not closely similar to any particular sparrow, they can cause temporary confusion. A "sparrow" that looks truly confusing could turn out to be an escaped cage bird or zoo bird of some kind — many exotic finches are kept in captivity — or even a stray individual of some migratory species from Eurasia.

33

CASSIN'S AND BOTTERI'S SPARROWS

BOTTERI'S SPARROW *Aimophila botterii*
CASSIN'S SPARROW *Aimophila cassinii*

The problem: These two sparrows of the desert grasslands are often considered to be practically identical in appearance, identifiable only by song. This is not really the case; there are several plumage differences between them. But they can still be genuinely difficult to identify, for three reasons:

1. Because of their secretive nature, they are difficult to see well when they are not singing (and when singing, of course, they are easily identified by song).
2. The plumage differences between them are mostly small-scale ones involving the patterns of individual feathers; so a good view, difficult or not, is necessary.
3. Because they molt in fall, they are in their freshest plumage in winter, when Botteri's and most Cassin's are absent from the United States. By late spring, abrasion of the plumage has made the pattern differences between them less obvious. Some very worn birds in late summer may appear to have no pattern at all.

Preliminary Points

Molt and wear: The timing of molt in these two species is still not thoroughly understood. The following summary is based on Arizona birds, but probably applies equally well in the rest of the birds' United States range.

Adult Cassin's Sparrows begin to molt by early September or a little earlier; molt of the body feathers begins at about the same time as molt of the flight feathers. The birds are in heavy molt in October, and the molt is essentially complete by late December, so that winter birds are in fresh plumage. There is only a partial molt in spring. The effects of wear on the plumage are noticeable first in reducing the pale edgings of the tertials and back feathers and in abrading the tail feathers. Most of the plumage characters useful for identification remain obvious at least through May, but by late July some individuals may be so worn and faded that they seem to have no pattern at all.

Adult Botteri's Sparrows may begin to molt the body feathers by August, with new back feathers appearing even while they are still caring for young. Molt of the flight feathers of the wings seems to start later — perhaps after the birds have left the United States (which may partly explain why their molt is not well known). There may be a partial body molt in spring. Although the effects of wear may be obvious on the tail feathers and edgings of the tertials by late spring, the back pattern is always fairly clear; Botteri's seem never to become as terribly worn and faded as some Cassin's Sparrows.

Postjuvenal molt in the two species differs in some ways; but by early fall, when the young birds have mostly finished molting the body feathers, they look similar to fresh-plumaged adults.

Migrations: The seasonal movements of Cassin's Sparrow are erratic and sometimes extensive. One side effect is that this species is capable of long-distance vagrancy; strays have turned up as far outside the "normal" range as Ontario and even Nova Scotia.

Botteri's Sparrow is apparently only a short-distance migrant (although its winter range is poorly known), is much more predictable in the timing of its migrations, and seems much less likely to show up far out of range. It would not be too surprising to find a few Botteri's wintering in Arizona or Texas; the lack of reliable records so far may be due partly to past difficulties in identification.

Geographic variation: No geographic variation has been fully established in Cassin's Sparrow, but the more sedentary Botteri's has developed a number of well-marked races in Mexico and Central America. The Arizona and Texas populations (races *A. b. arizonae* and *A. b. texana*, respectively) are noticeably different in overall color: *arizonae* tends toward warmer reddish brown above and buff on the breast, while *texana* is much grayer. Thus *texana* is closer to the general coloration of Cassin's Sparrow, and the two species may be more difficult to distinguish in Texas than in Arizona.

CASSIN'S SPARROW

BOTTERI'S SPARROW

Fig. 98. Sample feather patterns from the upper back, lower back, and scapulars. *Upper row:* Cassin's Sparrow. *Lower row:* Botteri's Sparrow. Although this degree of detail is rarely visible in the field, the overall patterns created are quite different.

Field Marks — Adults

Back pattern: In fresh plumage, the two species have very different back patterns because of the patterns of the individual feathers (Fig. 98). In Cassin's, most of the back feathers have broad gray edges and warm brown centers and are crossed by a *black crescent* or irregular black bar; the resulting variegated pattern is largely pale gray, partly warm brown, with conspicuous short black crossbars or spots. In Botteri's, each back feather is mostly reddish brown (Arizona) or grayish brown (Texas), with a broad, longitudinal *black stripe down the center* and a grayish edging that is very narrow if present at all; the resulting pattern is more evenly brown with conspicuous black streaks.

As the plumage becomes worn, the gray edgings on Cassin's become less obvious. Some very worn Cassin's in midsummer are entirely dingy pale gray-brown above with indistinct darker spots. The less complicated back pattern of Botteri's changes less with wear, and the black-streaked effect should always be apparent.

Uppertail coverts: The long uppertail coverts can be seen clearly in the field (beyond the tips of the short wings) on fresh-plumaged birds. On Cassin's, each feather has a gray edge, a brown center, and a *black subterminal crescent.* On

Botteri's, each feather is brown with a *black central streak.* These patterns are obvious at least through the spring, but they may be obscure on worn summer birds.

Tail pattern: Cassin's Sparrows have large pale gray or whitish tips to the outermost pair of tail feathers, with smaller pale areas at the tips of the next two pairs inward. These are sometimes noticeable on a bird flushing or flying away. However, they are not always apparent even on fresh-plumaged birds, and by late summer the pale tips may be partly or completely worn away. So, while the presence of pale corners on the tail is a good indication of Cassin's, lack of them does not necessarily indicate a Botteri's.

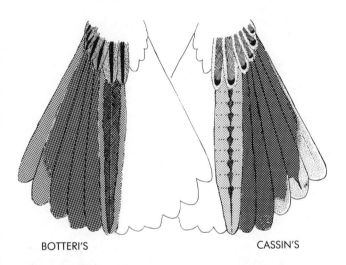

BOTTERI'S   CASSIN'S

Fig. 99. Tail patterns of sparrows in fresh plumage. On **Botteri's** the tail is mostly dark dusky brown, with the outer feathers only slightly paler; the central tail feathers are dusky brown with slightly paler brown edges; the uppertail coverts are brown with black central stripes. On **Cassin's** the outer tail feathers are dusky brown with pale gray tips; the central tail feathers are pale gray with a serrated dark central stripe and a hint of crossbars; the uppertail coverts are brown with pale gray edges and black subterminal crescents. Note that on very worn birds in mid- to late summer (especially Cassin's), all of these points may be obscure.

In both species, most of the upperside of the tail is dark dusky brown. But in Cassin's Sparrow the central pair of tail feathers is pale gray, with a serrated dark central stripe on each that spreads out into a suggestion of faint crossbars. In Botteri's Sparrow the central tail feathers are mostly dusky brown, somewhat paler brown along the edges. Sometimes there are "indentations" of gray along the edges, possibly creating the impression of dark crossbars in between them, but the effect is far less noticeable than in Cassin's (Fig. 99).

Flank pattern: Cassin's Sparrow has a few well-defined *dark brown streaks* on the whitish lower flanks. The streaks are usually visible in the field, but depending on the arrangement of the flank feathers, they are occasionally hidden by the wings. On Botteri's Sparrow the flanks are buffy brown, and although there may be a few narrow dark brown streaks in this area they are almost never visible in the field.

Breast color: Botteri's Sparrow has a fairly smooth, continuous wash of warm buff (Arizona) or grayish buff (Texas) from the sides of the neck across the breast and down the sides and flanks, paling to whitish on the throat and belly. Cassin's is duller and less evenly colored on the breast: pale brownish gray, mottled with brown toward the sides of the neck, fading to whitish at the center of the breast. Seen perched at a distance, when this kind of detail is not discernible, Cassin's looks noticeably paler-breasted than Botteri's.

Wing pattern: In Cassin's Sparrow the greater coverts are broadly tipped (and narrowly edged) with grayish white, forming a fairly conspicuous wing bar; a second wing bar (on the median coverts) is sometimes apparent. (On birds in very worn plumage, the wing bars may be obscure.) In Botteri's Sparrow the coverts are all broadly edged with dull buffy brown, so no wing-bar pattern is evident.

When the birds are in fresh plumage the blackish-centered tertials are broadly edged with whitish in Cassin's Sparrow, with brown in Botteri's Sparrow. This difference can be surprisingly noticeable in the field. The tertials are strongly affected by wear, however, and by summer their pale edgings may be entirely worn away (especially those of Cassin's).

Size and shape: Botteri's Sparrow is slightly larger and bulkier overall than Cassin's, and has a proportionately larger bill. Although Botteri's is the heavier bird, its wings are about

CASSIN'S (worn)

CASSIN'S (fresh)

BOTTERI'S

Fig. 100. Cassin's and Botteri's sparrows. The two Cassin's shown are one in very worn plumage (late summer) and one in fresh plumage (early winter). Most spring and summer birds are between these extremes. Of the **Cassin's Sparrow** field marks noted below, most are less obvious on worn birds. The back feathers and uppertail coverts are brown, with black subterminal crescents and gray edges; the breast is mottled at the sides, whitish toward the center; the flanks have a few streaks; the wings show one wing bar and pale edgings on the tertials; the central tail feathers are pale gray with faint crossbars. The **Botteri's Sparrow** shown is in fresh plumage (winter). Its back feathers and uppertail coverts are brown, with lengthwise black stripes; the breast has a relatively smooth wash of color; the wings are more uniform, with brown edgings; the central tail feathers are brown with paler edges. Botteri's is a slightly heavier bird, with a larger bill.

the same length as those of Cassin's, and its tail may be slightly shorter on average. This heavier wing loading usually gives Botteri's a more "labored" look in flight (but molting or very worn Cassin's may fly the same way).

Voice: The two species are easily identified by their typical songs.

CASSIN'S SPARROW: A soft double or single note, a long musical trill on one pitch, and (usually) two well-spaced musical notes, all with a slight minor-key quality (Fig. 101):

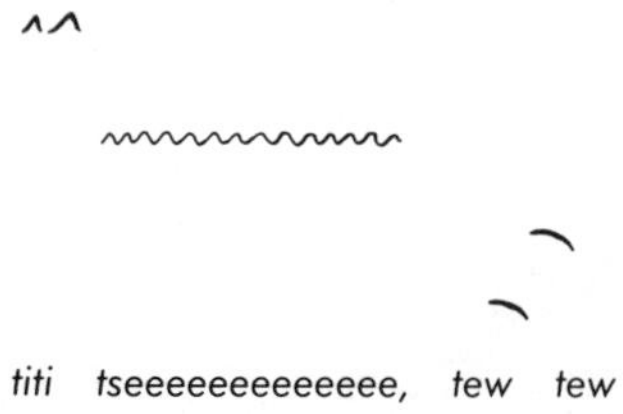

titi   tseeeeeeeeeeeee,   tew   tew

Fig. 101.

BOTTERI'S SPARROW: A long, well-spaced series of dry double and single notes, usually speeding up into a dry trill, all on about the same pitch (Fig. 102):

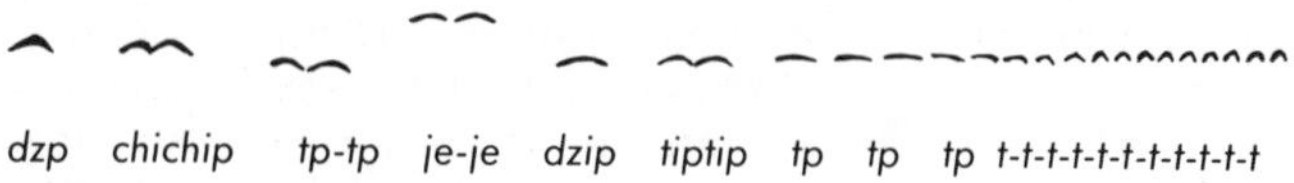

dzp   chichip   tp-tp   je-je   dzip   tiptip   tp   tp   tp t-t-t-t-t-t-t-t-t-t-t

Fig. 102.

Both species give some song variations. Cassin's has a potentially confusing alternate song: a series of chips ending in a warbling sound or rough trill, which could be interpreted as matching some voice descriptions of Botteri's. This song is heard most often during the latter part of the breeding season.

Cassin's Sparrow has a frequent "skylarking" display in which it gives the typical song while flying up from one perch and fluttering down to another. Botteri's apparently never gives this exaggerated display, but it may sing while flying from one perch to another, or it may begin its song in flight and complete it after landing.

Both species have chip notes of alarm while nesting but are relatively silent at other seasons. However, Cassin's Sparrow (which defends winter territories) may give a chittering note in territorial encounters; and unusual conditions may induce it to sing at unusual times of year.

Field Marks — Juveniles

Juveniles of both species have streaking on the upper breast; the streaks are usually darker, broader, and more extensive in Botteri's than in Cassin's. The edgings of the back feathers of juveniles tend to be buffier (Botteri's) or browner (Cassin's) than those of adults, but the patterns of the centers of these feathers are usually discernible: they are longitudinally striped in Botteri's, barred or scaled crosswise in Cassin's.

Although the young birds may not molt the flight feathers until late fall, the postjuvenal molt of the body plumage begins shortly after the birds leave the nest. When the body molt is complete, by late summer or early fall, young birds look like adults aside from a few dark spots on the chest. Juvenal-plumaged Cassin's and Botteri's sparrows are most unlikely to be seen away from the breeding grounds.

Comparison to Other Species

In plumage, Cassin's Sparrow is superficially similar to Brewer's Sparrow (*Spizella breweri*): both are mostly grayish brown, pale and plain. However, Brewer's is a smaller bird with a proportionately smaller bill and a slender tail that is notched at the tip, not rounded as in Cassin's. On close inspection there are also many plumage differences; for example, Brewer's has noticeable, regularly spaced black streaks on the back, unlike Cassin's.

Although their ranges do not overlap, Botteri's Sparrow is very similar — in size, shape, and plumage — to Bachman's Sparrow (*Aimophila aestivalis*) of the southeastern United States. Especially close is the resemblance between the western race of Bachman's (found from southern Illinois to eastern Texas) and the Arizona race of Botteri's, since both are relatively reddish brown above and buffy on the underparts.

There are few concrete differences in appearance between the species. Botteri's usually has well-defined black streaks on the crown, while Bachman's has a plainer reddish brown crown with no more than a small amount of blackish mottling. Bachman's usually has a brighter shade of buff on the breast, contrasting more with the white belly. These points are so subtle, however, that if either species were found far out of range it would have to be photographed, at least, to document the record.

34

THE SPIZELLA SPARROWS

CHIPPING SPARROW *Spizella passerina*
CLAY-COLORED SPARROW *Spizella pallida*
BREWER'S SPARROW *Spizella breweri*

The problem: These three *Spizella* sparrow species present little difficulty in spring, when they can be named at a glance by the color patterns of their crowns: mostly solid rufous in Chipping Sparrow; heavily streaked with black, with a pale median crown stripe, in Clay-colored Sparrow; sandy brown, finely and evenly streaked with black, in Brewer's Sparrow. Their face patterns are also helpful in spring, when Chipping has a bold black eyestripe, Clay-colored has brown ear coverts sharply set off by a blackish brown outline, and Brewer's has a pattern like Clay-colored but less contrasty and less colorful.

Autumn birds, however, can be much more difficult. Most immatures and many autumn adults converge on a generalized head pattern: their ear coverts have brown patches with moderately distinct dark outlines, and their crowns are finely streaked, with ill-defined pale median stripes.

Preliminary Points

Geographic variation: In Brewer's and Clay-colored sparrows there is not enough geographic variation to be apparent in the field (despite the fact that an isolated race of Brewer's, *S. b. taverneri*, breeds only above timberline in the Canadian Rockies). But in Chipping Sparrow, birds from western populations average slightly larger, longer-tailed, and paler than those found farther east. If a western Chipping strayed to the Atlantic seaboard and was seen in the company of local birds it might appear noticeably different, tempting birders to call it one of the other two species.

Juvenal plumage: Brewer's and Clay-colored sparrows wear juvenal plumage only briefly, molting into their first basic plumage before they leave the breeding grounds; but in Chipping Sparrow the first prebasic molt is often later, and some birds are seen in partial juvenal plumage as late as October, when they may be some distance away from the breeding range. The juvenile Chipping is very different in appearance from the spring adult — its crown is streaked black on dull brown, its rump is brown instead of gray at first, and its breast is heavily marked with fine streaks — and birders may be mystified by it on first encounter. However, its shape and behavior should clearly mark it as a *Spizella* rather than any of the other small streak-breasted sparrows.

Tail length: Although this difference in proportions is only occasionally helpful in identification, these three species differ in average tail length — Brewer's has the longest tail, Chipping has the shortest, and Clay-colored is intermediate.

Field Marks — Chipping Sparrows vs. Others

Because Chipping Sparrow is the most distinctive of these three species, it is useful to isolate it first, before considering how to separate the other two.

Rump color: In Brewer's and Clay-colored sparrows, the rump is always dull brown (with fine dark streaks in juvenal plumage). In all Chipping Sparrows past the first prebasic molt, the rump is *gray*. Juvenile Chippings have finely streaked brown rumps, but this area of the plumage begins to change rather early in the first prebasic molt and most individuals probably have completely gray rumps by the time they lose the streaking on the breast.

Rump color is usually difficult to see on *Spizellas* when they are feeding on the ground, but when perched upright they often hold the wings slightly drooped so that their rump color is easily discerned. On Chipping Sparrows, the contrast between the brown back and gray rump may be conspicuous even in flight.

Lores: Most Chipping Sparrows have a distinct dark line from the eye to the bill — i.e., through the lores — and virtually all Chippings (past the juvenile stage) have at least a vague dark line there. In Clay-colored and Brewer's sparrows the lores are usually pale, hardly contrasting with the tone of the supercilium, all the way down to where the moustachial stripe begins. In most cases this character will let you rapidly separate Chipping from the other two species; but some individuals have an intermediate appearance, so if you cannot decide that the lores are distinctly pale or dark you should ignore this point.

Crown pattern: In Chipping Sparrow the crown is nearly solid rufous on spring and summer adults, but on fall and winter birds it is quite variable. Most immatures lack any rufous on the crown until late fall; their crowns are medium brown with fine black streaks and usually a poorly defined pale median crown stripe. This pattern is also seen on some fall and winter adults, but most have at least a small amount of visible rufous, and on some the crown is almost solid rufous even in fall. There may be a tendency for eastern Chipping Sparrows to show more rufous on the crown in fall, on average, than those in the West.

Brewer's Sparrows and many Clay-colored Sparrows in fall have much the same crown pattern as the immature Chip-

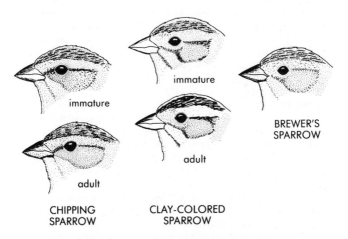

Fig. 103. Face patterns of *Spizella* sparrows. These are all typical individuals as they would appear in mid-autumn. The differences between adult and immature Brewer's Sparrows are not apparent at that season.

ping Sparrow. Some Clay-coloreds continue to have heavier black streaks toward the sides of the crown, and a more clearly defined pale median crown stripe, than any Chipping.

Outline of ear coverts: A contrasting brown patch on the ear coverts is a feature of Brewer's and Clay-colored sparrows all year, and of immature and many adult Chipping Sparrows in fall and winter. In the first two species, most of the edge of this patch is traced by a dark outline. This outline is darker on some individuals than on others, but the *moustachial stripe* (which forms the forward part of the lower border of the patch) is always as distinct as the *eyestripe* (which forms the upper border). In Chipping Sparrow, the very distinct eyestripe is always darker and more obvious than any part of the lower border of the ear coverts.

Field Marks — Brewer's Sparrow vs. Clay-colored Sparrow

The pale median crown stripe of Clay-colored Sparrow — often quoted as *the* field mark separating these two — is not diagnostic by itself, because many Brewer's have at least a suggestion of such a stripe. Clay-colored Sparrow tends to be more strongly patterned and more colorful than Brewer's Sparrow, but this generalization is not always enough for identification: there are some "borderline" birds. You need to make a point-by-point analysis to name these sparrows correctly.

Crown pattern: There is little variation in the crown pattern of Brewer's Sparrow. At all ages its crown is sandy brown with fine black streaks; often there are fewer streaks down the center (especially toward the forehead), and sometimes the ground color is paler there also, creating a vague pale median crown stripe that is more noticeable from the front than from the sides.

On adult Clay-colored Sparrows in spring and summer the sides of the crown are rich brown, and this color is heavily overlaid by wide black streaks; from a distance the total effect is of very dark, broad lateral crown stripes, contrasting sharply with the pale supercilium and median crown stripe. Fall and winter adults may have slightly thinner black streaks on the brown lateral areas of the crown, but they still have stronger crown patterns than any Brewer's.

On immature Clay-coloreds in their first fall and winter, the black streaks on the crown may be still thinner, and the pale median crown stripe may be less clearly defined. Although the color toward the sides of the crown on these birds is still a richer brown than on Brewer's Sparrow, some Clay-coloreds may look identical in crown pattern to some Brewer's under field conditions.

Supercilium: In Clay-colored Sparrow, the color of the pale stripe over the eye is variable. On adults it ranges from white (mostly males) through grayish white to brownish white (mostly females); on immatures, it is usually a warm, rich buff. The supercilium of Brewer's Sparrow is always some shade of pale brownish gray. It appears less "clean" — more invaded by fine streaking or mottling — than the supercilium of Clay-colored, and usually contrasts less with the crown and ear coverts.

Malar region: In Clay-colored Sparrow the thin, dark malar stripe is usually noticeable, and it helps to set off the pale submoustachial stripe just above it; this pale stripe often seems to be a slightly different color (more clearly whitish or buffy) than the throat. In Brewer's Sparrow the dark malar stripe tends to be less distinct, so that the dull pale stripe above it is rarely made more conspicuous.

Gray side of neck: All three species in this group have a gray "collar" on the sides of the neck, extending up onto the nape. This gray area is most noticeable on Clay-colored Sparrow because it contrasts strongly with the colors of the face, especially on immatures. It is *least* noticeable on Brewer's Sparrow, hardly contrasting at all.

Breast color: Immature Clay-colored Sparrows usually have a warm buffy wash across the upper breast, strongest toward the sides, while adults are usually grayish white in this area. Brewer's Sparrows are dingy grayish below, often washed with brown on the flanks and at the sides of the upper breast, but rarely with any warm buff.

Outline of ear coverts: Although many Brewer's Sparrows have the brown ear coverts just as distinctly outlined as the typical Clay-colored, a bird with a very *indistinct* outline to this patch is almost certain to be a Brewer's, not a Clay-colored.

Quick Summary

Among birds of this group that are past the juvenile stage, i.e., without any breast streaking, Chipping Sparrow is the most distinctive. Any individual with obvious rufous on the crown is a Chipping; so is any bird of this group with a gray rump, a distinct dark line through the lores, and an eyestripe that is much darker and more obvious than any part of the lower border of the ear coverts.

In separating Brewer's and Clay-colored sparrows, the first point to check is the crown pattern. A bird with a rich brown crown very heavily streaked with black and divided by an obvious pale median crown stripe is a Clay-colored, probably an adult. If the crown is medium brown with finer black streaks and only an indistinct pale median stripe, the bird could be either a Brewer's or an immature Clay-colored, and you must check a number of characters, as outlined below.

Clay-colored (immature)	Brewer's
Supercilium unmarked warm buff	Supercilium pale gray-brown with mottled effect
Narrow dark malar stripe sets off conspicuous white or buffy white submoustachial stripe	Malar stripe often less distinct, and submoustachial stripe dull, less conspicuous
Gray side of neck contrasts sharply with colorful face	Almost no contrast between gray side of neck and dull face
Outline of brown ear coverts distinct	Outline of ear coverts sometimes indistinct
Breast washed with buff	Breast dull grayish

35

THE CARPODACUS FINCHES

PURPLE FINCH *Carpodacus purpureus*
CASSIN'S FINCH *Carpodacus cassinii*
HOUSE FINCH *Carpodacus mexicanus*

The problem: Cassin's Finch, of the mountainous West, is very similar in all plumages to the more widespread Purple Finch. The field marks usually suggested for separating them (brightness of cap in males, sharpness of breast streaking in females) are only relative; they can be difficult to judge for birders who have not had a lot of experience with one or both species. The related House Finch is more distinctive but may sometimes be a source of confusion, particularly as the introduced population in the East expands into new areas.

Preliminary Points

Color variation: The precise shade of red or reddish on various parts of the plumage can be helpful in identifying adult males. But although the great majority of birds will have the colors described here, some odd color variants turn up. Especially in House Finch, the red may be replaced partially or entirely by orange, or even by yellow. Some Purple Finches (mainly young males?) may be a much paler and pinker shade than normal. And at least in the eastern populations of Purple Finch, older females often develop some pink on the breast; they may be bright enough to be mistaken for young males. In the discussions of field marks below, these color variations are mostly ignored. In the unlikely event that you see an aberrantly colored finch all by itself, not associating with a flock, you will have to identify it by other characteristics.

Subspecies: Geographic variation in these three finches in North America is not very great and is mostly overshadowed by individual variation. Some of the supposed subspecies are probably not valid. The only racial variation that could have an effect on field identification is in Purple Finch: birds of far western Canada and the Pacific states tend to have slightly less contrast in their overall pattern than those found farther east, and they differ in other minor ways to be noted below.

General Field Marks — Carpodacus Finches (All Ages)

Bill shape: The bill of the House Finch appears short and stubby, relatively smaller than those of the other two species. Cassin's often has a proportionately *longer bill* than Purple Finch, with the *culmen* (ridge of the upper mandible) *relatively straight* except near the tip (the culmen tends to be more evenly curved in Purple Finch). Notice, however, that Purple Finches of the far western races have slightly longer bills than do those farther east (although they don't approach the long-billed extremes of Cassin's) (Fig. 104). Also, there is individual variation in both species, and occasional Cassin's have bills not very different in shape from those of typical Purple Finches. Therefore, while bill shape is often a helpful clue in identifying these two species, it is probably never diagnostic except for classic long-billed Cassin's Finches.

Flight calls: The call is one of the easiest and best field marks for Purple and Cassin's finches. Cassin's Finch gives a musical, two- or three-syllabled *chidiup* or *chidilip*. Purple Finch gives a light, dry, slightly metallic *pick*. However, the Purple also has a rich clear note, *cheeyew* or *chewee*, usually given from a perch but also occasionally used in flight; this may be confused with the typical flight note of Cassin's by observers unfamiliar with either call.

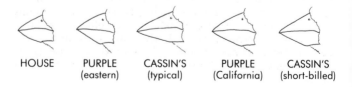

HOUSE   PURPLE   CASSIN'S   PURPLE   CASSIN'S
        (eastern)   (typical)   (California) (short-billed)

Fig. 104. Bill shapes of *Carpodacus* finches.

The House Finch has a variety of harsher chirping notes, many of which suggest softer renditions of House Sparrow calls.

Size and body shape: Purple and Cassin's finches are both chunky birds, with rather large heads and heavy bills; Cassin's is slightly larger overall than Purple. House Finch is slimmer and smaller, with a proportionately smaller head.

Tail shape: Tails of Purple and Cassin's finches look short and are deeply notched at the tip. That of House Finch looks longer in proportion to its body size and is not so deeply notched.

Wing length: Purple and Cassin's finches look relatively long-winged (which helps to emphasize their short-tailed appearance); House Finch does not. Of the two larger species, Cassin's has longer wings: the measured length of the folded wing averages about 11 percent greater, but the difference in *relative* length would be a little less, considering the slightly larger body size of Cassin's. You can sometimes see this difference in proportions in the field, but only after some experience with both species.

Field Marks — Females and Immatures

All of the field marks discussed below for female and immature finches (Fig. 105) are subject to some variation, so there is no single point that could be considered diagnostic by itself. Always use these field marks in combination, along with bill shape and voice.

Breast pattern: With practice, the ground color of the breast and the pattern of streaking on it can provide good quick clues to identification, although the differences are of the general-impression sort, easier to see than to describe adequately. In female or immature Purple Finch the breast is dull white or pearly grayish white, without any brown tinge. Its streaks are heavy, broad but short, creating a blotchy or almost spotted effect on the upper breast; the streaks are fairly sharply defined but a little blurry at the edges (and tend to be a little less sharply defined in the West than in the East). In Cassin's Finch the breast is paler (i.e., a cleaner white, but sometimes with a faint yellowish tinge toward the sides of the chest); the streaks are narrower and more sharply defined. Note that birds of either species can have an intermediate appearance, so this is a good field mark only for the two extremes.

In female House Finch the breast is a dusty brownish white; the streaks are long, broad, blurry, and not as contrastingly dark as in the other two species.

Face pattern: Female Purple Finch has a strong pattern on the face, House Finch has practically none at all, and Cassin's is somewhere in between. A heavy dark malar stripe, typical of Purple Finch, is rarely evident on Cassin's. Purple Finch has a heavy dark patch on the ear coverts, sharply set off by whitish lines above and below. Cassin's has a similar patch but it is *usually* far less conspicuous, since it is paler and not so sharply defined at the edges. Many Cassin's Finches are so indistinctly marked that they approach the blank-faced expression of House Finch. However, Cassin's often shows a complete pale *eye-ring*, usually lacking on the other two species.

HOUSE FINCH

PURPLE FINCH

CASSIN'S FINCH

Fig. 105. Adult females of the three North American species of *Carpodacus* finches, to compare overall proportions, face patterns, and pattern of the underparts.

Undertail coverts: In the female House Finch, the undertail coverts have broad dark streaks. Cassin's Finch also has streaks, narrower than in House Finch but very dark and sharply defined against a clean white background, and generally obvious with a good view from below. Occasionally these streaks are very narrow, and although they are still sharply defined they may be apparent only at close range.

Purple Finch *usually* has no streaks on the undertail coverts, but (contrary to some published statements) this is not always true. In at least some parts of its range, the majority of juveniles and a significant minority of first-winter immatures have narrow dark streaks on some of the undertail coverts; this character even turns up regularly in a small percentage of adult females.

Pattern of upperparts: The general tone of the upperparts is slightly grayer in Cassin's Finch females and immatures, slightly browner in Purple Finch (tending toward olive-brown in its western populations). The ground color of the upperparts (behind the streaks) is *paler* in Cassin's — this in itself is not easy to discern, but it makes the dark streaks stand out much more contrastingly on Cassin's than on Purple Finch, especially on the nape and upper back. The House Finch is a medium dusty brown above (paler than Purple Finch), with broad streaks that are not very conspicuous.

A Note on Juveniles

Although first-winter immature *Carpodacus* finches look very much like adult females, juveniles may show more noticeable differences. These finches remain in full juvenal plumage only briefly — a couple of months or so — and these young birds are likely to be seen with adults, so only rarely will they cause any identification problems.

Juveniles resemble adult females but have slightly looser and fluffier plumage, and their bills may be smaller at first. In Purple and House finches, the breast streaks of juveniles are more sharply defined than those of adults (this difference is not apparent in Cassin's Finch, in which the adult females are also sharply streaked). Confusion is most likely with recently fledged juvenile Purple Finches: they can differ from adult females in being smaller, smaller-billed, more sharply and continuously streaked on the underparts, and less strongly patterned on the face; superficially, they can look quite similar to juvenile House Finches. Juvenile Purples, however, have more deeply notched tails than House Finches, and darker tips to the median and greater coverts (rufous-chestnut rather than pale buff).

Field Marks — Adult Males

Head pattern: In both Purple and Cassin's finch males the entire head is colored (or at least tinged) with some shade of reddish. Purple Finch has a rather evenly colored head, dull purplish rose, varying only with the underlying brown pattern of darker ear coverts, nape, and crown. By comparison, the male Cassin's has a paler throat and a paler and browner nape, but a more richly colored crown. The shade of red on the crown may vary (with wear) from dark to bright, but it always *contrasts* sharply with the nape, face, and throat; Purple Finch never duplicates (and rarely even approaches) this pattern. (Inexperienced birders seeing male Cassin's Finches for the first time have even called them redpolls because of this pattern, although redpolls are much smaller and have black chins.) In addition, the male Cassin's Finch often raises its crown feathers slightly, producing a spiky, crested appearance.

House Finch has a very different pattern, its bright red throat, supercilium, and forehead contrasting with the duller and browner crown, nape, and ear coverts.

Breast pattern: Male House Finches have conspicuous streaks on the lower breast and flanks, male Purple and Cassin's finches do not. Actually, on close inspection many male Cassin's will be seen to have a few narrow dark streaks on the flanks, and male Purples can also have some vague streaking in this area; but they never duplicate the pattern of House Finch, in which bold dark streaks start immediately below the sharp cutoff of red at midbreast. Be aware, however, that when House Finches are in very worn plumage, the streaks on the underparts can become indistinct.

Comparing Purple and Cassin's, the breast color of the male Purple Finch is a darker, more purplish red (as opposed to paler rosy red) and tends to extend farther down the breast than in Cassin's Finch.

Back color and pattern: In male Purple Finch the ground color of the back is usually reddish, varying from deep maroon to pale rosy (the latter being achieved on birds in very worn plumage); the broad streaking on the back is usually not very conspicuous (becoming a little more apparent on very worn birds). In male Cassin's Finch the ground color of the back tends toward medium brown or pale brown, and the streaks on the upper back tend to be narrower, darker, and more sharply defined than those of Purple Finch, so they stand out much more conspicuously. In male House Finch the back is dull brownish (sometimes washed with reddish) with broad blurry streaks that rarely show much contrast.

Comparison to Other Species

Juvenile crossbills (especially Red Crossbill, *Loxia curvirostra*, but also White-winged Crossbill, *Loxia leucoptera*) can look surprisingly similar to female-plumaged Purple and Cassin's finches; they are brown-backed, streaked below, and approximately the same overall shape. Birders who are aware of this superficial similarity are unlikely to be misled, however.

Bibliography

Index

BIBLIOGRAPHY

The birder who develops a particular interest in one of the challenging groups presented in this field guide — through discovery of some really perplexing individual bird, or through simple curiosity — may want information even more detailed than what is offered in this book. The following section is a guide to further references.

Major Book References

Some bird books contain so much detailed information that they are always worth consulting, even if field identification is not their primary subject. The following are a few such books that I consider especially helpful.

Handbook of North American Birds. Edited by Ralph S. Palmer. Yale University Press. Volume 1 (1962): Loons to Flamingos. Volumes 2 and 3 (1976): Waterfowl. Volumes 4 and 5 (1988): Raptors. Detailed account of many aspects of bird biology. Its treatment of molts and plumages can be useful.

Handbook of the Birds of Europe, the Middle East, and North Africa: The Birds of the Western Palearctic. Edited by Stanley Cramp and K. E. L. Simmons. Oxford University Press. For North American species that also occur in Europe, this multivolume work is an excellent reference.

Identification Guide to North American Passerines. By Peter Pyle, Steve N. G. Howell, Robert P. Yunick, and David F. DeSante. 1987. Slate Creek Press, Bolinas, California. Written for banders and focusing on details for identifying, aging, and sexing birds in the hand, this book contains many points that can be gleaned for use in the field.

Magazines and Journals

Hardly a week goes by without the publication of some piece of information that will be useful in recognizing difficult species. Articles on field identification often appear in the birding magazines. Notes on taxonomy, distribution, hybridization, and numerous other more technical topics that might affect field birding are frequently published in the ornithological journals. The list below features those periodicals that regularly carry articles relating directly to field identification.

American Birds, published by the National Audubon Society. Four seasonal issues plus the annual Christmas Bird Count results. Notes on identification in almost every issue.

Birding, published by the American Birding Association. Bimonthly. Notes on identification in almost every issue.

Western Birds, published by Western Field Ornithologists. A quarterly (originally published as *California Birds*) that has carried a number of outstanding identification articles.

British Birds, published by British Birds Ltd. Despite its geographic scope, this first-class monthly is read by many North American birders. Every issue has something on identification, often relevant on this side of the Atlantic as well.

Journal of Field Ornithology, published by the Association of Field Ornithologists. Until 1980 this journal was published under the title *Bird-Banding*, and it still includes results of many banding studies, which can sometimes be applicable to field identification.

Understanding Literature Citations

Birders without academic backgrounds sometimes ignore the lists of "literature cited" at the end of scholarly articles because these listings look complicated. But they are not difficult to interpret.

Here is an example of a typical periodical literature citation:

Binford, Laurence C. 1978. Lesser Black-backed Gull in California, with notes on field identification. *Western Birds* 9: 141–150.

Here the first thing listed is the name of the author, and the second is the year that the article was actually published. If I were writing a piece on gulls, and I wanted to let you know that my source for some fact had been this particular article, I would mention it this way: "The first Lesser Black-backed Gull found in California was an adult (Binford 1978) . . ." and then give the full citation in a listing at the end of my article. After the author and year, the next thing in the citation is the title of the article. Following that, usually in *italic* type, is the name of the journal or magazine in which it was published: *Western Birds.* The numbers after the journal name indicate the volume and page numbers of the article. Volume 9 of *Western Birds* includes all four issues published in 1978; this article occupied pages 141 to 150. Most specialized journals number all the pages for a given volume (year) consecutively — thus, the first issue of the *Auk* this year might end with page 141, so the second issue this year would begin with page 142. On the other hand, many popular magazines start over with page 1 at the beginning of each issue, so the same page numbers will crop up multiple times in each volume. In these cases, to indicate which issue contained a particular article, it is necessary to give the number of the issue in parentheses: an article in the March issue of a popular magazine might be cited as "*Birdtime* 10 (3): 26–31."

Further References on Identification of Specific Groups

This is not an attempt at a complete bibliography. I have included only those papers that, in my opinion, will provide genuinely useful information for the person who is researching one of these identification problems. I have not included older papers if the information contained has been superseded or completely updated by a more recent publication. In general I have also excluded articles that simply review well-known field marks, unless they provide exceptionally good illustrations or some other special advantage.

Many of the technical journals cited here may not seem to be easily accessible to birders. However, for anyone who might be discouraged, I offer these suggestions: (1) The person who lives near a major university will find that a serious amateur can almost always make arrangements to use the university library facilities. (2) Although few public libraries (except the largest ones) subscribe to scientific journals, many of them can provide a service called "interlibrary loan." One facet of this service will allow you to get photo-copies of papers published in practically any journal — for a fee, and with some delay — as long as you have the detailed citation of the paper you want.

Much of the information published in the major ornithol-ogical journals (like *Auk, Condor,* or *Wilson Bulletin*) is be-yond the interest of field birders. But if you have a chance to sift through these journals, you may run across tidbits about avian biology that will expand the horizons of your interest in birds.

Loons

Appleby, R. H., S. C. Madge, and Killian Mullarney. 1986. Identification of divers in immature and winter plum-ages. *British Birds* 79: 365–391.

Binford, Laurence C., and J. V. Remsen, Jr. 1974. Identifica-tion of the Yellow-billed Loon (*Gavia adamsii*). *Western Birds* 5: 111–126.

Walsh, Terry. 1988. Identifying Pacific Loons: some old and new problems. *Birding* 20(1): 12–28.

Western and Clark's Grebes

Neuchterlein, Gary L. 1981. Courtship behavior and repro-ductive isolation between Western Grebe color morphs. *Auk* 98: 335–349. Good discussion of vocal differences.

Ratti, John T. 1979. Reproductive separation and isolating mechanisms between sympatric dark- and light-phase Western Grebes. *Auk* 96: 573–586.

Storer, Robert W. 1965. The color phases of the Western Grebe. *Living Bird* 4: 59–63.

Storer, Robert W., and Gary L. Neuchterlein. 1985. An anal-ysis of plumage and morphological characters of the two color forms of the Western Grebe (*Aechmophorus*). *Auk* 102: 102–119. The best information on seasonal varia-tion.

Medium-sized Herons

Cardillo, Robert, Alec Forbes-Watson, and Robert Ridgely. 1983. The Western Reef-Heron (*Egretta gularis*) at Nan-tucket Island, Massachusetts. *American Birds* 37: 827–829.

Dickerman, Robert W., and Kenneth C. Parkes. 1968. Notes on the plumages and generic status of the Little Blue Heron. *Auk* 85: 437–440.

Wassink, A. 1978. Some additional field characters of the

Western Reef Heron *Egretta gularis*. *Ardea* 66: 123–124.

Wilds, Claudia. 1984. ID Points: Snowy Egret/Little Blue Heron/Reddish Egret (white phase). *Birding* 16: 15.

Dark Ibises

Pratt, H. Douglas. 1976. Field identification of White-faced and Glossy ibises. *Birding* 8: 1–5.

Scaup

Anderson, Bertin W., and Richard L. Timken. 1969. A hybrid Lesser Scaup × Ring-necked Duck. *Auk* 86: 556–557.

Trauger, David L. 1974. Eye color of female Lesser Scaup in relation to age. *Auk* 91: 243–254.

Other Ducks

Haramis, G. M. 1982. Records of Redhead × Canvasback hybrids. *Wilson Bulletin* 94: 599–602.

Lehman, Paul. 1986. ID Point: Female Surf vs. White-winged Scoters. *Birding* 18: 76–77.

Madge, Steve, and Hilary Burn. 1988. *Waterfowl: An Identification Guide to the Ducks, Geese, and Swans of the World*. Boston: Houghton Mifflin.

Stallcup, Rich. 1983. Focus: Female Ducks. *Pt. Reyes Bird Observatory Newsletter* No. 63, Autumn 1983, pp. 6–7.

Accipiters

Clark, William S. 1984. Field identification of accipiters in North America. *Birding* 16: 251–263.

Clark, William S., and Brian K. Wheeler. 1987. *A Field Guide to Hawks of North America*. Boston: Houghton Mifflin.

Dunne, Pete, David Sibley, and Clay Sutton. 1988. *Hawks in Flight*. Boston: Houghton Mifflin.

Kaufman, Kenn. 1986. ID counterpoint: more on accipiters. *Birding* 18: 208–209.

Mueller, Helmut C., Daniel D. Berger, and George Allez. 1976. Age and sex variations in the size of Goshawks. *Bird-Banding* 47: 310–318.

Mueller, Helmut C., Daniel D. Berger, and George Allez. 1979. Age and sex differences in size of Sharp-shinned Hawks. *Bird-Banding* 50: 34–44.

Mueller, Helmut C., Daniel D. Berger, and George Allez. 1981. Age, sex, and seasonal differences in size of Cooper's Hawks. *Journal of Field Ornithology* 52: 112–126.

Shorebirds — General

Hayman, Peter, John Marchant, and Tony Prater. 1986. *Shorebirds: An Identification Guide to the Waders of the*

World. Boston: Houghton Mifflin. This book is an outstanding reference, thoroughly researched and very well illustrated. Indispensable.

Dowitchers
Conover, H. B. 1941. A study of the dowitchers. *Auk* 58: 376–380. Compares Long-billed Dowitcher and the *griseus* and *hendersoni* races of Short-billed Dowitcher.

Newlon, Michael C., and Thomas H. Kent. 1980. Speciation of dowitchers in Iowa. *Iowa Birdlife* 50: 59–68. Compares Long-billed with *hendersoni* race of Short-billed Dowitcher.

Pitelka, Frank A. 1950. Geographic variation and the species problem in the shorebird genus *Limnodromus. University of California Publications in Zoology* 50: 1–108. The most complete study of Short-billed and Long-billed dowitchers, based on skins in museums across the country.

Wilds, Claudia, and Mike Newlon. 1983. The identification of dowitchers. *Birding* 15: 151–165. Field identification and distribution of dowitchers in North America. Color photos of all forms in breeding plumage, and of juveniles.

Sharp-tailed and Pectoral Sandpipers
American Birds Volume 41, No. 5 (Winter 1987) has extensive material on Cox's Sandpiper, as well as a comparison of Sharp-tailed and Pectoral sandpipers.

Britton, David. 1980. Identification of Sharp-tailed Sandpipers. *British Birds* 73: 333–345.

Webb, Bruce E., and Jeanne A. Conry. 1979. A Sharp-tailed Sandpiper in Colorado, with notes on plumage and behavior. *Western Birds* 10: 86–91.

Semipalmated and Western Sandpipers
Grant, P. J. 1981. Identification of Semipalmated Sandpiper. *British Birds* 74: 505–509.

Grant, P. J. 1986. Four problem stints. *British Birds* 79: 609–621. Photos, discussion of some difficult individuals.

Page, G., and B. Fearis. 1971. Sexing Western Sandpipers by bill length. *Bird-Banding* 42: 297–298.

Phillips, Allan R. 1975. Semipalmated Sandpiper: identification, migrations, summer and winter ranges. *American Birds* 29: 799–806.

Veit, Richard R., and Lars Jonsson. 1984. Field identification of smaller sandpipers within the genus *Calidris. Ameri-*

can Birds 38: 853–876. Reprinted in *American Birds* 41: 212–236 (Summer 1987 issue). Thorough text, and brilliant paintings by Jonsson, make this the standard reference on "peeps" and stints. Note that the same paintings were published (accompanied by an equally good text by P. J. Grant) in *British Birds* 77: 293–315.

Jaegers

British Birds Volume 77, Number 9 (September 1984) has three excellent short notes discussing identification of juvenile jaegers (written by Lars Jonsson, Magnus Ullman, and Klaus Malling Olsen and Steen Christensen). Included are a painting by Jonsson and some photos.

Kaufman, Kenn. In press. Juvenile Pomarine Jaegers: exceptionally late fall migrants? *American Birds.*

Kaufman, Kenn. In press. Two notable Long-tailed Jaeger records, with comments on identification of the species inland. *American Birds.*

Southern, H. N. 1943. The two phases of *Stercorarius parasiticus. Ibis* 85: 443–485.

Southern, H. N. 1944. Dimorphism in *Stercorarius pomarinus. Ibis* 86: 1–16.

Veit, Richard R. 1985. Long-tailed Jaegers wintering along the Falkland Current. *American Birds* 39: 873–878.

Skuas

Balch, Lawrence G. 1981. Identifying skuas in the ABA area. *Birding* 13: 190–201.

Devillers, Pierre. 1977. The skuas of the North American Pacific coast. *Auk* 94: 417–429.

Devillers, Pierre. 1978. Distribution and relationships of South American skuas. *Le Gerfaut* 68: 374–417.

Parmelee, David F. 1988. The hybrid skua: a southern ocean enigma. *Wilson Bulletin* 100: 345–356. Hybrids between *maccormicki* and *lonnbergi.*

Gulls — General
Major references:

Dwight, Jonathan. 1925. The gulls (Laridae) of the world: their plumages, moults, variations, relationships and distribution. *Bulletin of the American Museum of Natural History* 52: 63–401. A few details have proven to be incorrect, but this is still a valuable reference.

Grant, P. J. 1986. *Gulls — A Guide to Identification*. 2nd ed.

Calton, England: T. & A. D. Poyser. Although aimed primarily at a British/European audience, this excellent book covers all North American gulls: eastern species in great detail, western ones more briefly. An essential field reference.

Other references:

Andrle, Robert F. 1980. Three more probable hybrids of *Larus hyperboreus* and *L. argentatus*. *Wilson Bulletin* 92: 389–393.

Binford, Laurence C. 1978. Lesser Black-backed Gull in California, with notes on field identification. *Western Birds* 9: 141–150. Compares adults of all "black-backed" species.

Devillers, Pierre, Guy McCaskie, and Joseph R. Jehl, Jr. 1971. The distribution of certain large gulls (*Larus*) in southern California and Baja California. *California Birds* 2: 11–26. Notes on identification as well as seasonal occurrence.

Foxall, Roger A. 1979. Presumed hybrids of the Herring Gull and the Great Black-backed Gull — a new problem of identification. *American Birds* 33: 838.

Fussell, John O., III, Michael J. Tove, and Harry E. LeGrand, Jr. 1982. Report on six recent sightings of the Iceland Gull in North Carolina with comments on problems of field identification. *Chat* 46: 57–71.

Gosselin, Michel, and Normand David. 1975. Field identification of Thayer's Gull (*Larus thayeri*) in eastern North America. *American Birds* 29: 1059–1066.

Harris, M. P., C. Morley, and G. H. Green. 1978. Hybridization of Herring and Lesser Black-backed gulls in Britain. *Bird Study* 25: 161–166.

Hoffman, Wayne, John A. Wiens, and J. Michael Scott. 1978. Hybridization between gulls (*Larus glaucescens* and *L. occidentalis*) in the Pacific Northwest. *Auk* 95: 441–458.

Ingolfsson, Agnar. 1969. Sexual dimorphism of large gulls (*Larus* spp.). *Auk* 86: 732–737.

Ingolfsson, Agnar. 1970. Hybridization of Glaucous Gulls (*Larus hyperboreus*) and Herring Gulls (*L. argentatus*) in Iceland. *Ibis* 112: 340–362.

Lauro, Anthony J., and Barbara J. Spencer. 1980. A method for separating juvenal and first-winter Ring-billed Gulls (*Larus delawarensis*) and Common Gulls (*Larus canus*). *American Birds* 34: 111–117.

Lehman, Paul. 1980. The identification of Thayer's Gull in the field. *Birding* 12: 198–210. This remains the best single treatment of issues involved in identifying this difficult gull.

MacPherson, A. H. 1961. Observations on Canadian arctic *Larus* gulls, and on the taxonomy of *L. thayeri* Brooks. *Arctic Institute of North America, Technical Paper* No. 7.

Monaghan, P., and N. Duncan. 1979. Plumage variation of known-age Herring Gulls. *British Birds* 72: 100–103. Evidence from banding that in large gulls, some older immatures may actually be a year older or younger than suggested by their plumage.

Patten, S., and A. R. Weisbrod. 1974. Sympatry and interbreeding of Herring and Glaucous-winged gulls in southeastern Alaska. *Condor* 76: 343–344.

Smith, Neal G. 1966. Evolution of some arctic gulls (*Larus*): an experimental study of isolating mechanisms. *Ornithological Monographs* No. 4. A controversial study.

Medium-sized Terns

Cormons, Grace D. 1976. Roseate Tern bill color change in relation to nesting status and food supply. *Wilson Bulletin* 88: 377–389.

Grant, P. J., and R. E. Scott. 1969. Field identification of juvenile Common, Arctic, and Roseate Terns. *British Birds* 62: 297–299.

Grant, P. J., R. E. Scott, and D. I. M. Wallace. 1971. Further notes on the 'portlandica' plumage phase of terns. *British Birds* 64: 19–22.

Hays, Helen. 1975. Probable Common × Roseate Tern hybrids. *Auk* 92: 219–234.

Hume, R. A., and P. J. Grant. 1974. The upperwing pattern of adult Common and Arctic terns. *British Birds* 67: 133–136.

Kaufman, Kenn. 1987. The practiced eye:. terns overhead. *American Birds* 41: 184–187.

Kirkham, Ian R., and Ian C. T. Nisbet. 1987. Feeding techniques and field identification of Arctic, Common and Roseate terns. *British Birds* 80: 41–47.

Palmer, Ralph S. 1941. 'White-faced' terns. *Auk* 58: 164–178. A dated but still valuable study of subadult plumages of Common and Arctic terns.

Other Terns

Davis, A. H., and K. E. Vinicombe. 1978. Field identification of Gull-billed Terns. *British Birds* 71: 466–468.

Escalante, Rodolfo. 1970. Notes on the Cayenne Tern in Uruguay. *Condor* 72: 89–94. With information on plumages, molts, bill color, etc.

Gantlett, S. J. M., and Alan Harris. 1987. Identification of large terns. *British Birds* 80: 257–276.

Massey, B. W., and J. L. Atwood. 1978. Plumages of the Least Tern. *Bird-Banding* 49: 360–371.

Screech-Owls

Marshall, Joe T. 1967. Parallel variation in the screech owls of North and Middle America. *Western Foundation for Vertebrate Zoology, Memoir* 1: 1–72.

Miller, Alden H., and Loye Miller. 1951. Geographic variation in the screech owls of the deserts of western North America. *Condor* 53: 154–178.

Owen, Dennis F. 1963. Polymorphism in the Screech Owl, *Otus asio*, in eastern North America. *Wilson Bulletin* 75: 183–190.

Hummingbirds

Baldridge, Frank A. 1983. Plumage characteristics of juvenile Black-chinned Hummingbirds. *Condor* 85: 102–103.

Baltosser, William H. In press. Age, species, and sex determination of four North American hummingbirds. *North American Bird Bander*. Very detailed information on in-hand identification of Anna's, Costa's, Black-chinned, and Ruby-throated hummingbirds.

Banks, Richard C., and Ned K. Johnson. 1961. A review of North American hybrid hummingbirds. *Condor* 63: 3–28.

Phillips, Allan R. 1975. The migrations of Allen's and other hummingbirds. *Condor* 77: 196–205.

Short, Lester L., and Allan R. Phillips. 1966. More hybrid hummingbirds from the United States. *Auk* 83: 253–265.

Stiles, F. Gary. 1971. On the field identification of California hummingbirds. *California Birds* 2: 41–54.

Stiles, F. Gary. 1972. Age and sex determination in Rufous and Allen hummingbirds. *Condor* 74: 25–32. Essential for anyone banding these species or trying to identify them in the hand.

Wells, Shirley, Richard A. Bradley, and Luis F. Baptista. 1978

Hybridization in *Calypte* hummingbirds. *Auk* 95: 537–549.

Sapsuckers
Including references on the distribution of the different forms and the hybridization among them as well as on their identification.

Browning, M. Ralph. 1977. Interbreeding members of the *Sphyrapicus varius* group (Aves: Picidae) in Oregon. Southern California Academy of Sciences, *Bulletin* 76: 38–41.

DeBenedictis, Paul. 1979. Gleanings from the technical literature. *Birding* 11: 178–181. Includes information from the author's own examination of specimens, as well as notes from the literature.

Devillers, Pierre. 1970. The identification and distribution in California of the *Sphyrapicus varius* group of sapsuckers. *California Birds* 1: 47–76; reprinted in *Birding* 11: 181–199. Very detailed; its usefulness is not limited to California.

Dunn, Jon. 1978. The races of the Yellow-bellied Sapsucker. *Western Tanager* 44, no. 7; reprinted in *Birding* 10: 142–149. Good summary of plumage characters, plus details of status in southern California.

Howell, Thomas R. 1952. Natural history and differentiation in the Yellow-bellied Sapsucker (*Sphyrapicus varius*). *Condor* 54: 237–282.

Howell, Thomas R. 1953. Racial and sexual differences in migration in *Sphyrapicus varius*. *Auk* 70: 118–126.

Scott, D. M., C. Davison Ankney, and C. H. Jarosch. 1976. Sapsucker hybridization in British Columbia: changes in 25 years. *Condor* 78: 253–257.

Short, Lester L., Jr. 1969. Taxonomic aspects of avian hybridization. *Auk* 86: 84–105. Provides some of the rationale for recognizing Red-breasted, Red-naped, and Yellow-bellied as three full species of sapsucker.

Short, Lester L., and John J. Morony, Jr. 1970. A second hybrid Williamson's × Red-naped Sapsucker and an evolutional history of sapsuckers. *Condor* 72: 310–315.

Wood-Pewees
Phillips, Allan R., Marshall A. Howe, and Wesley E. Lanyon. 1966. Identification of the flycatchers of eastern North America, with special emphasis on the genus *Empi-*

donax. Bird-Banding 37: 153–171. Includes a discussion of distinguishing the two wood-pewees in the hand.

Rising, James D., and Frederick W. Schueler. 1980. Identification and status of wood pewees (*Contopus*) from the Great Plains: what are sibling species? *Condor* 82: 301–308. A study based mostly on measurements, but includes some good miscellaneous information.

Empidonax Flycatchers

Hussell, David J. T. 1980. The timing of fall migration and molt in Least Flycatchers. *Journal of Field Ornithology* 51: 65–71.

Johnson, Ned K. 1963. Biosystematics of sibling species of flycatchers in the *Empidonax hammondii–oberholseri–wrightii* complex. *University of California Publications in Zoology* 66: 79–238. The classic study of Hammond's, Dusky, and Gray flycatchers, crammed with information.

Johnson, Ned K. 1980. Character variation and evolution of sibling species in the *Empidonax difficilis–flavescens* complex (Aves: Tyrannidae). *University of California Publications in Zoology* 112: 1–151. Originally presented the case for splitting Western Flycatcher into two species.

Phillips, Allan R., Marshall A. Howe, and Wesley E. Lanyon. 1966. Identification of the flycatchers of eastern North America, with special emphasis on the genus Empidonax. *Bird-Banding* 37: 153–171. Written for identification in the hand, but provides some insight for field study.

Phillips, Allan R., and Wesley E. Lanyon. 1970. Additional notes on the flycatchers of eastern North America. *Bird-Banding* 41: 190–197. Includes some notes on western Empids.

Stein, Robert C. 1963. Isolating mechanisms between populations of Traill's Flycatchers. *Proceedings of the American Philosophical Society* 107: 21–50. Presented the case for splitting Willow and Alder flycatchers.

Whitney, Bret, and Kenn Kaufman. 1985–1987. The *Empidonax* challenge. Part I: Introduction. *Birding* 17: 151–158. Part II: Least, Hammond's, and Dusky flycatchers. *Birding* 17: 277–287. Part III: Willow and Alder flycatchers. *Birding* 18: 153–159. Part IV: Acadian, Yellow-bellied, and Western flycatchers. *Birding* 18: 315–327. Part V: Buff-breasted and Gray flycatchers. *Birding* 19 (5): 7–

15. A detailed treatment of field identification, with many photos.

Chickadees

Balch, Lawrence G. 1980. Mystery bird of the North: the Gray-headed Chickadee. *Birding* 12: 126–131. Includes an extensive discussion of habitat preference and field identification.

Banks, Richard C. 1970. Re-evaluation of two supposed hybrid birds. *Wilson Bulletin* 82: 331–332. An aberrant Black-capped, with partial white supercilium, was previously identified as a hybrid with Mountain Chickadee.

Dixon, Keith L., and Dennis J. Martin. 1979. Notes on the vocalizations of the Mexican Chickadee. *Condor* 81: 421–423.

Ficken, Millicent S., Robert W. Ficken, and Steve R. Witkin. 1978. Vocal repertoire of the Black-capped Chickadee. *Auk* 95: 34–48.

Gochfeld, Michael. 1977. Plumage variation in Black-capped Chickadees: is there sexual dimorphism? *Bird-Banding* 48: 62–66. Concludes that the sexes cannot be identified by plumage characters, contrary to an earlier report (*Bird-Banding* 43: 139–140).

Lunk, William A. 1952. Notes on variation in the Carolina Chickadee. *Wilson Bulletin* 64: 7–21. Plumage and size variation.

McLaren, Margaret A. 1976. Vocalizations of the Boreal Chickadee. *Auk* 93: 451–463.

Merritt, Peter G. 1978. Characteristics of Black-capped and Carolina chickadees at the range interface in northern Indiana. *Jack-Pine Warbler* 56: 171–179.

Merritt, Peter G. 1981. Narrowly disjunct allopatry between Black-capped and Carolina chickadees in northern Indiana. *Wilson Bulletin* 93: 54–66.

Robbins, Mark B., Michael J. Braun, and E. A. Tobey. 1986. Morphological and vocal variation across a contact zone between the chickadees *Parus atricapillus* and *P. carolinensis*. *Auk* 103: 655–666.

Smith, Susan T. 1972. Communication and other social behavior in *Parus carolinensis*. *Publications of the Nuttall Ornithological Club*, No. 11.

Thormin, Terry W., and C. Eric Tull. 1980. The ex-Gray-headed Chickadee. *Birding* 12: 62–64. Describes a leucistic Black-capped Chickadee in Alberta that was misidentified as a Gray-headed.

Ward, Rodman. 1966. Regional variation in the song of the Carolina Chickadee. *Living Bird* 5: 127–150.

Vireos

Terrill, Scott B., and Linda S. Terrill. 1981. On the field identification of Yellow-green, Red-eyed, Philadelphia and Warbling vireos. *Continental Birdlife* 2: 144–149.

Blackpoll and Similar Warblers

Howard, Deborah V. 1968. Criteria for aging and sexing Bay-breasted Warblers in the fall. *Bird-Banding* 39: 132.

Waterthrushes

Binford, Laurence C. 1971. Identification of Northern and Louisiana waterthrushes. *California Birds* 2: 1–10. Thorough discussion, including in-hand details.

Miscellaneous Warblers

Hubbard, John P. 1970. Geographic variation in the *Dendroica coronata* complex. *Wilson Bulletin* 82: 355–369.

Kaufman, Kenn. 1979. Identifying "Myrtle" and "Audubon's" warblers out of breeding plumage. *Continental Birdlife* 1: 89–92.

Raveling, Dennis G., and Dwain W. Warner. 1965. Plumages, molt and morphometry of Tennessee Warblers. *Bird-Banding* 36: 169–179.

Cassin's and Botteri's Sparrows

Borror, Donald J. 1971. Songs of *Aimophila* sparrows occurring in the United States. *Wilson Bulletin* 83: 132–151.

Dickerman, Robert W., and Allan R. Phillips. 1967. Botteri's Sparrows of the Atlantic coastal lowlands of Mexico. *Condor* 69: 596–600.

Hubbard, John P. 1977. The status of Cassin's Sparrow in New Mexico and adjacent states. *American Birds* 31: 933–941.

Webster, J. Dan. 1959. A revision of the Botteri Sparrow. *Condor* 61: 136–146. With comparisons of various subspecies.

Wolf, Larry L. 1977. Species relationships in the avian genus *Aimophila*. *Ornithological Monographs* No. 23, viii + 220 pp. Contains much useful information.

***Spizella* Sparrows**

Knapton, R. W. 1978. Sex and age determination in the Clay-colored Sparrow. *Bird-Banding* 49: 152–156.

***Carpodacus* Finches**

Aldrich, John W., and John S. Weske. 1978. Origin and evolution of the eastern House Finch population. *Auk* 95: 528–536. Includes information on geographical variation in western North America and on the introduced population in the East.

Blake, Charles H. 1955. Notes on the eastern Purple Finch. *Bird-Banding* 26: 89–116.

Blake, Charles H. 1957. Female eastern Purple Finches. *Bird-Banding* 28: 26–29.

Blake, Charles H. 1957. Notes on juvenal Purple Finches. *Bird-Banding* 28: 29–40. These three papers by Blake provide a detailed analysis of the variation of this species in the East.

Duvall, A. J. 1945. Variation in *Carpodacus purpureus* and *Carpodacus cassinii. Condor* 47: 202–204.

Samson, F. B. 1974. On determining sex and age in the Cassin's Finch. *Western Bird-Bander* 49 (3): 4–7.

INDEX

Page numbers in *italics* refer to illustrations.

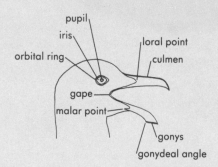

EYE AND BILL TERMS

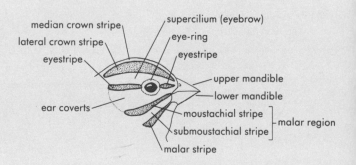

HEAD-PATTERN TERMS

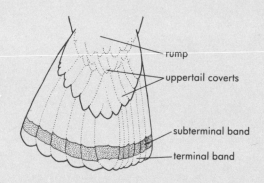

UPPERSIDE OF TAIL

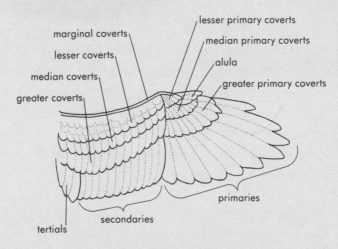

UPPERSIDE OF WING

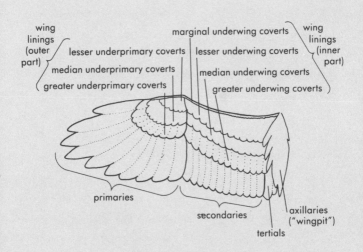

UNDERSIDE OF WING